# Cartoons That Fit

— For Angus —
With Best Wishes...

JRROSE!

10 - '96

Clinton has made thousands of
new jobs — I met an ex - doctor
with three of them yesterday!

TWO BILLS THAT CONTINUE TO REACH RECORD LOWS...
FEDERAL RESERVE NOTE
THE UNITED STATES OF AMERICA
D 38493830 A
ONE DOLLAR
POPULARITY
©1995 BYRD NEWSPAPERS
J.R.ROSE!

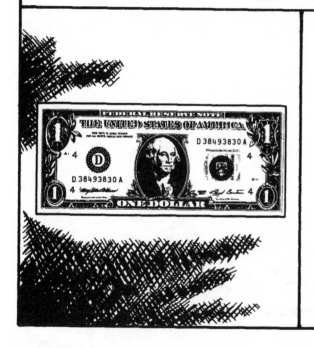

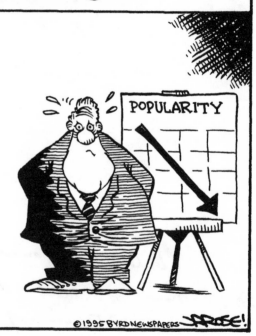

# Cartoons That Fit the Bill

## An Editorial Cartoon Collection about Washington and Beyond

John R. Rose

Foreword by George Allen

PELICAN PUBLISHING COMPANY
Gretna 1996

*For Karen and our two little rosebuds, Meredith and Sarah*

Thanks to the following for their support and encouragement: my wife, parents, and brothers; my editors/managers Richard Morin, Dale McConnaughay, Linda Swecker, Ken Mink, Bob Cramer, Tom Byrd, and Rebecca Poe. Also thanks to Amerallus Teter, Penny Anderson, Jeremy Downey, and David Shiplett for their help in producing this book.

*The word "Pelican" and the depiction of a pelican are trademarks of Pelican Publishing Company, Inc., and are registered in the U.S. Patent and Trademark Office.*

**Library of Congress Cataloging-in-Publication Data**

Rose, John (John Robert)
    Cartoons that fit the bill : an editorial  cartoon book about
Washington and beyond / John R. Rose ; foreword by George Allen.
        p.    cm.
    ISBN 1-56554-215-0 (pbk. : alk. paper)
    1. United States—Politics and government—1993- ——Caricatures
and cartoons. 2. Virginia—Politics and government—1951- -
-Caricatures and cartoons. 3. American wit and humor, Pictorial.
4. Editorial cartoons—Virginia—Harrisonburg. I. Title.
E885.R67 1996
320.973'0207—dc20                                          96-17501
                                                              CIP

Manufactured in the United States of America

Published by Pelican Publishing Company
1101 Monroe Street, Gretna, Louisiana 70053

# Contents

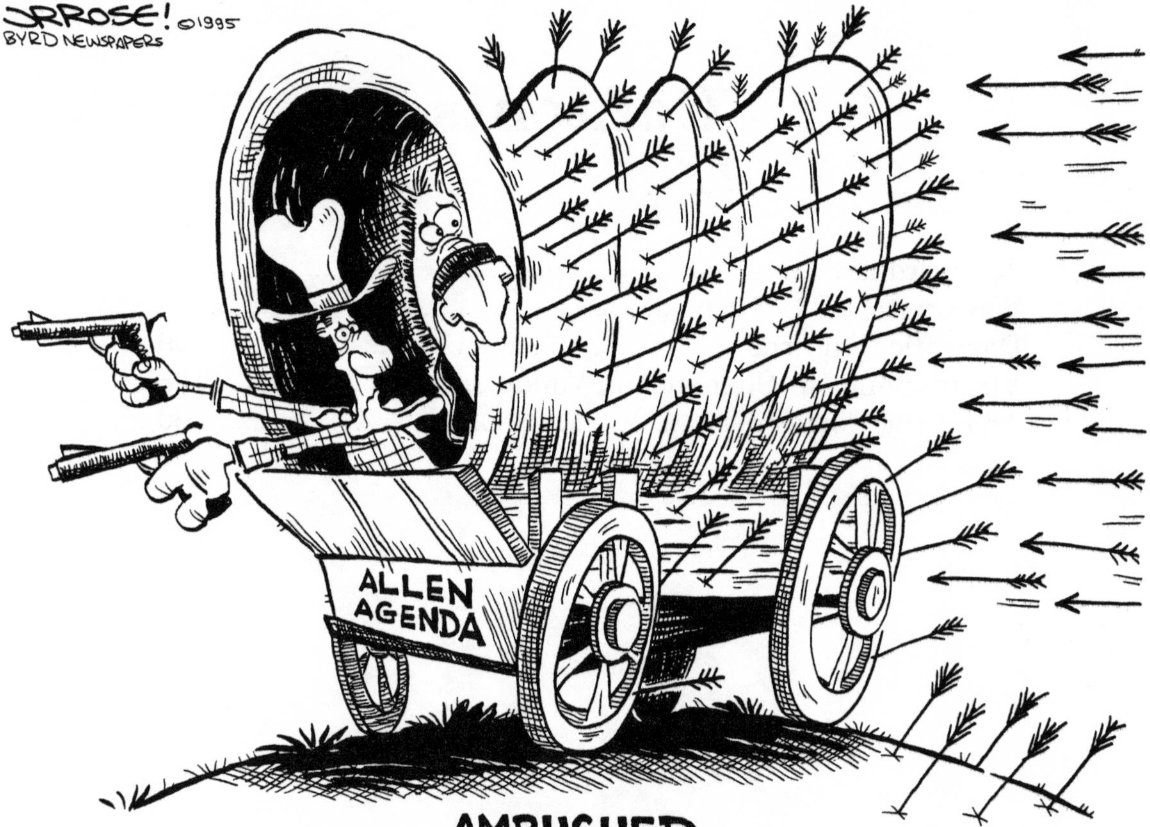
JRROSE! ©1995
BYRD NEWSPAPERS
ALLEN AGENDA

AMBUSHED

# Foreword

Throughout history, satirists have used political cartoons to poke fun at newsworthy events and notable personalities. Anyone who has been their subject can certainly lend insight into what makes an effective cartoonist great. While their work can run the gamut from good-natured ribbing to scathing ridicule, only the best can creatively and effectively combine satire with an accurate and informed perspective, while simultaneously conveying a message that is current and informative.

Virginia is fortunate to be home to a number of such fine cartoonists, and among them is one of my favorites—John Rose. John's musings on federal, state, and local concerns always entertain, but, more importantly, they educate his readers about the issues that directly impact their lives.

In the age of the soundbyte, many of us have come to rely heavily upon a brief, efficient means of acquainting ourselves with the news. In such a demanding environment, John has mastered the art of relaying a point with good-natured humor and thought-provoking insight. Whether you are discovering John's cartoons for the first time or are a veteran fan of his work, I know that you will enjoy being reminded, once again, of the personalities and issues that have shaped our Commonwealth and our nation over the past several years.

GEORGE ALLEN
Governor, Commonwealth of Virginia

# Washington, D.C.

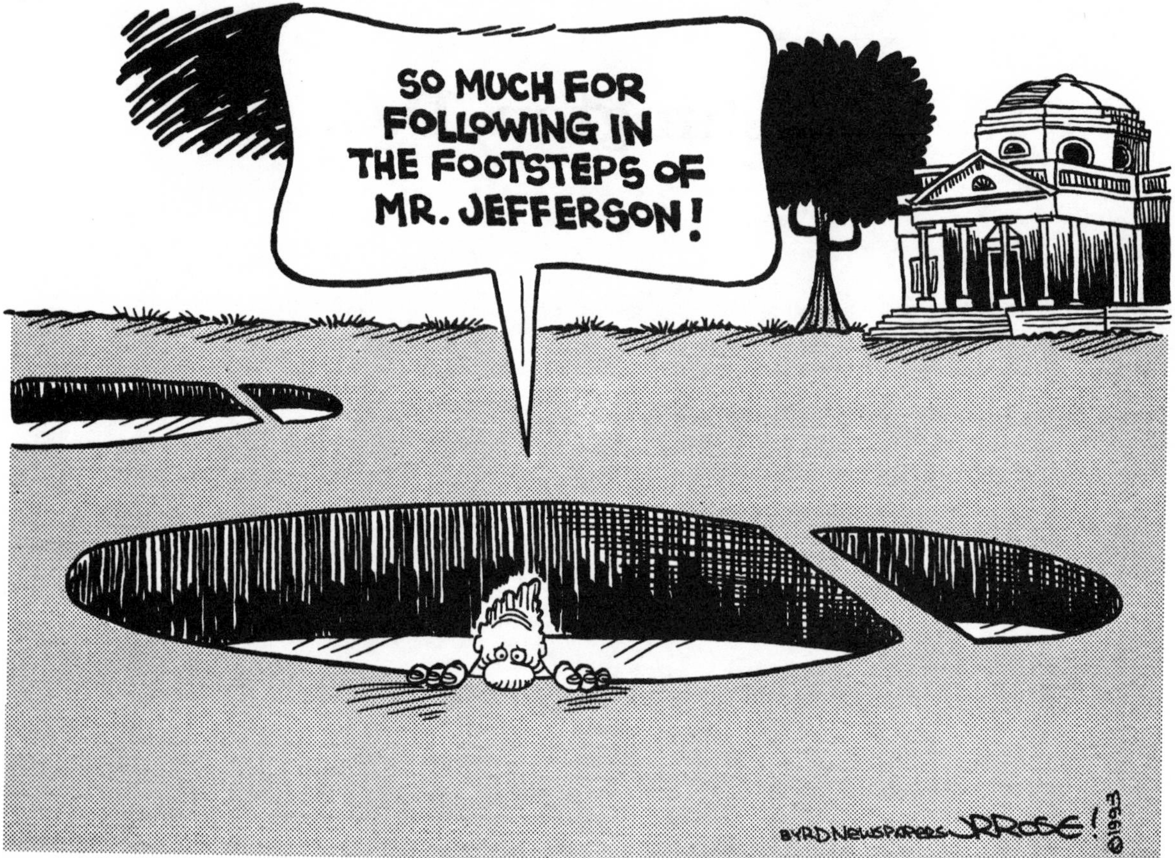
SO MUCH FOR FOLLOWING IN THE FOOTSTEPS OF MR. JEFFERSON!
BYRD NEWSPAPERS
RROSE!
©1993

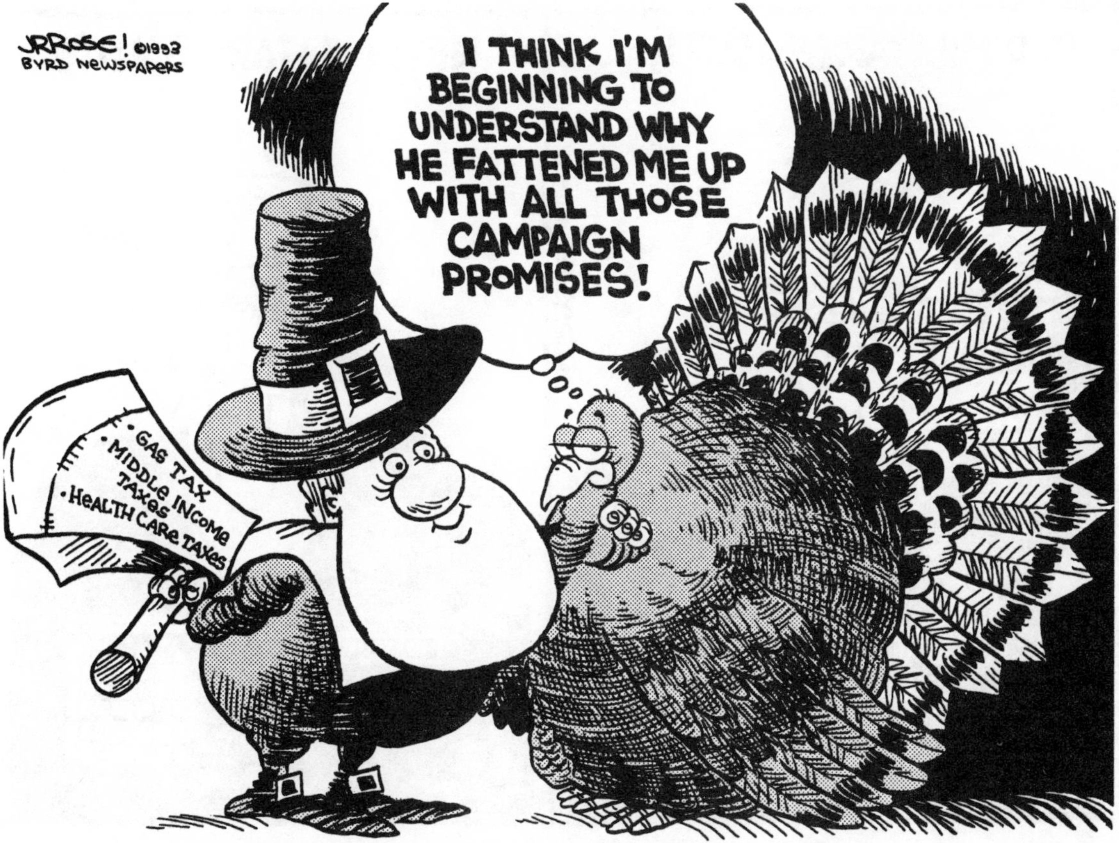
JRROSE! ©1993
BYRD NEWSPAPERS
I THINK I'M BEGINNING TO UNDERSTAND WHY HE FATTENED ME UP WITH ALL THOSE CAMPAIGN PROMISES!
• GAS TAX
• MIDDLE INCOME TAXES
• HEALTH CARE TAXES

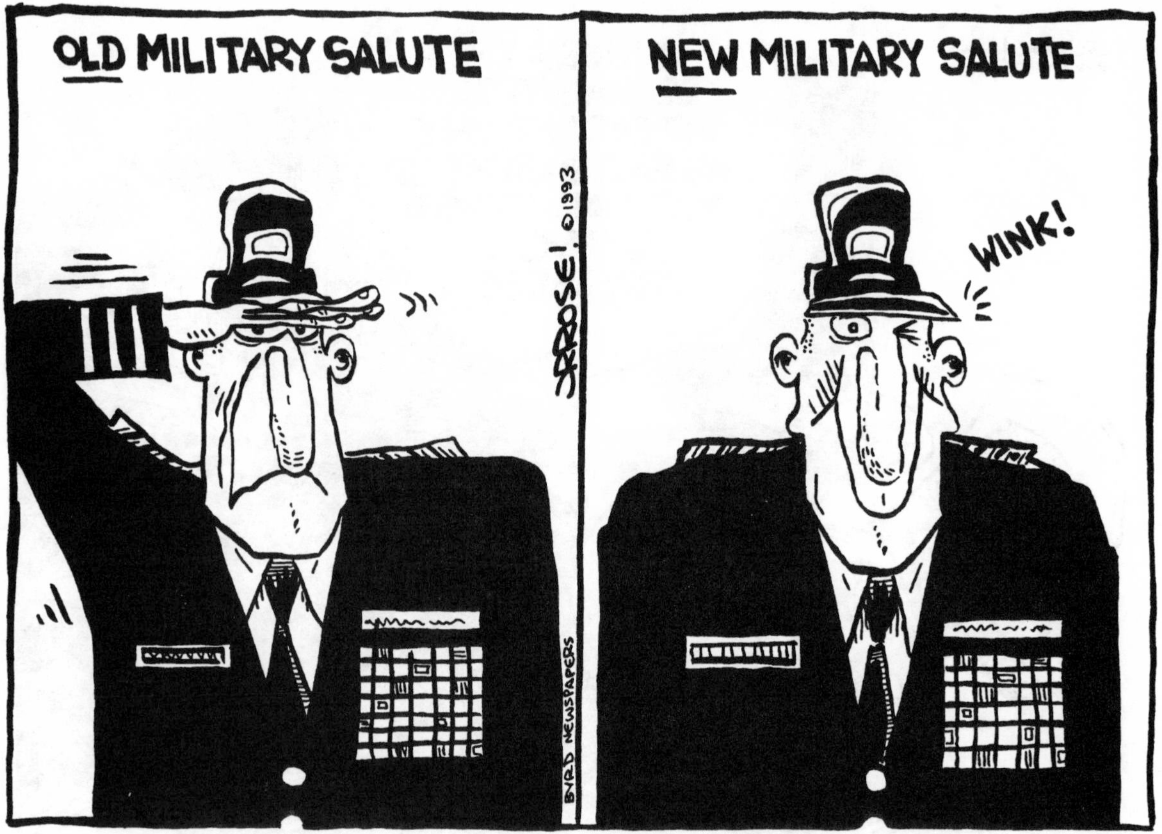
OLD MILITARY SALUTE
NEW MILITARY SALUTE
WINK!
JD ROSE! ©1993
BYRD NEWSPAPERS

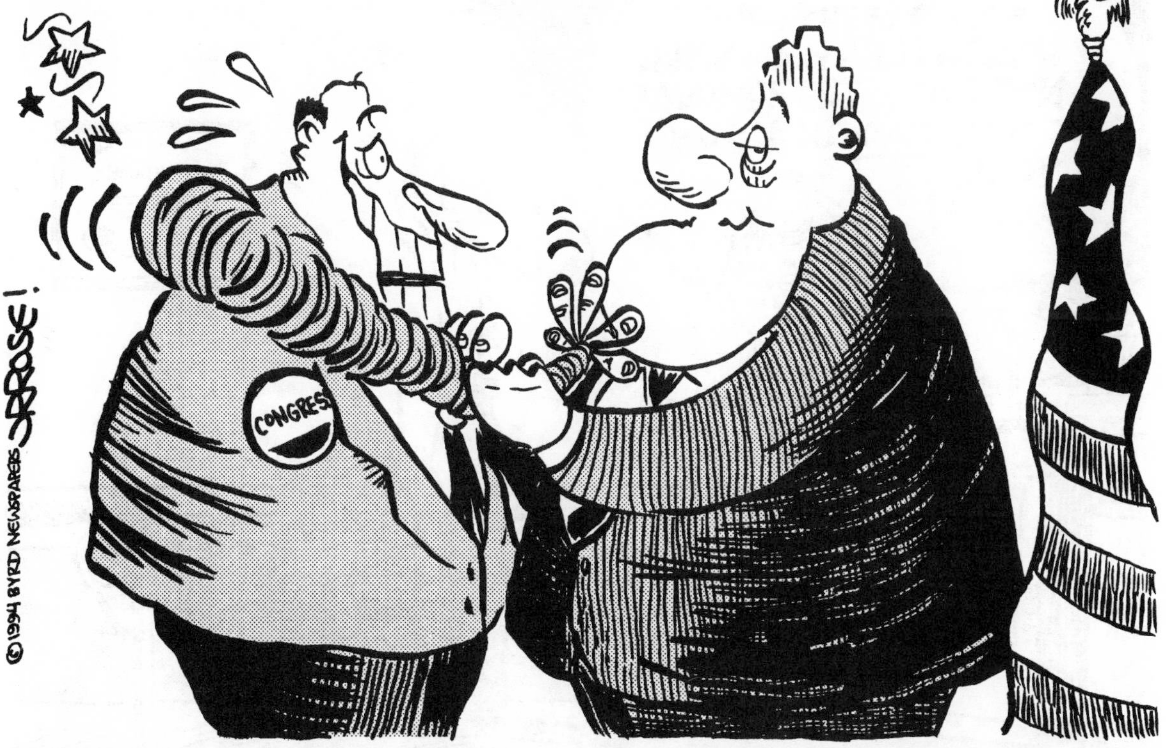
CONGRES
©1994 BYRD NEWSPAPERS

IS ARM-TWISTING COVERED IN THE 'CLINTON HEALTH PLAN' MR. PRESIDENT?

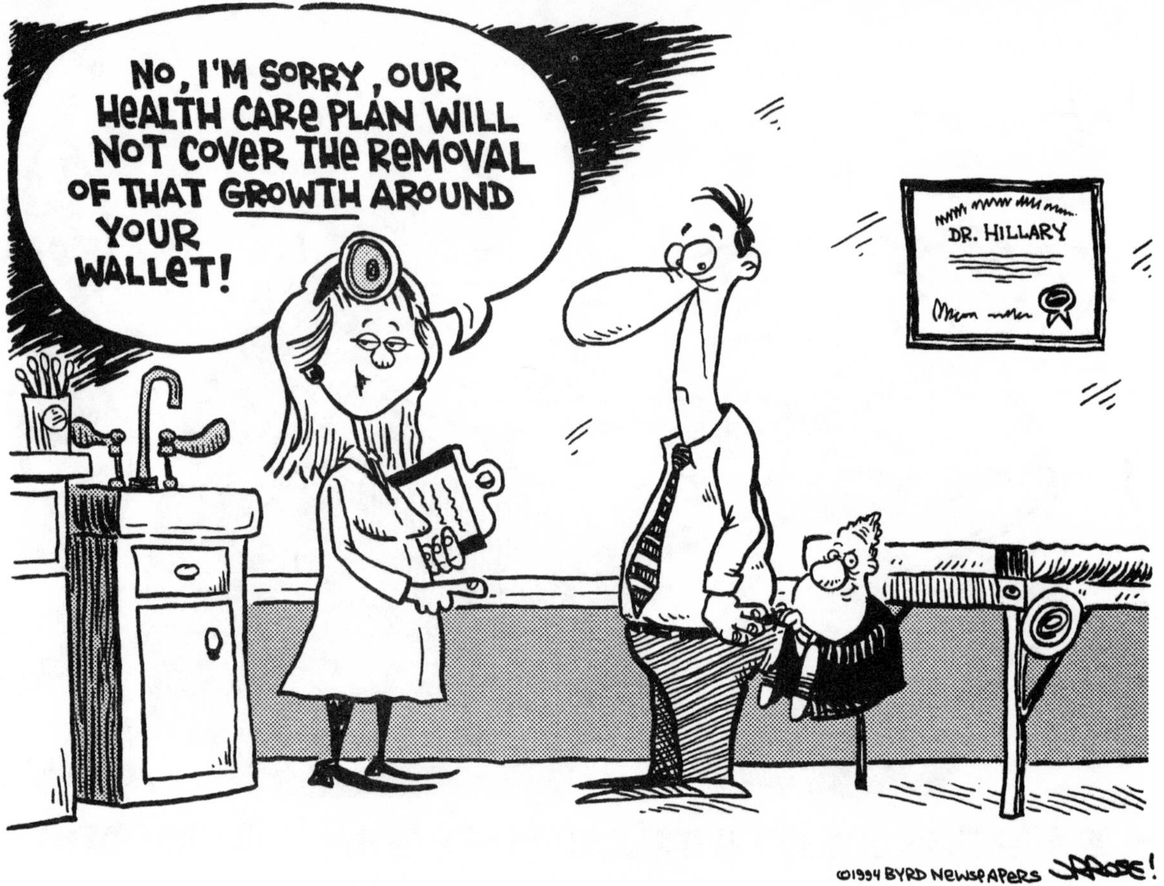
NO, I'M SORRY, OUR HEALTH CARE PLAN WILL NOT COVER THE REMOVAL OF THAT GROWTH AROUND YOUR WALLET!
DR. HILLARY
©1994 BYRD NEWSPAPERS J.ROSE!

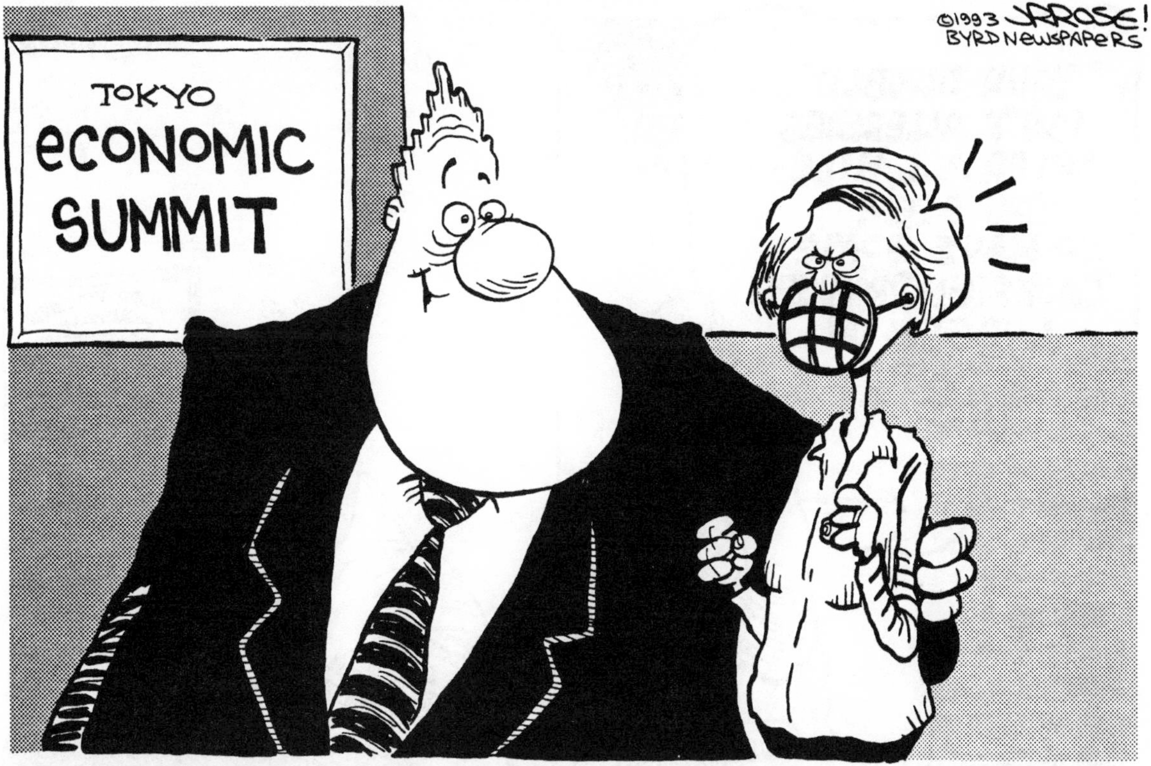
©1993 JRROSE!
BYRD NEWSPAPERS
TOKYO
ECONOMIC
SUMMIT

DON'T WORRY HIL ... AS SOON AS WE GET BACK IN THE STATES, I PROMISE WE'LL REMOVE THAT MUZZLE!

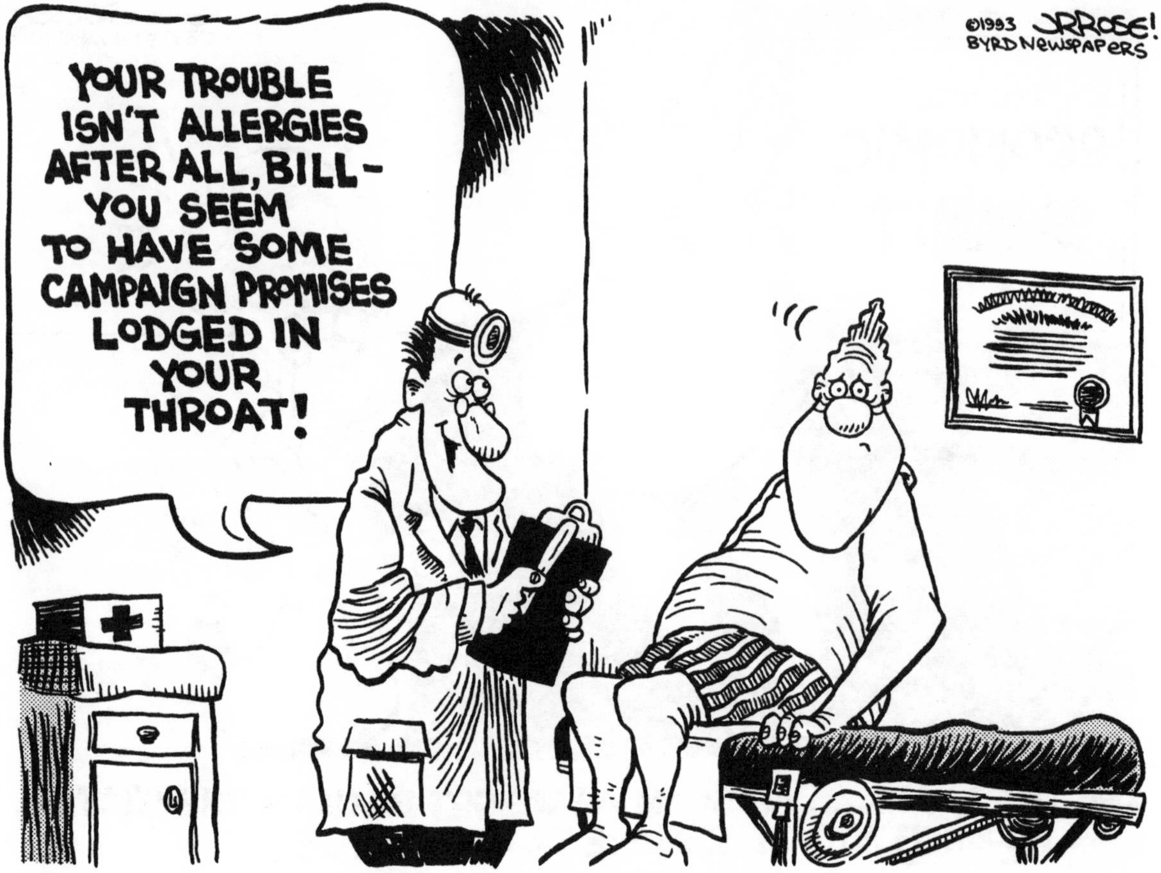
YOUR TROUBLE ISN'T ALLERGIES AFTER ALL, BILL - YOU SEEM TO HAVE SOME CAMPAIGN PROMISES LODGED IN YOUR THROAT!
©1993 JRROSE!
BYRD NEWSPAPERS

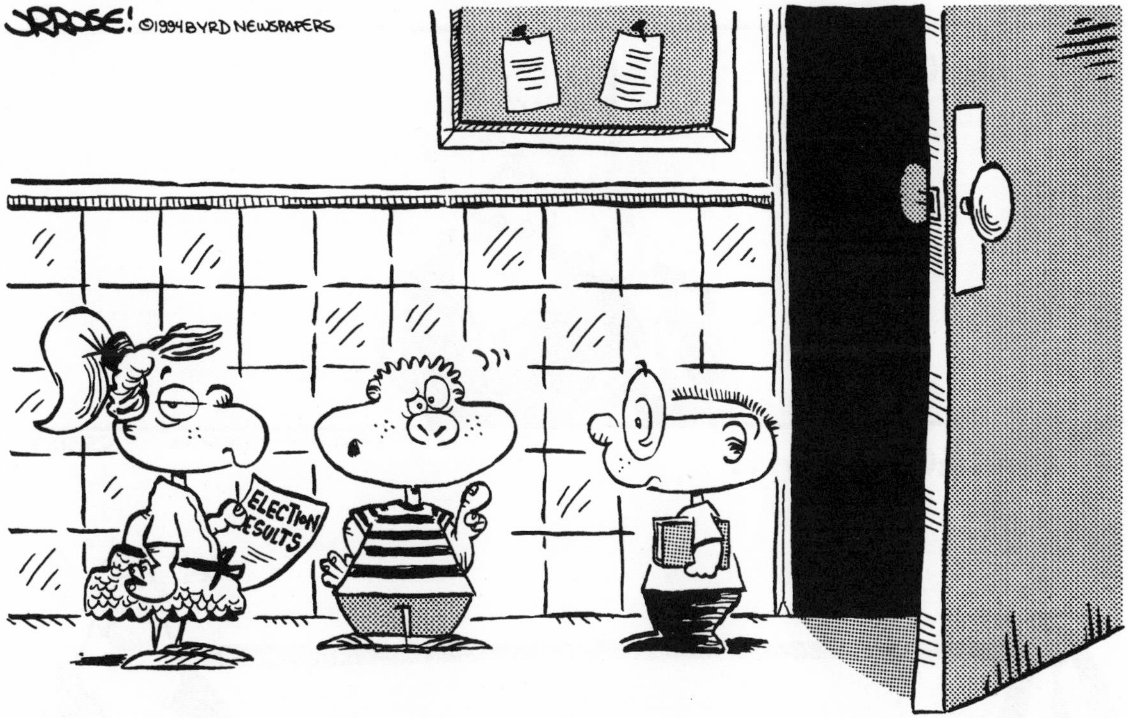
JRROSE! ©1994 BYRD NEWSPAPERS
ELECTION RESULTS

IF I HADN'T GOTTEN THAT ENDORSEMENT FROM BILL CLINTON, I REALLY THINK I WOULD'VE WON THE ELECTION FOR CLASS PRESIDENT!

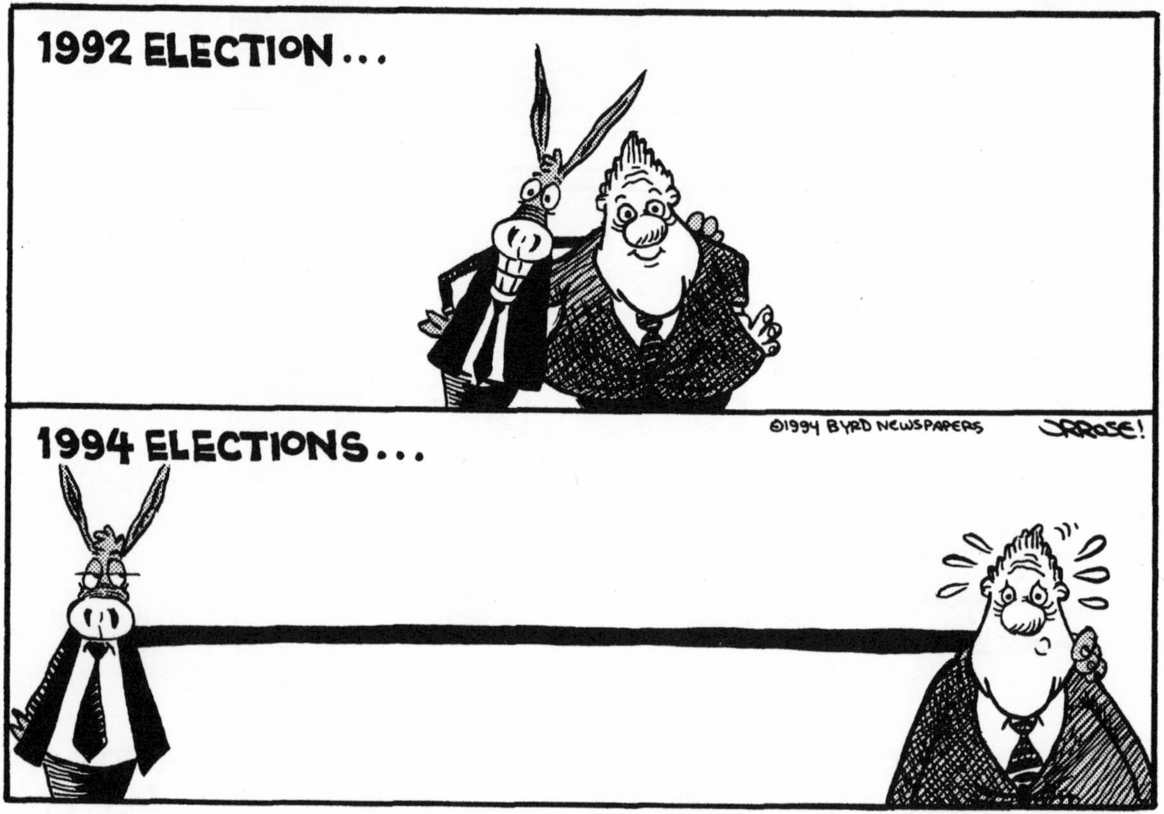
1992 ELECTION...
1994 ELECTIONS...
©1994 BYRD NEWSPAPERS
JRROSE!

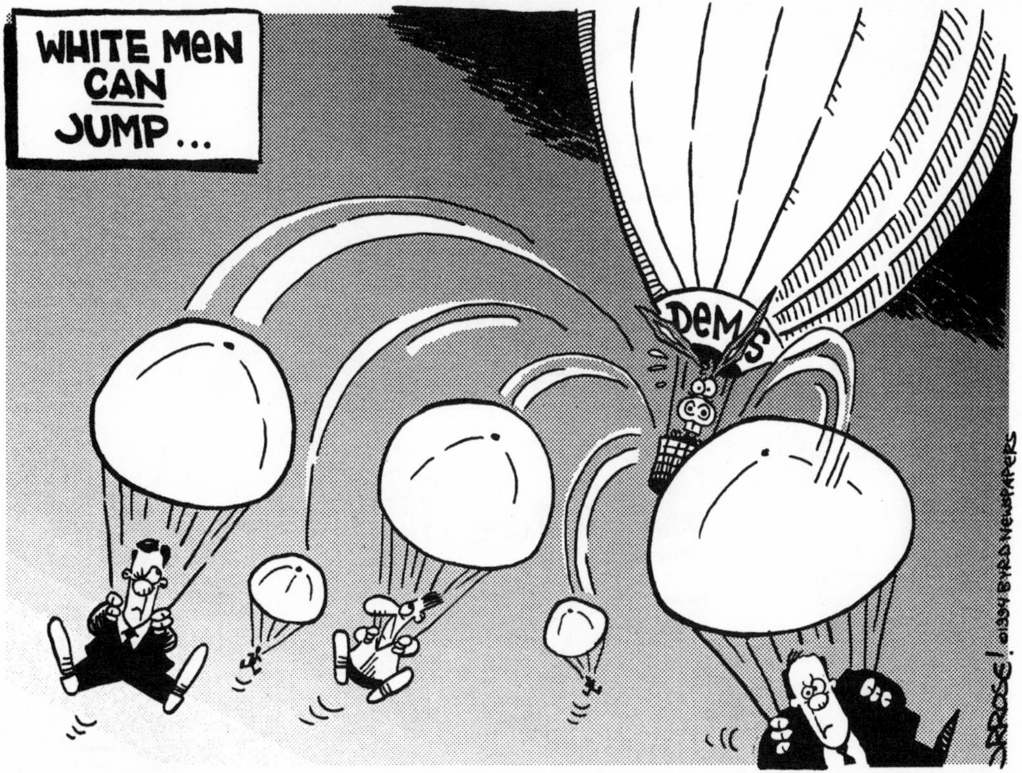
WHITE MEN CAN JUMP...
DEMS
©1994 BYRD NEWSPAPERS

News Item: Election exit polls show white males led the exodus from the Democratic Party.

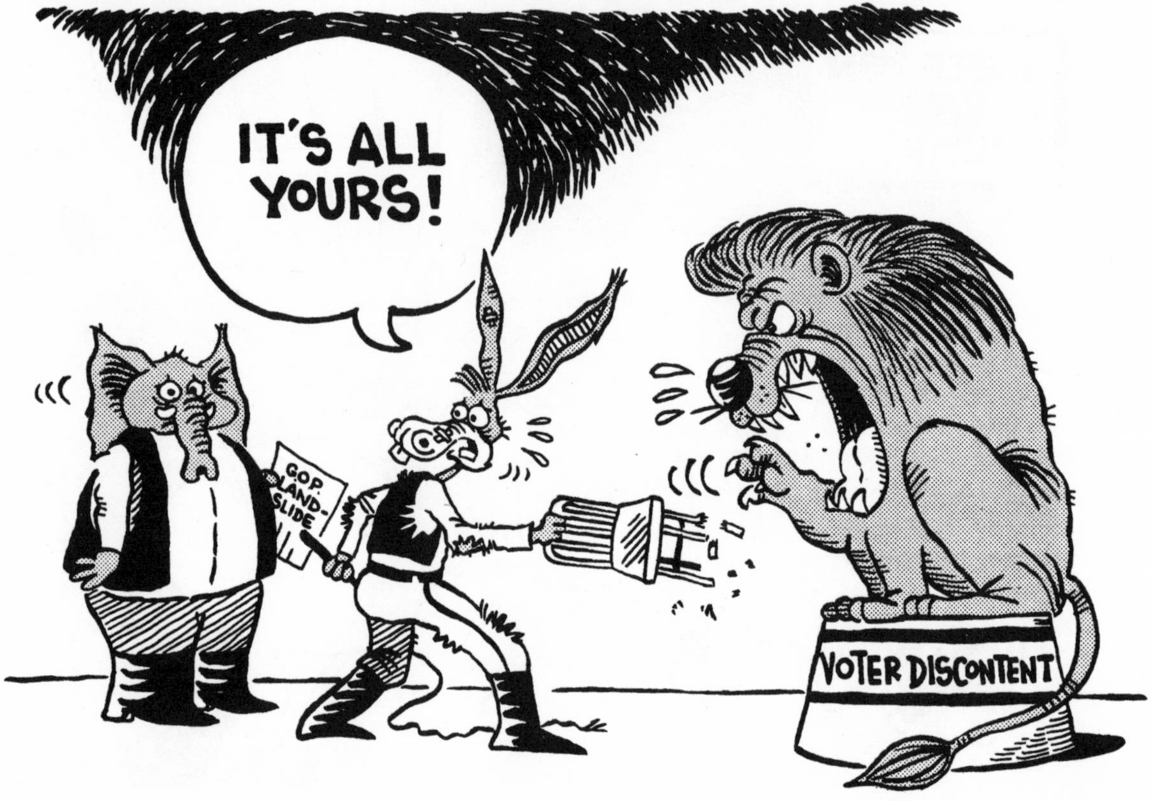
IT'S ALL YOURS!
G.O.P. LAND-SLIDE
VOTER DISCONTENT

 JRROSE!

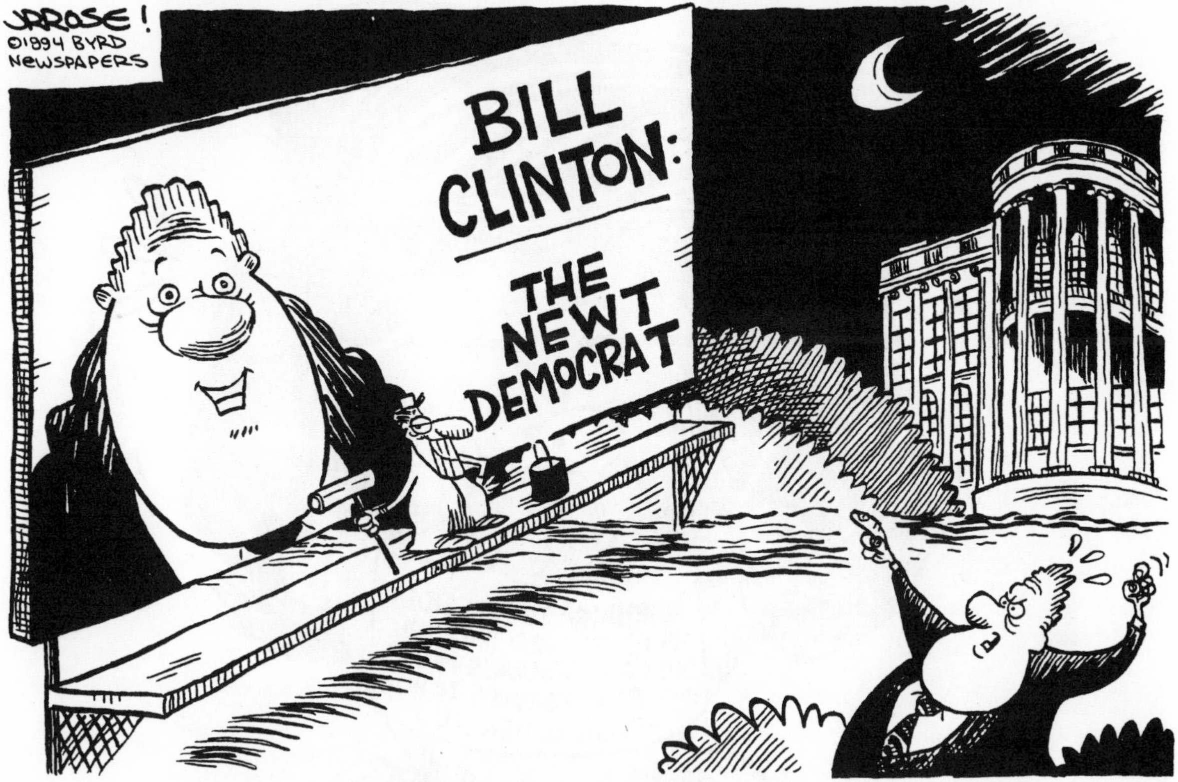
JRROSE!
©1994 BYRD
NEWSPAPERS
BILL CLINTON:
THE NEWT DEMOCRAT

THAT'S NEW DEMOCRAT, YOU IDIOT!

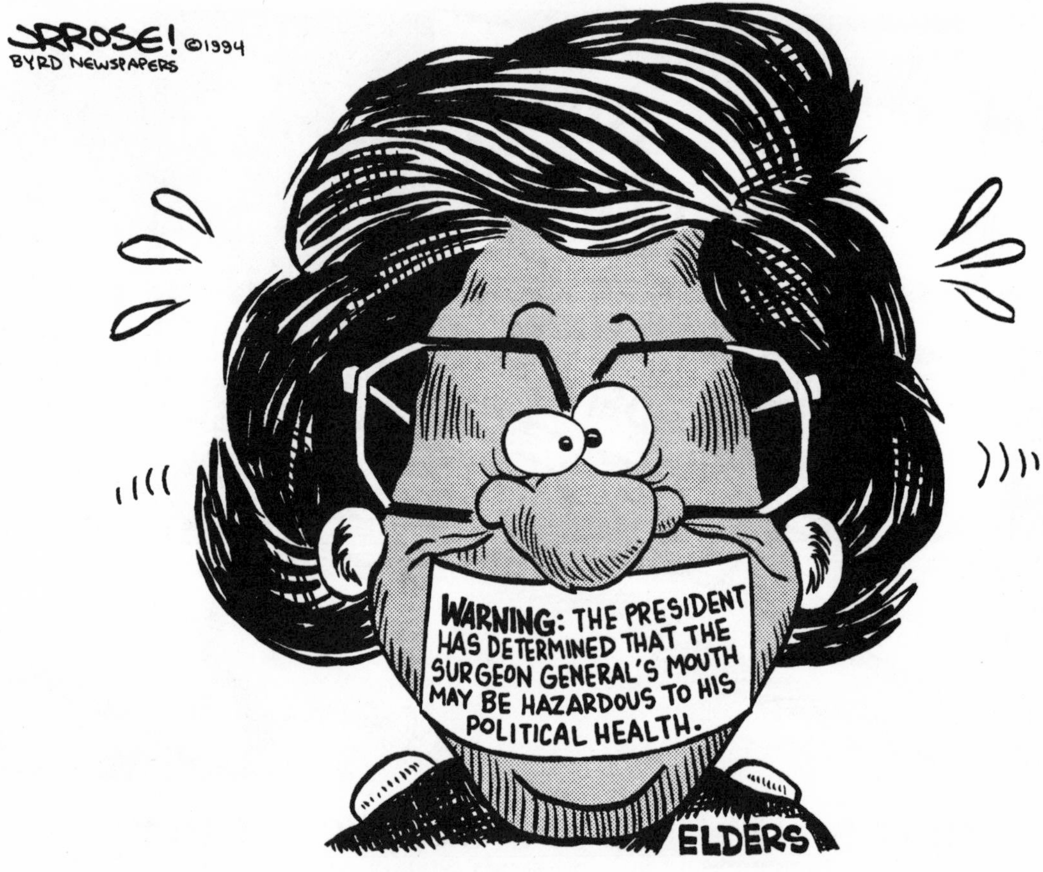
JRROSE! ©1994
BYRD NEWSPAPERS
WARNING: THE PRESIDENT HAS DETERMINED THAT THE SURGEON GENERAL'S MOUTH MAY BE HAZARDOUS TO HIS POLITICAL HEALTH.
ELDERS

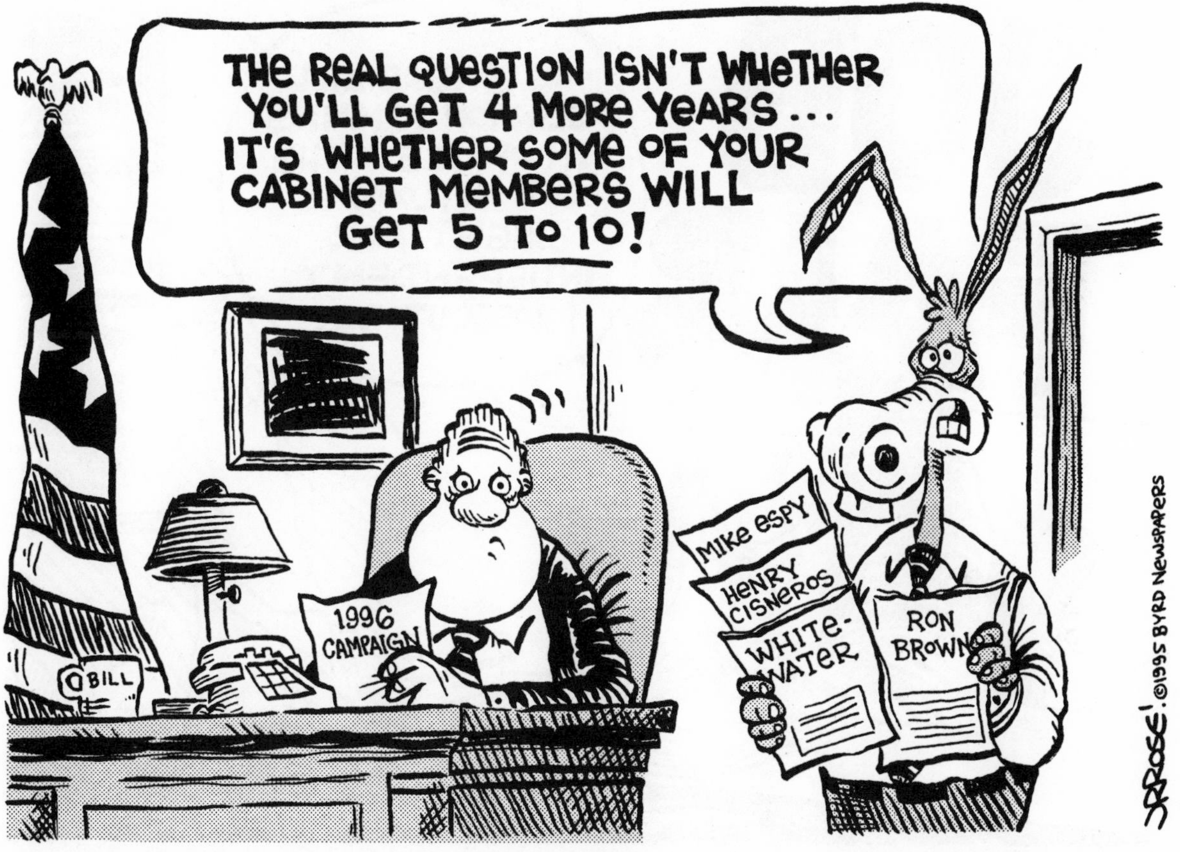
THE REAL QUESTION ISN'T WHETHER YOU'LL GET 4 MORE YEARS... IT'S WHETHER SOME OF YOUR CABINET MEMBERS WILL GET 5 TO 10!
1996 CAMPAIGN
BILL
MIKE ESPY
HENRY CISNEROS
WHITE-WATER
RON BROWN
JRROSE! ©1995 BYRD NEWSPAPERS

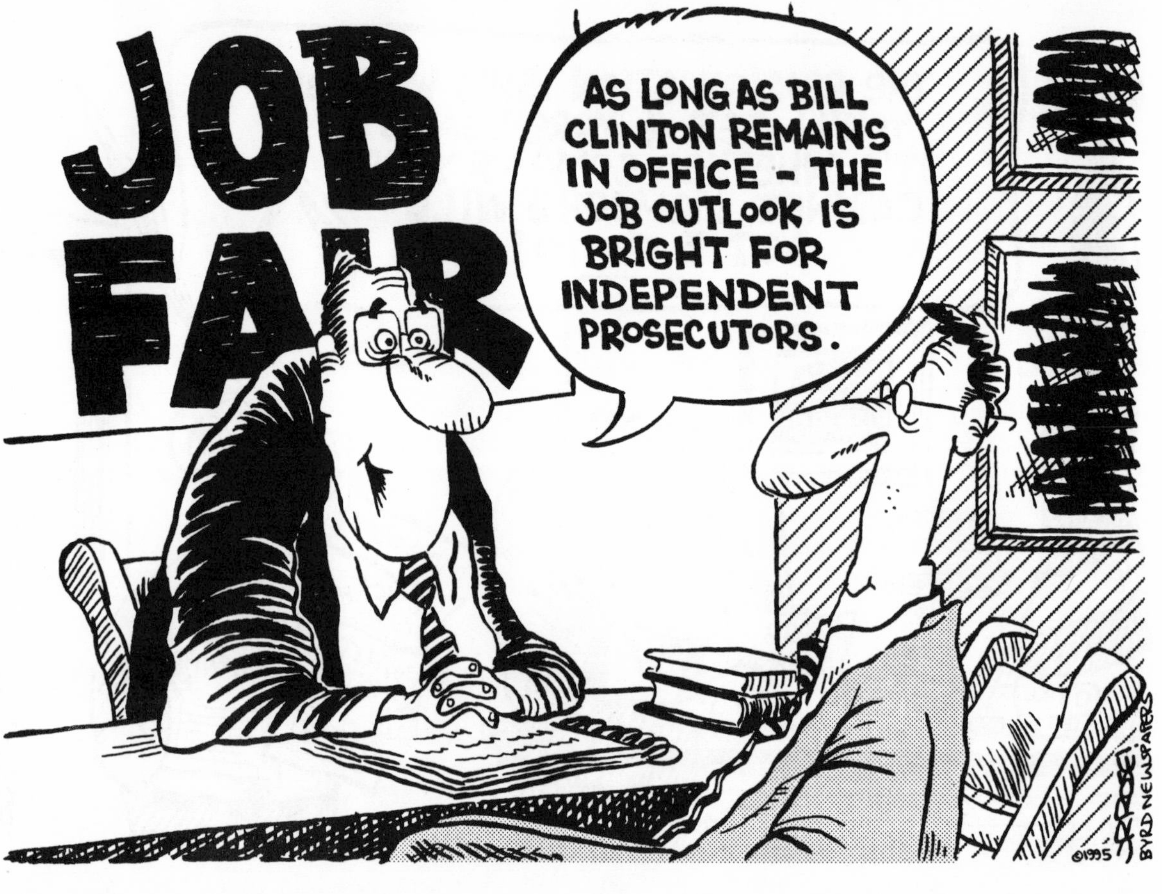
JOB FAIR
AS LONG AS BILL CLINTON REMAINS IN OFFICE - THE JOB OUTLOOK IS BRIGHT FOR INDEPENDENT PROSECUTORS.
©1995
BYRD NEWSPAPERS

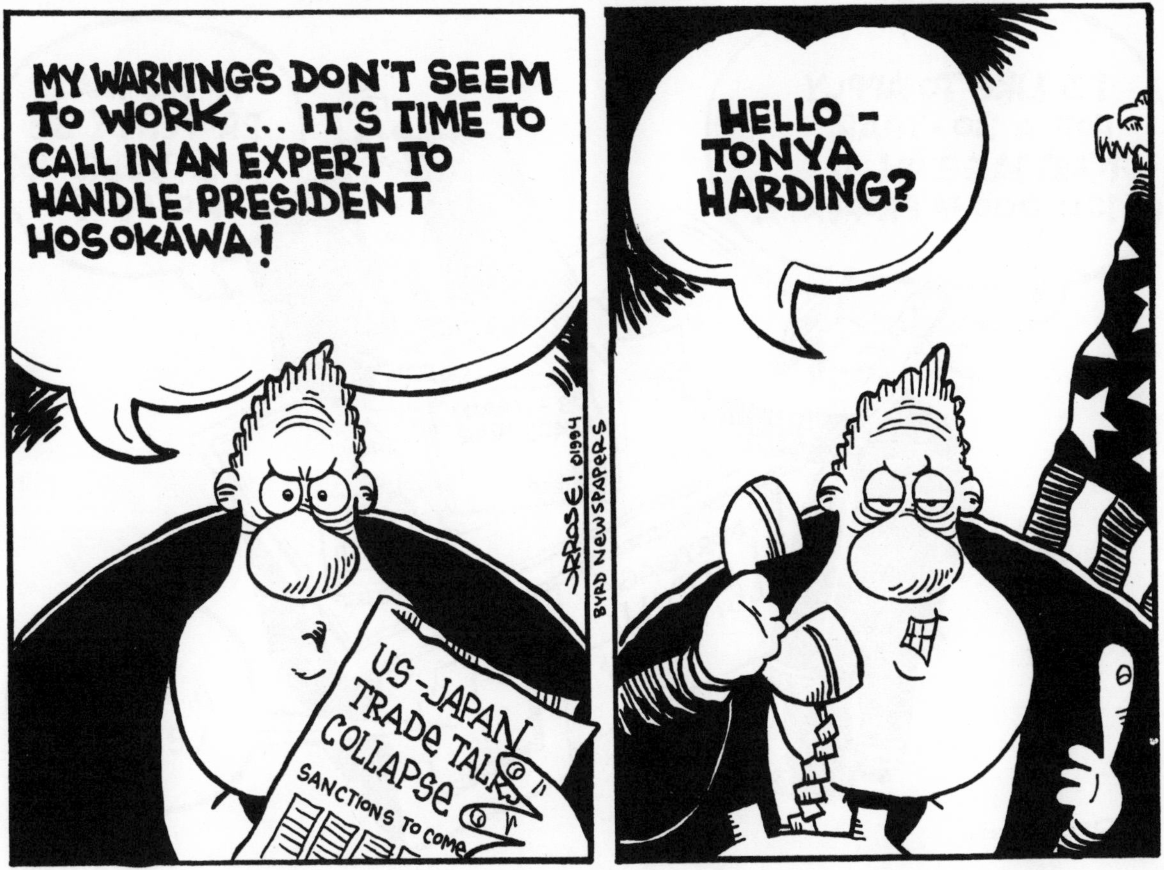
MY WARNINGS DON'T SEEM TO WORK ... IT'S TIME TO CALL IN AN EXPERT TO HANDLE PRESIDENT HOSOKAWA!
US-JAPAN TRADE TALKS COLLAPSE
SANCTIONS TO COME
BYRD NEWSPAPERS
HELLO - TONYA HARDING?

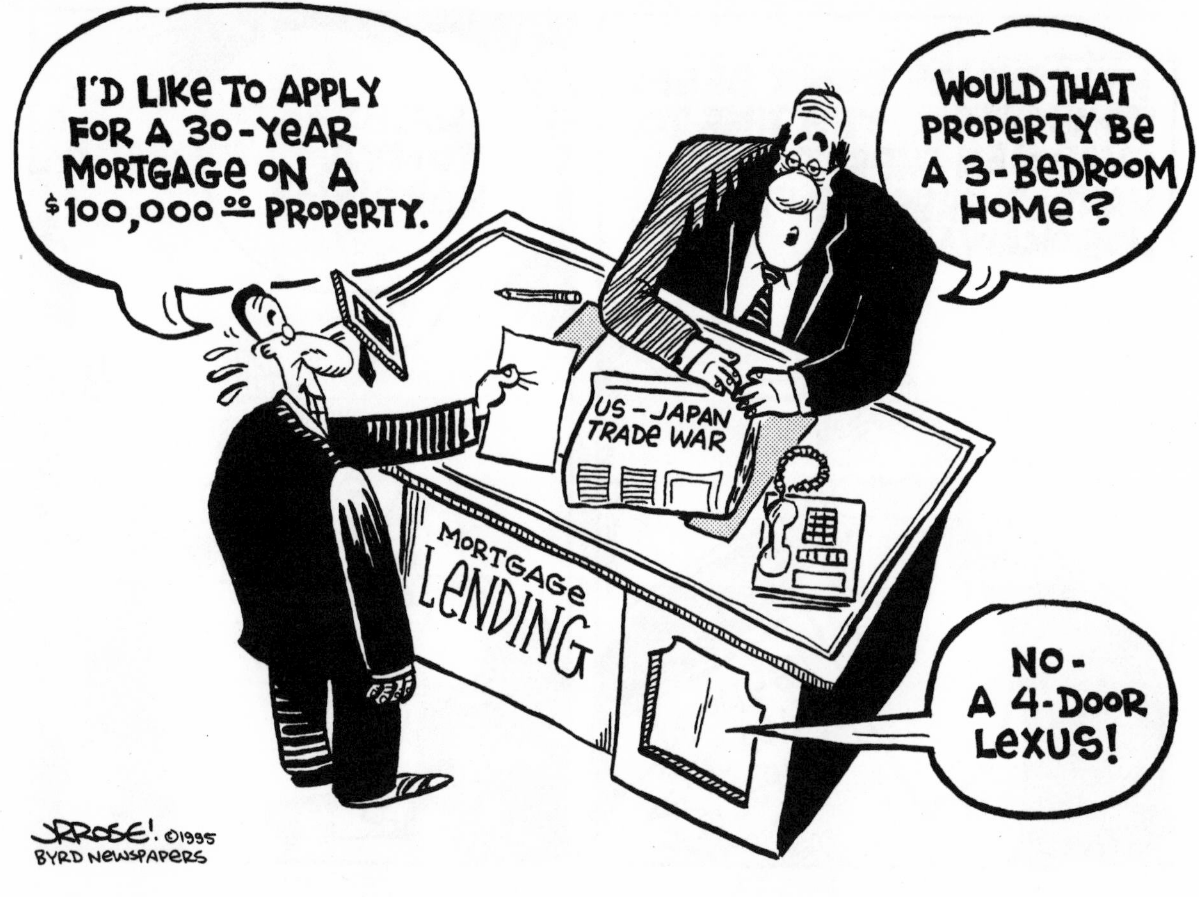
I'D LIKE TO APPLY FOR A 30-YEAR MORTGAGE ON A $100,000.00 PROPERTY.
WOULD THAT PROPERTY BE A 3-BEDROOM HOME?
NO - A 4-DOOR LEXUS!
US - JAPAN TRADE WAR
MORTGAGE LENDING
JRROSE! ©1995 BYRD NEWSPAPERS

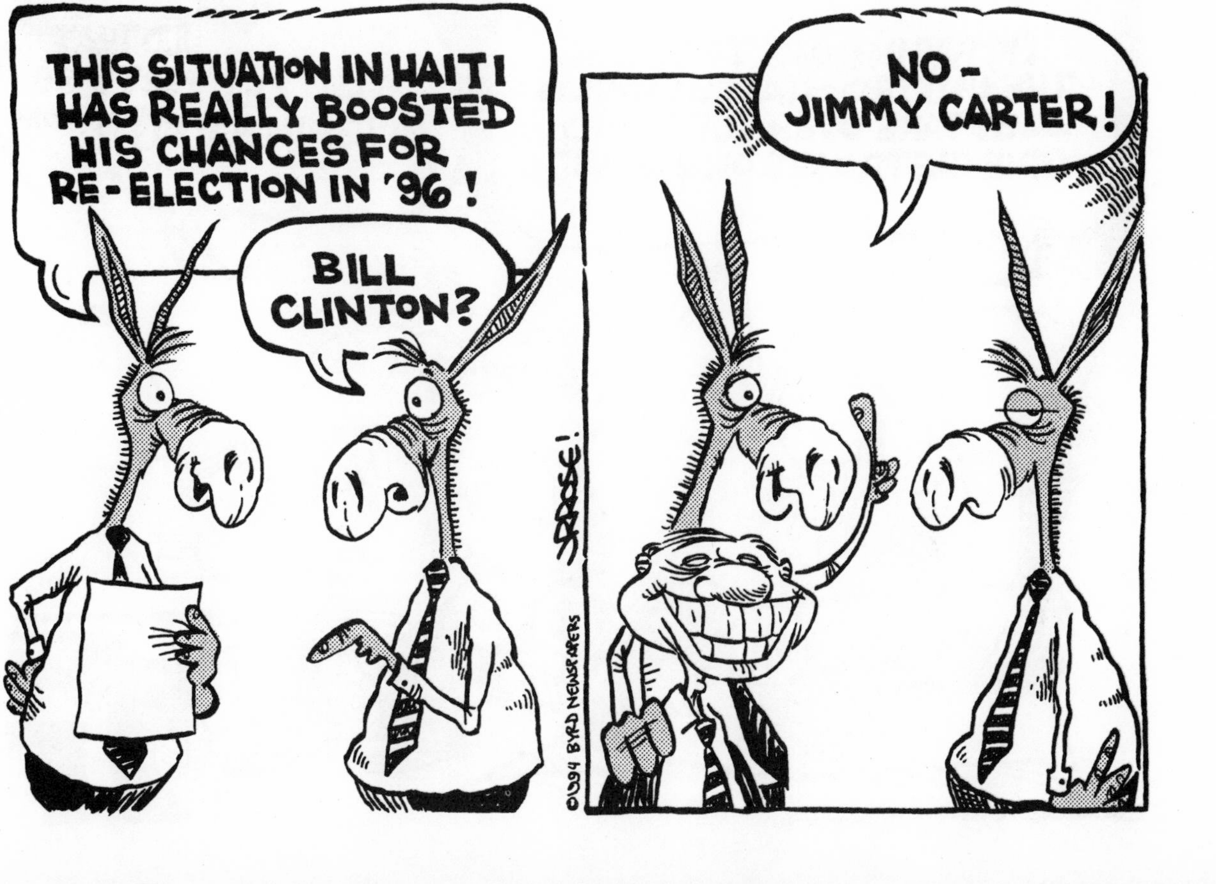
THIS SITUATION IN HAITI HAS REALLY BOOSTED HIS CHANCES FOR RE-ELECTION IN '96!
BILL CLINTON?
NO - JIMMY CARTER!
©1994 BYRD NEWSPAPERS

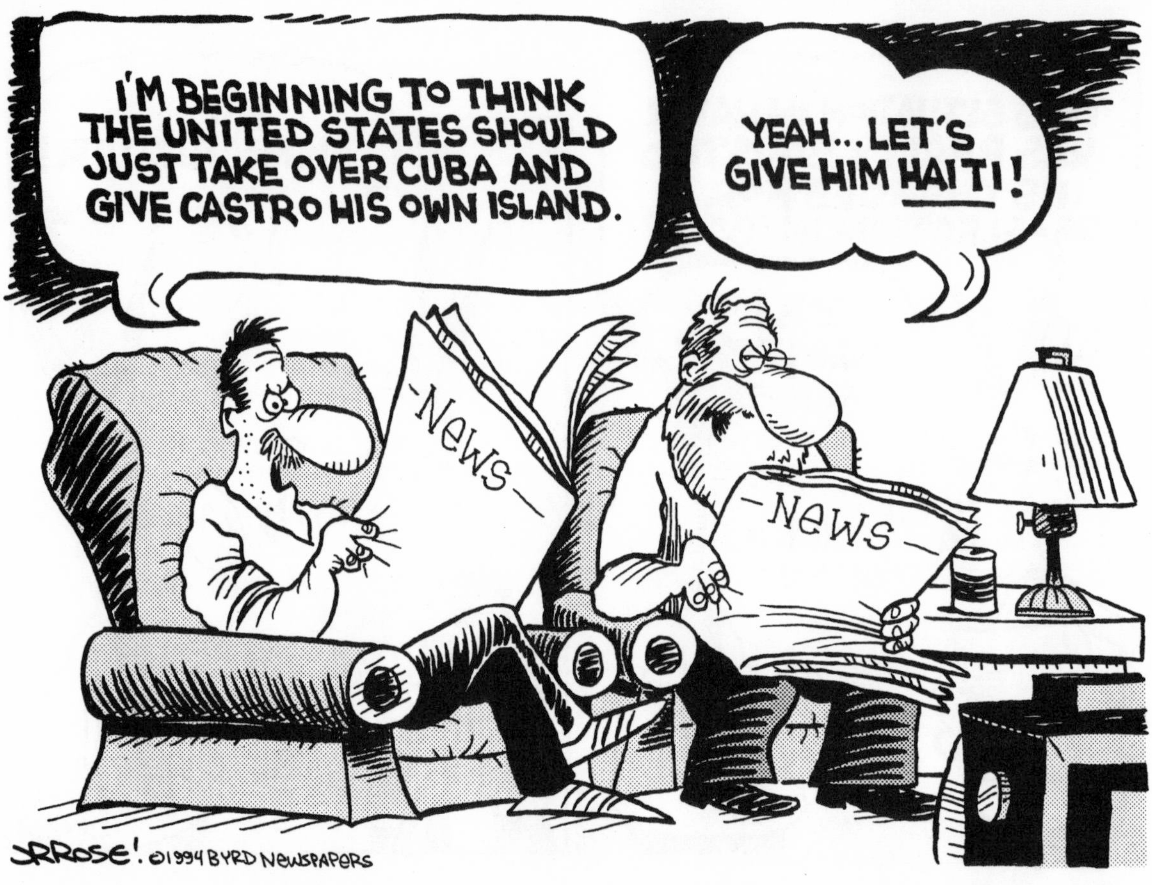
I'M BEGINNING TO THINK THE UNITED STATES SHOULD JUST TAKE OVER CUBA AND GIVE CASTRO HIS OWN ISLAND.
YEAH... LET'S GIVE HIM HAITI!
-News-
-News-
JRROSE! ©1994 BYRD NEWSPAPERS

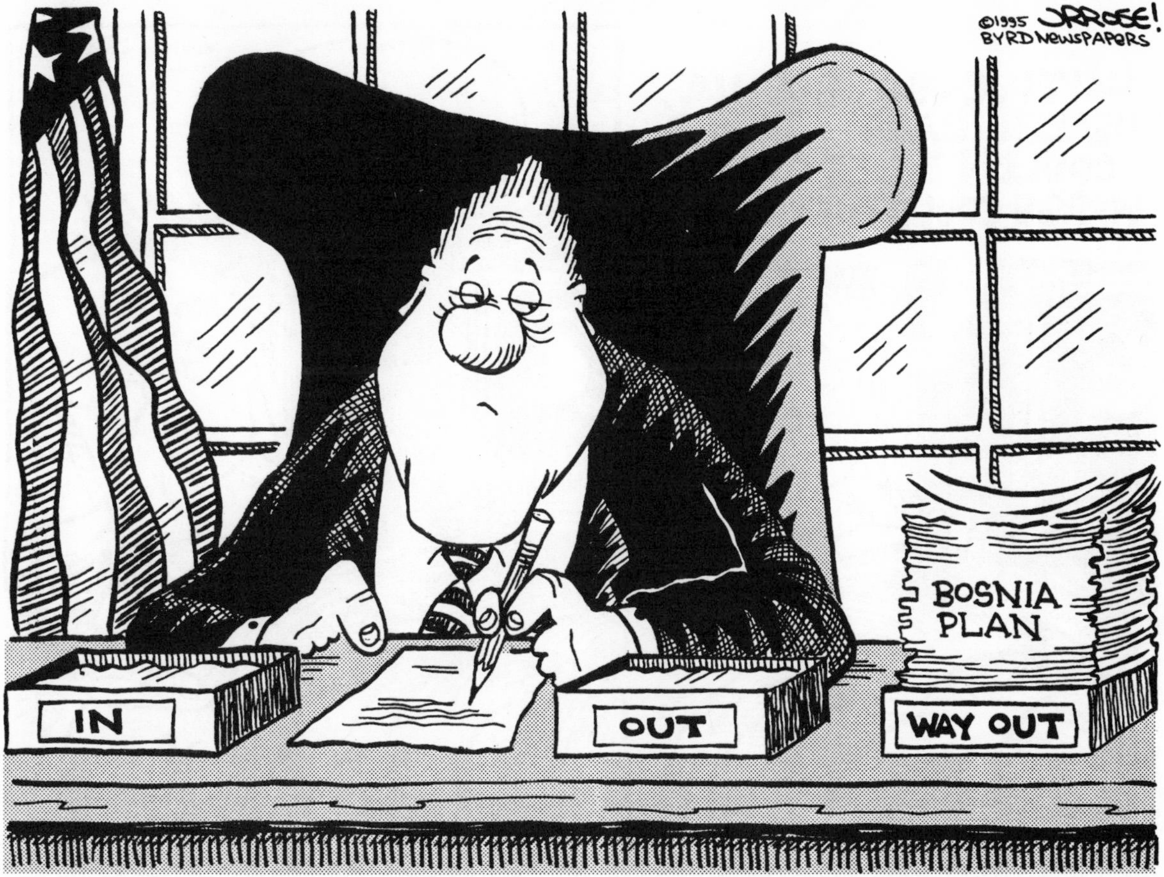
©1995 JRROSE!
BYRD NEWSPAPERS
BOSNIA PLAN
IN
OUT
WAY OUT

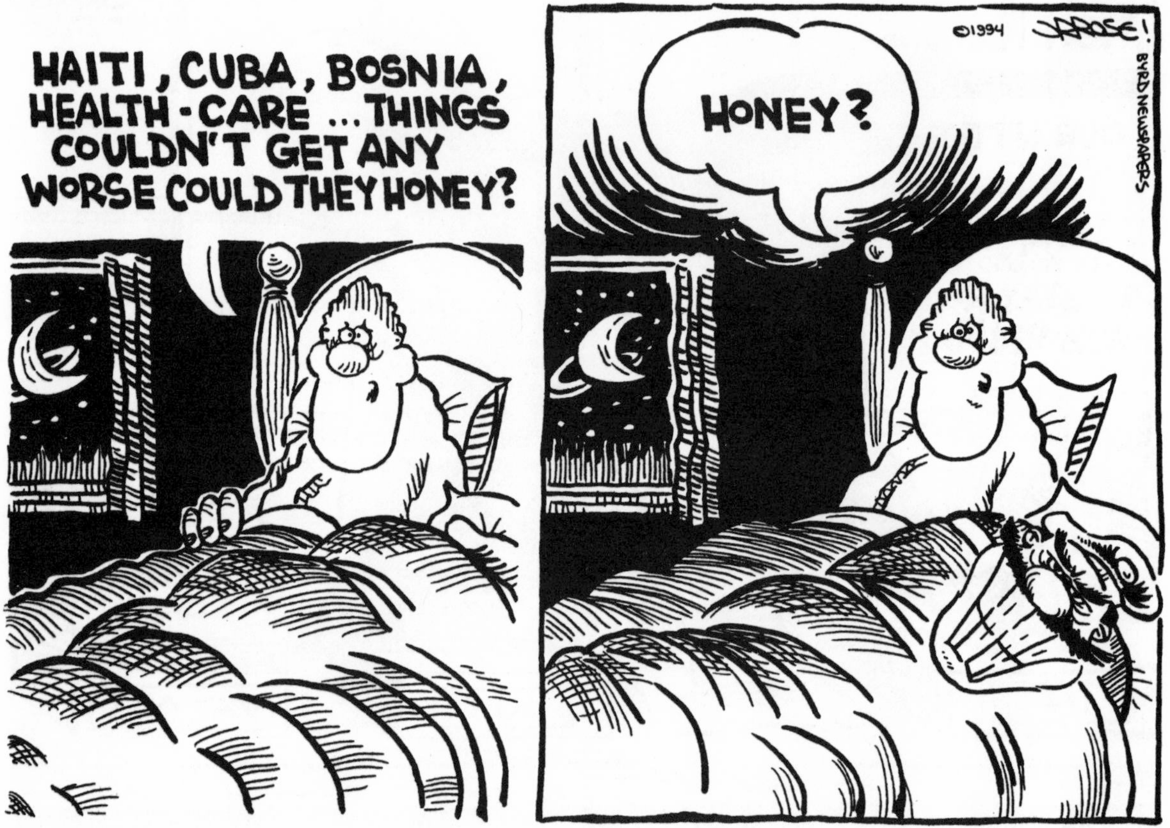
HAITI, CUBA, BOSNIA, HEALTH-CARE ... THINGS COULDN'T GET ANY WORSE COULD THEY HONEY?
HONEY?
©1994 JRROSE!
BYRD NEWSPAPERS

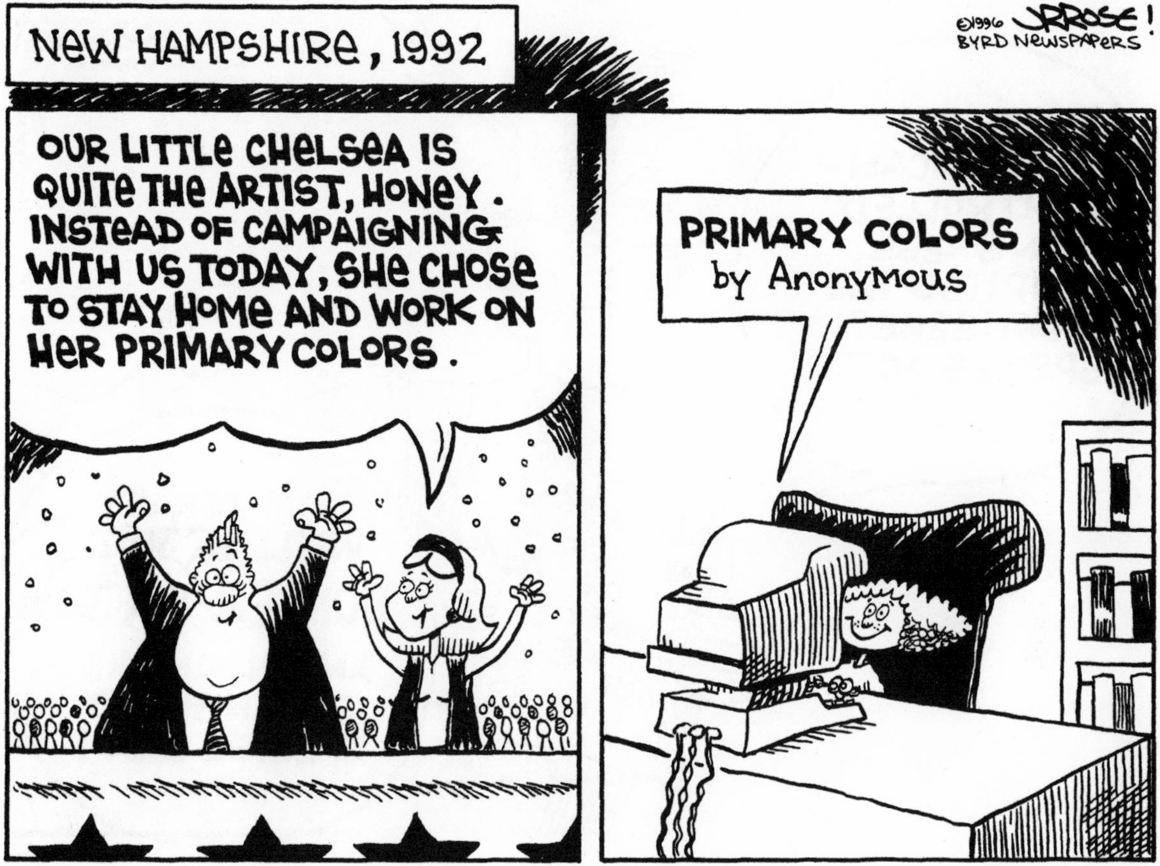
NEW HAMPSHIRE, 1992
©1996 JRROSE!
BYRD NEWSPAPERS
OUR LITTLE CHELSEA IS QUITE THE ARTIST, HONEY. INSTEAD OF CAMPAIGNING WITH US TODAY, SHE CHOSE TO STAY HOME AND WORK ON HER PRIMARY COLORS.
PRIMARY COLORS by Anonymous

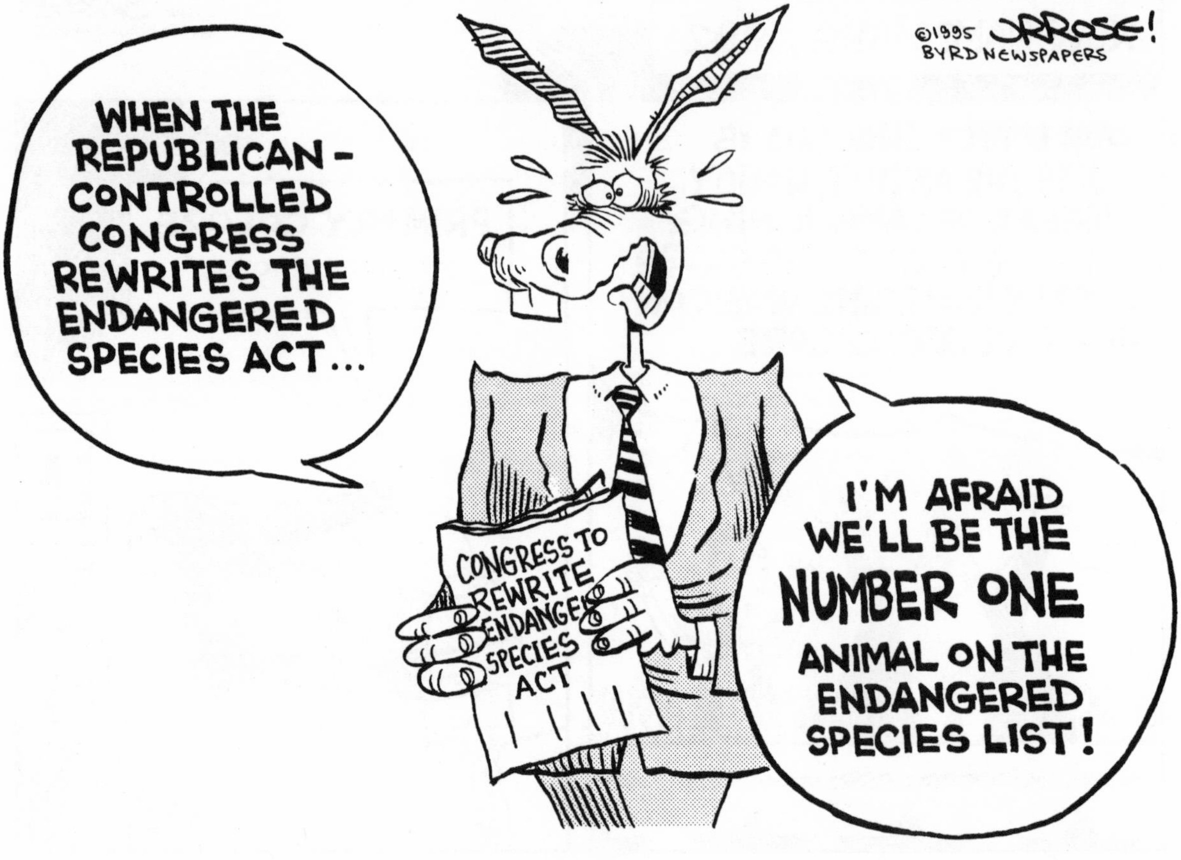
©1995 JRROSE!
BYRD NEWSPAPERS
WHEN THE REPUBLICAN-CONTROLLED CONGRESS REWRITES THE ENDANGERED SPECIES ACT...
CONGRESS TO REWRITE ENDANGE ENDANGE SPECIES ACT
I'M AFRAID WE'LL BE THE NUMBER ONE ANIMAL ON THE ENDANGERED SPECIES LIST!

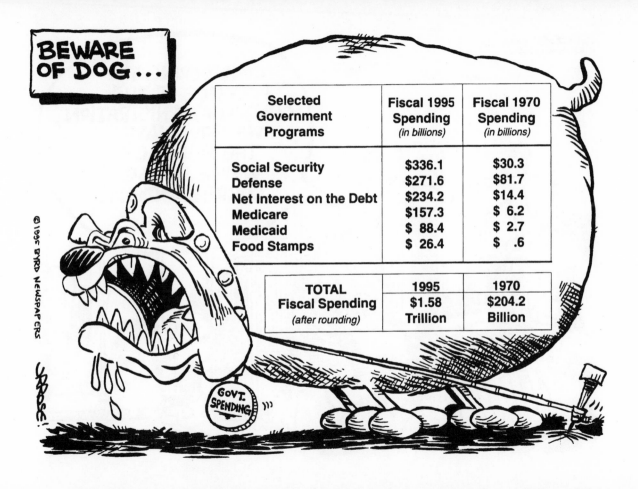

BEWARE OF DOG...

| Selected Government Programs | Fiscal 1995 Spending (in billions) | Fiscal 1970 Spending (in billions) |
|---|---|---|
| Social Security | $336.1 | $30.3 |
| Defense | $271.6 | $81.7 |
| Net Interest on the Debt | $234.2 | $14.4 |
| Medicare | $157.3 | $ 6.2 |
| Medicaid | $ 88.4 | $ 2.7 |
| Food Stamps | $ 26.4 | $ .6 |

| TOTAL Fiscal Spending (after rounding) | 1995 | 1970 |
|---|---|---|
| | $1.58 Trillion | $204.2 Billion |

© 1995 BYRD NEWSPAPERS

GOVT. SPENDING

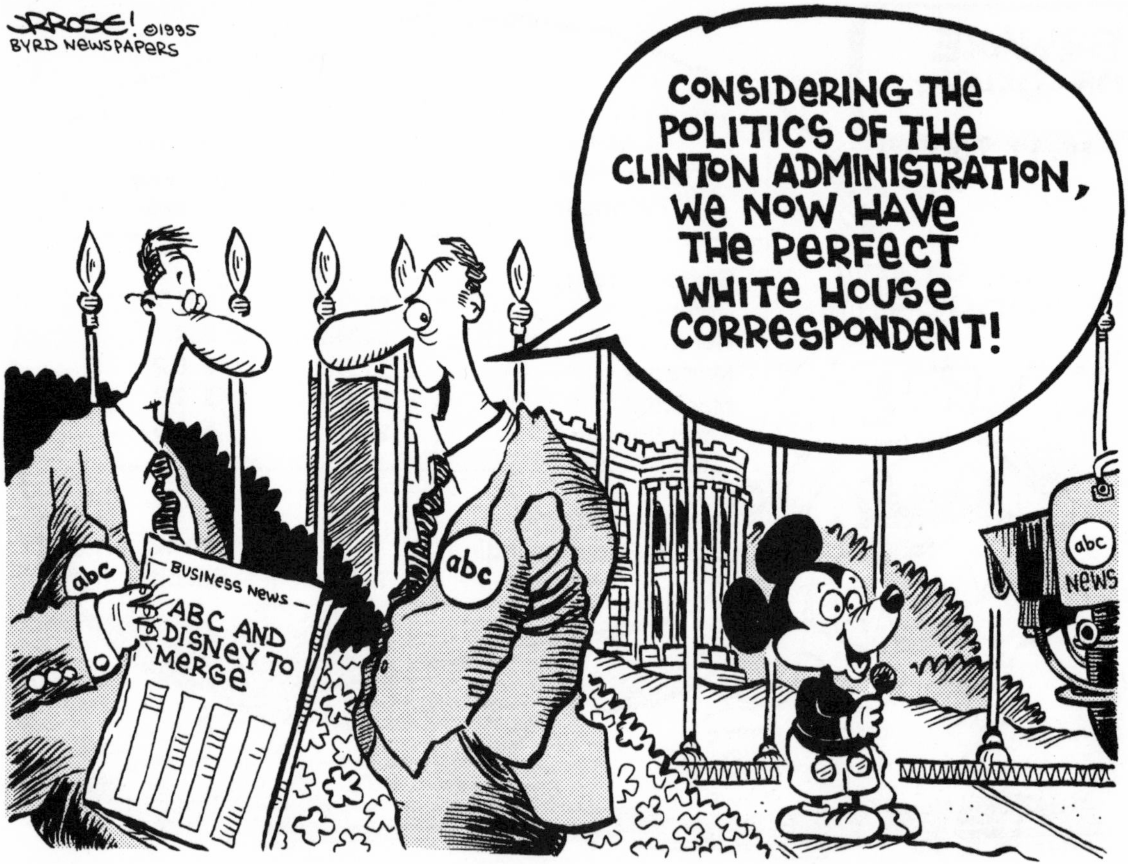
J.R.ROSE! ©1995
BYRD NEWSPAPERS
CONSIDERING THE POLITICS OF THE CLINTON ADMINISTRATION, WE NOW HAVE THE PERFECT WHITE HOUSE CORRESPONDENT!
abc
BUSINESS NEWS
ABC AND DISNEY TO MERGE
abc
abc
NEWS

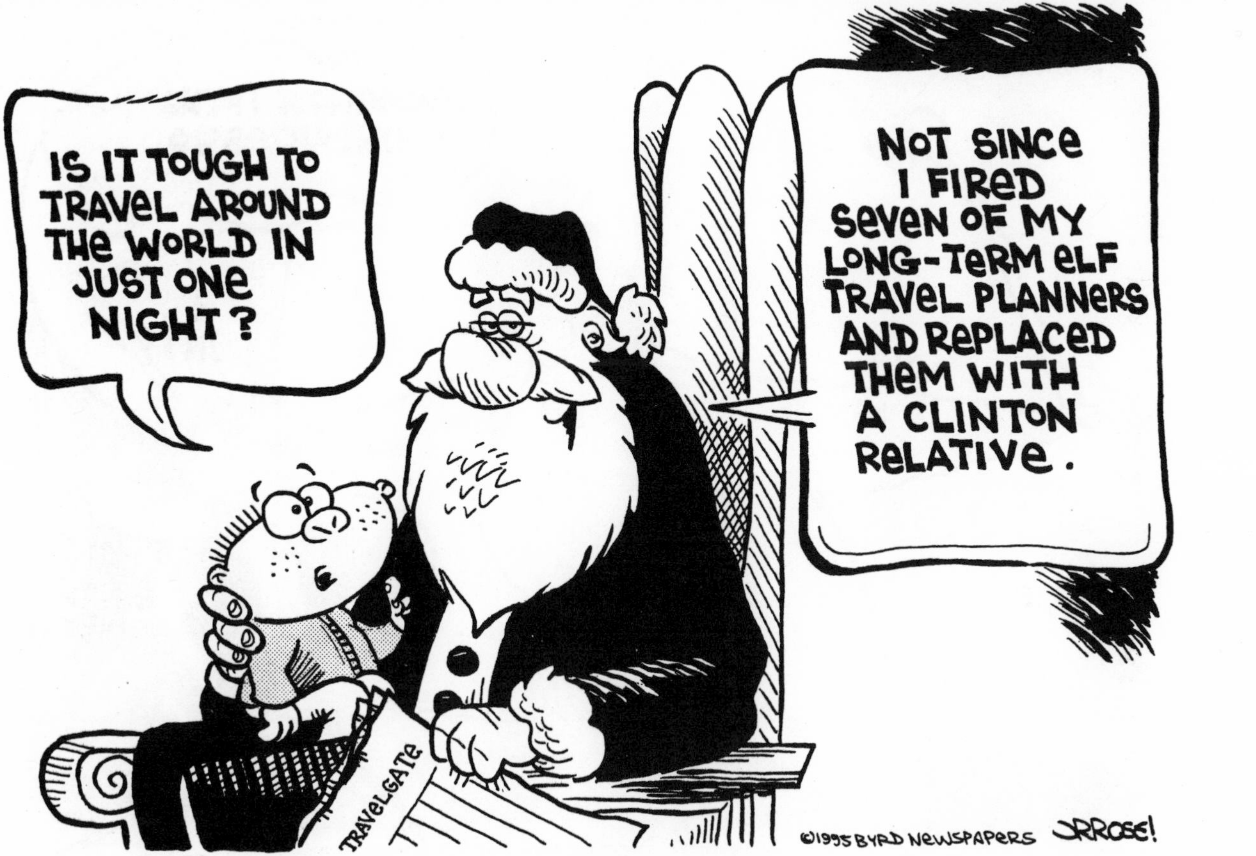

IS IT TOUGH TO TRAVEL AROUND THE WORLD IN JUST ONE NIGHT?
NOT SINCE I FIRED SEVEN OF MY LONG-TERM ELF TRAVEL PLANNERS AND REPLACED THEM WITH A CLINTON RELATIVE.
TRAVELGATE
©1995 BYRD NEWSPAPERS
JRROSE!

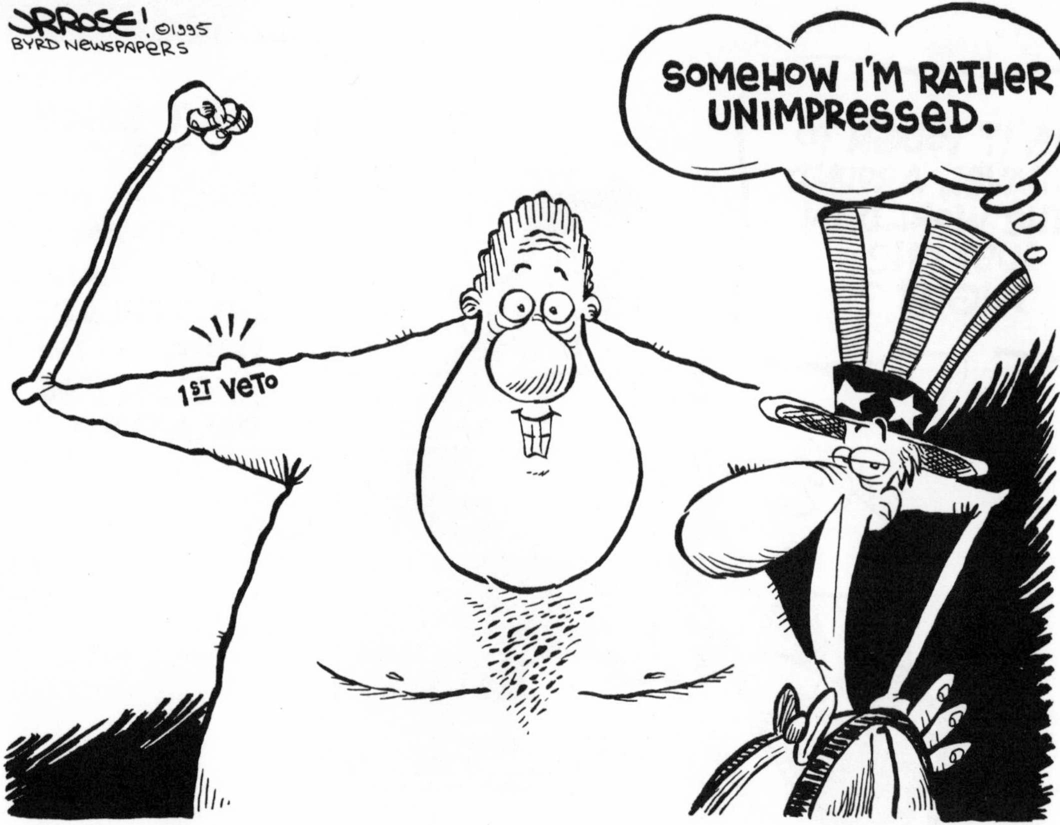
JRROSE! ©1995
BYRD NEWSPAPERS
SOMEHOW I'M RATHER UNIMPRESSED.
1ST VETO

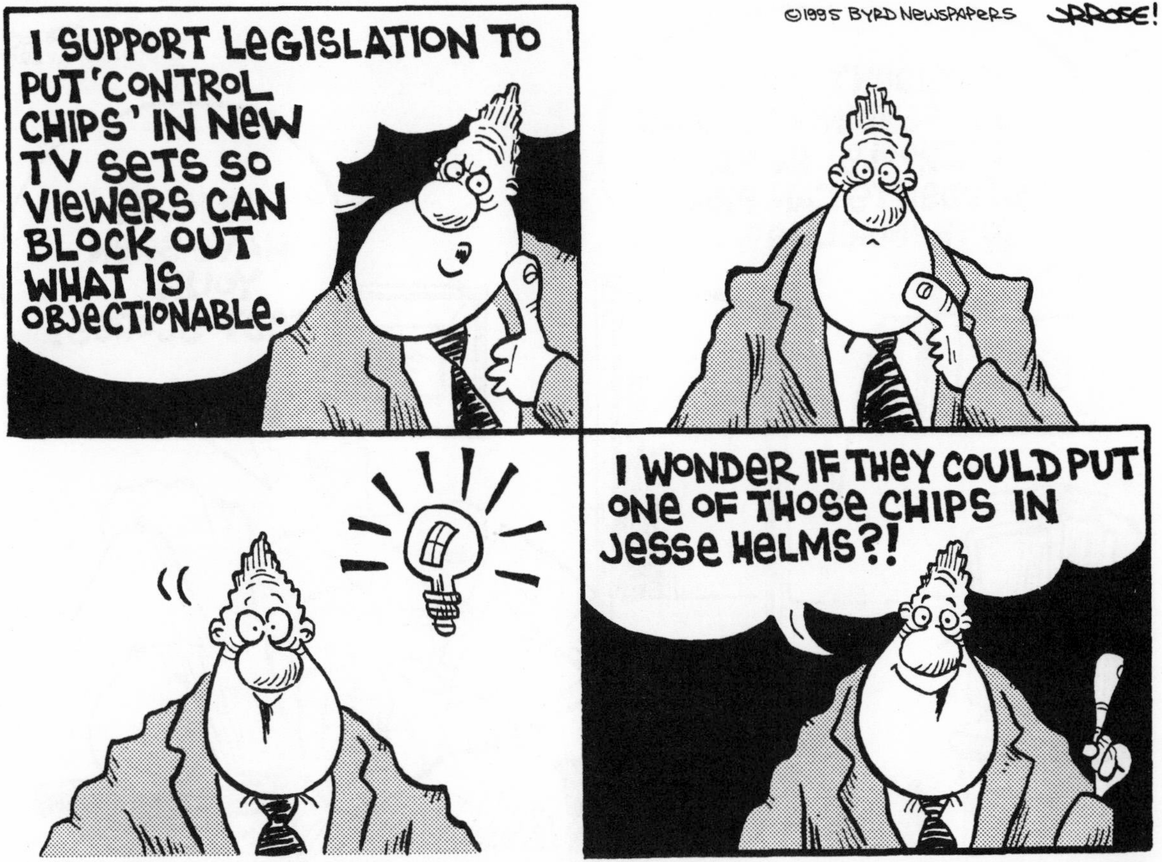
©1995 BYRD NEWSPAPERS
JRROSE!
I SUPPORT LEGISLATION TO PUT 'CONTROL CHIPS' IN NEW TV SETS SO VIEWERS CAN BLOCK OUT WHAT IS OBJECTIONABLE.
I WONDER IF THEY COULD PUT ONE OF THOSE CHIPS IN JESSE HELMS?!

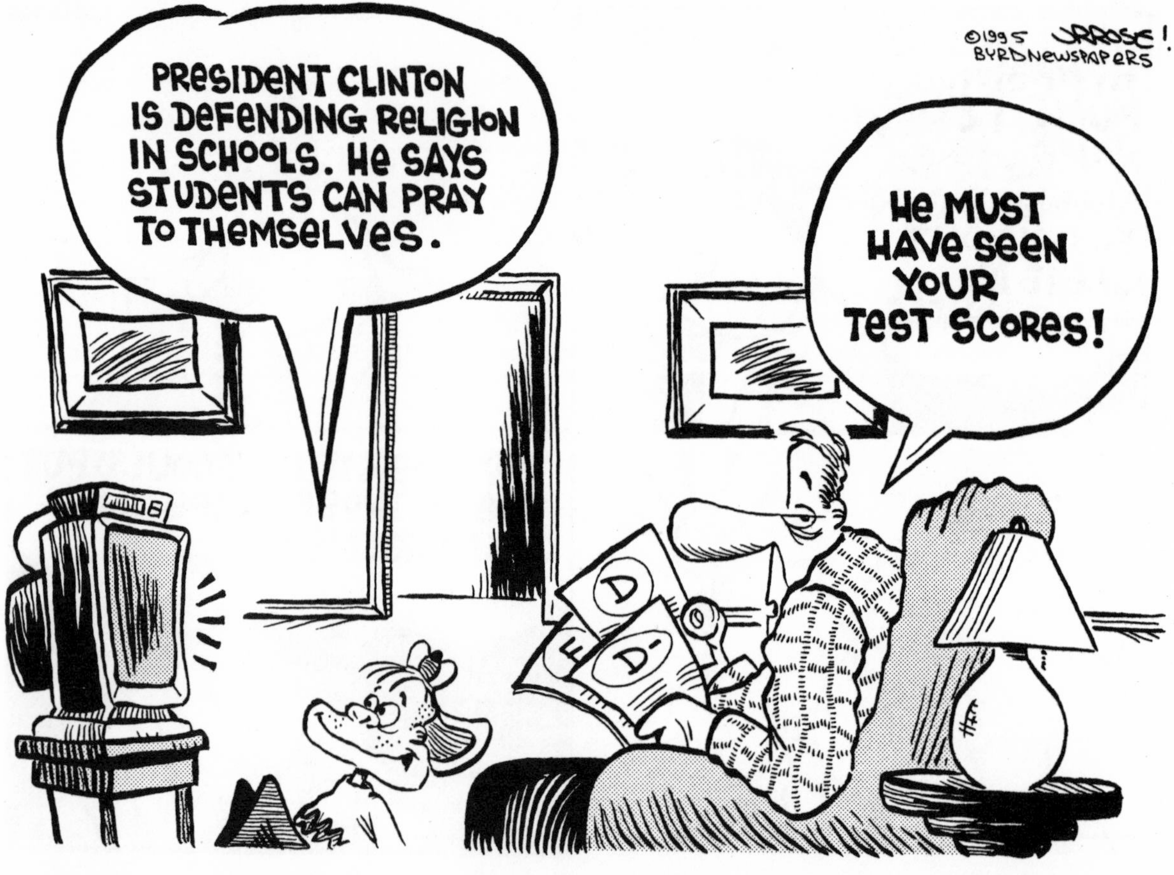
©1995 JRROSE!
BYRDNEWSPAPERS
PRESIDENT CLINTON IS DEFENDING RELIGION IN SCHOOLS. HE SAYS STUDENTS CAN PRAY TO THEMSELVES.
HE MUST HAVE SEEN YOUR TEST SCORES!
D
F
D-

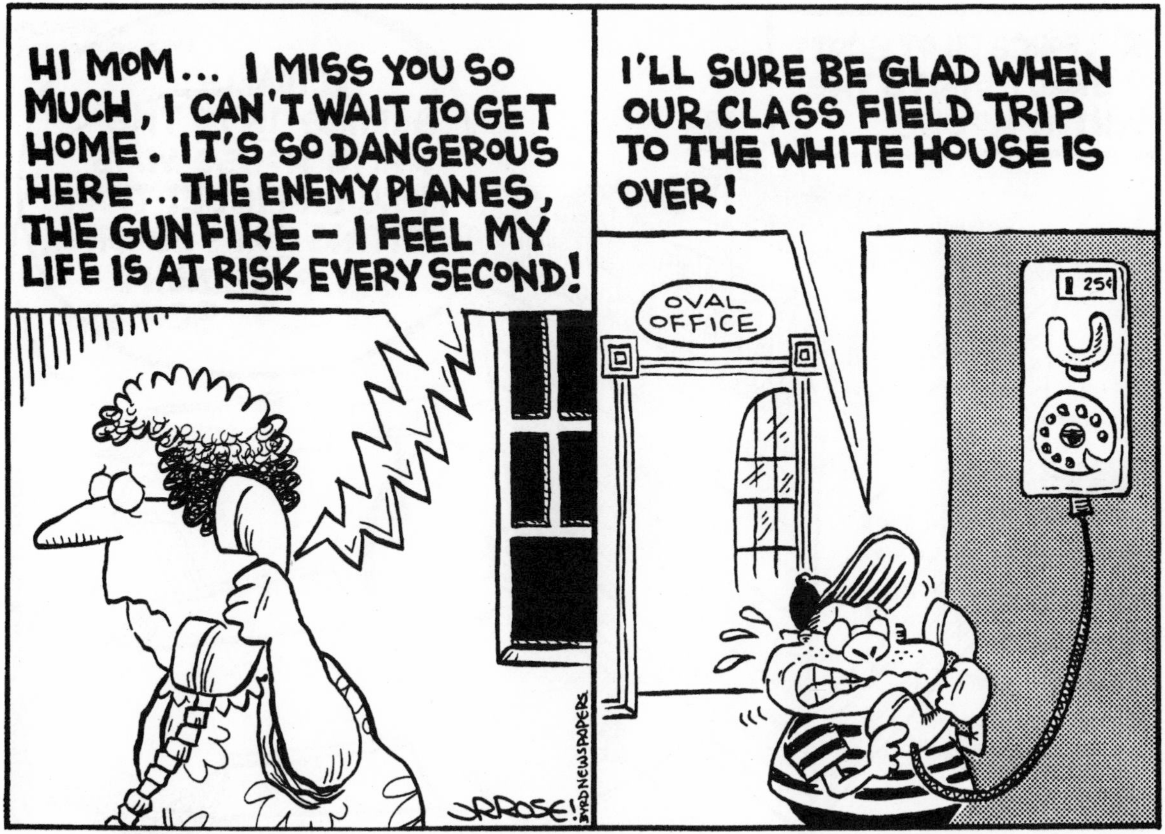
HI MOM... I MISS YOU SO MUCH, I CAN'T WAIT TO GET HOME. IT'S SO DANGEROUS HERE ... THE ENEMY PLANES, THE GUNFIRE – I FEEL MY LIFE IS AT RISK EVERY SECOND!
JRROSE!
BYRD NEWSPAPERS
I'LL SURE BE GLAD WHEN OUR CLASS FIELD TRIP TO THE WHITE HOUSE IS OVER!
OVAL OFFICE
25¢

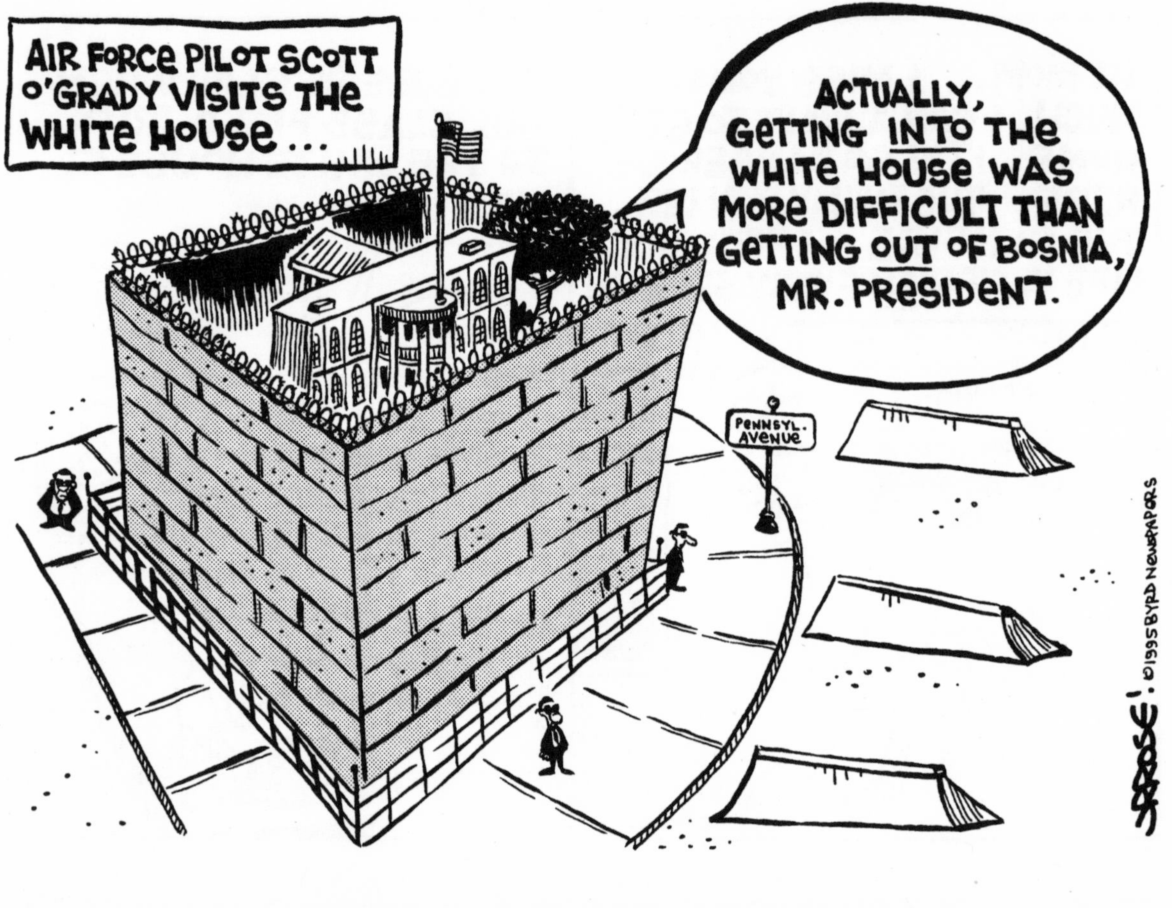
AIR FORCE PILOT SCOTT O'GRADY VISITS THE WHITE HOUSE...
ACTUALLY, GETTING INTO THE WHITE HOUSE WAS MORE DIFFICULT THAN GETTING OUT OF BOSNIA, MR. PRESIDENT.
PENNSYL. AVENUE
©1995 BYRD NEWSPAPERS

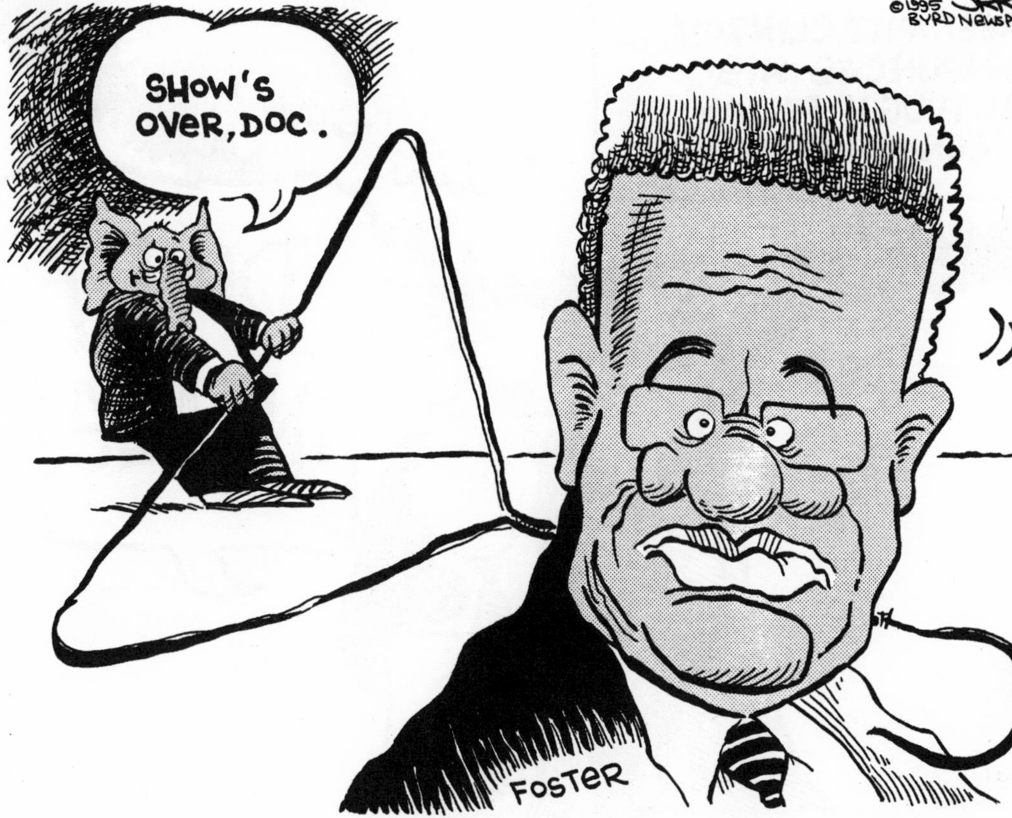
SHOW'S OVER, DOC.
©1995 JRROSE! BYRD NEWSPAPERS
FOSTER

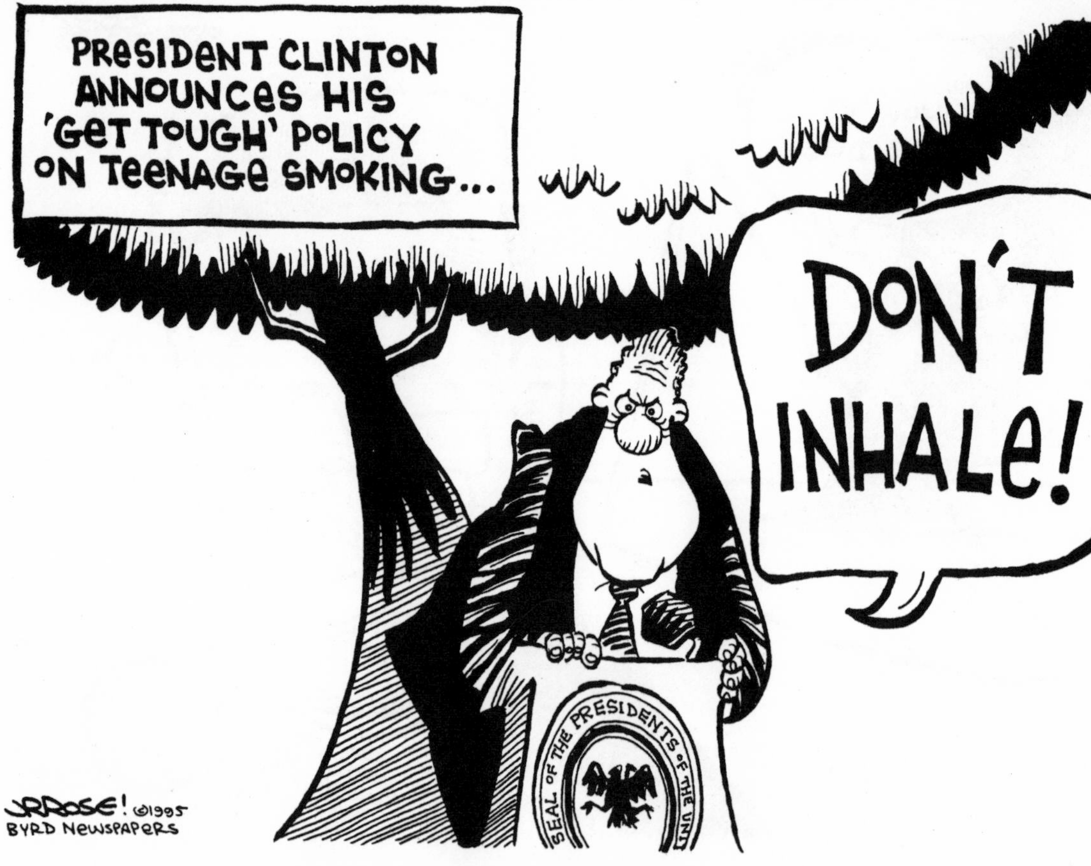
PRESIDENT CLINTON ANNOUNCES HIS 'GET TOUGH' POLICY ON TEENAGE SMOKING...
DON'T INHALE!
SEAL OF THE PRESIDENTS OF THE UNI
JRROSE! ©1995
BYRD NEWSPAPERS

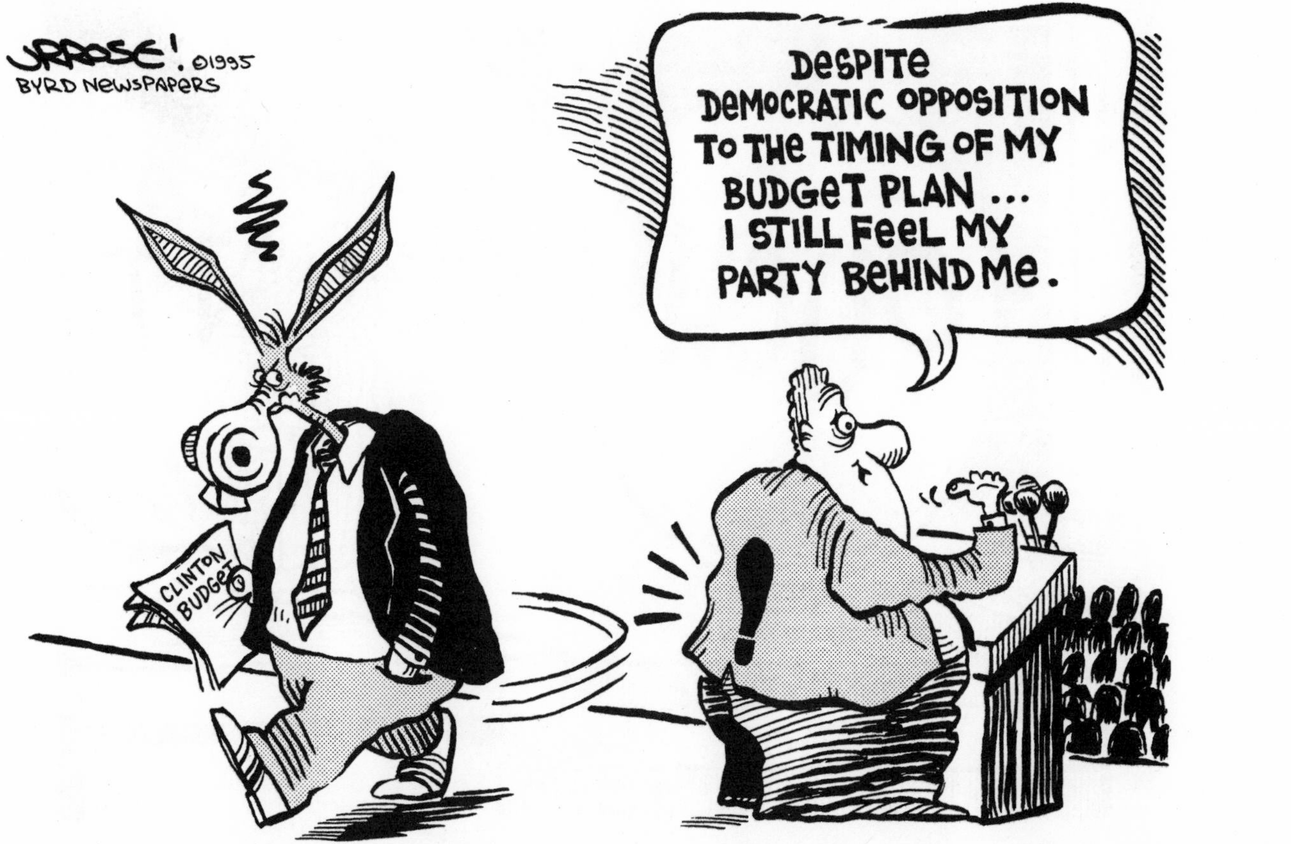
JRROSE! ©1995
BYRD NEWSPAPERS
DESPITE DEMOCRATIC OPPOSITION TO THE TIMING OF MY BUDGET PLAN ... I STILL FEEL MY PARTY BEHIND ME.
CLINTON BUDGET

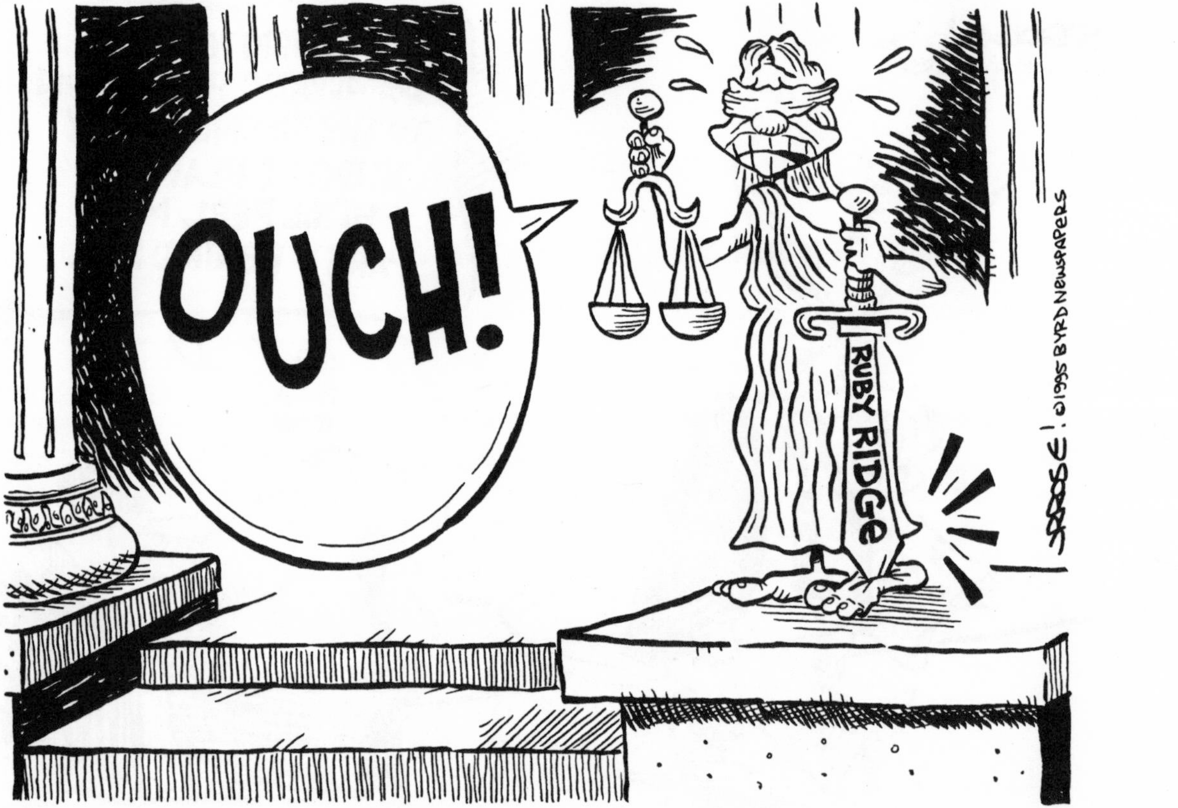

OUCH!
RUBY RIDGE
SARGE!
©1995 BYRD NEWSPAPERS

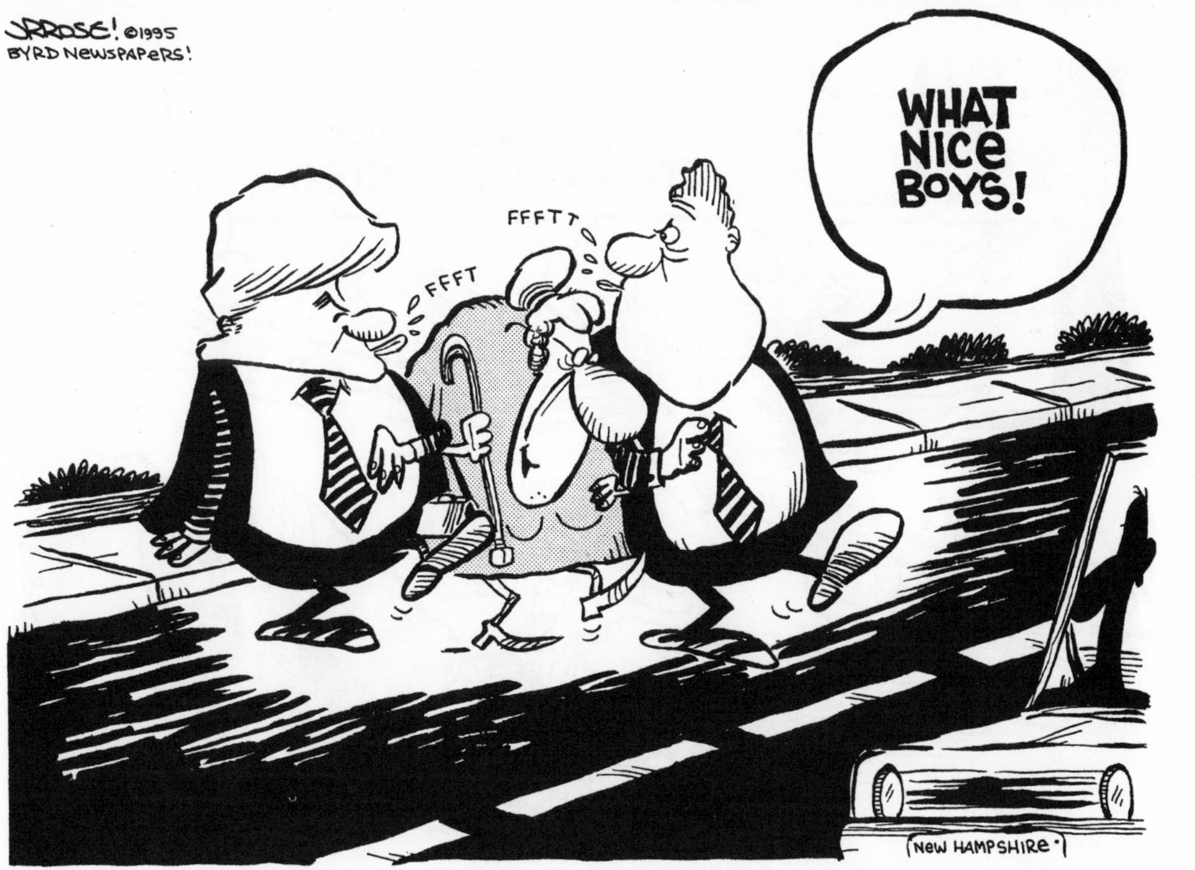

JRROSE! ©1995
BYRD NEWSPAPERS!
WHAT NICE BOYS!
FFFT
FFFTT
NEW HAMPSHIRE

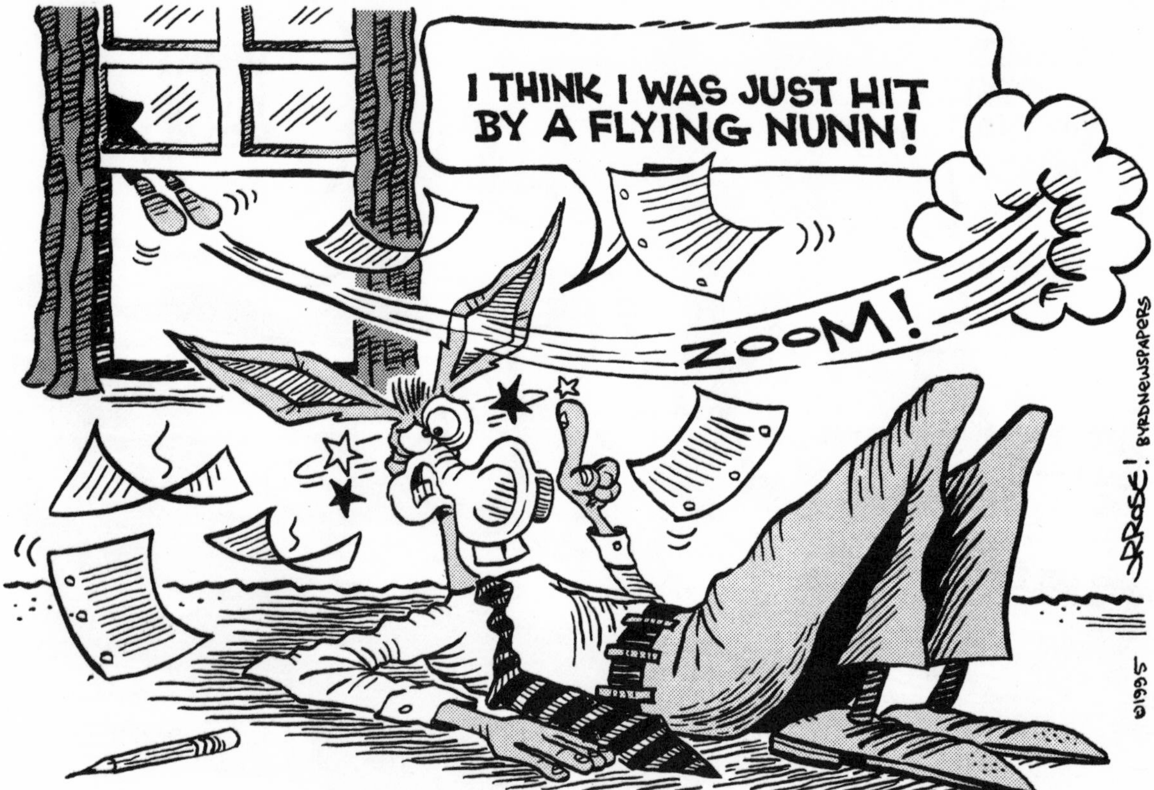
I THINK I WAS JUST HIT BY A FLYING NUNN!
ZOOM!
©1995
BYRDNEWSPAPERS

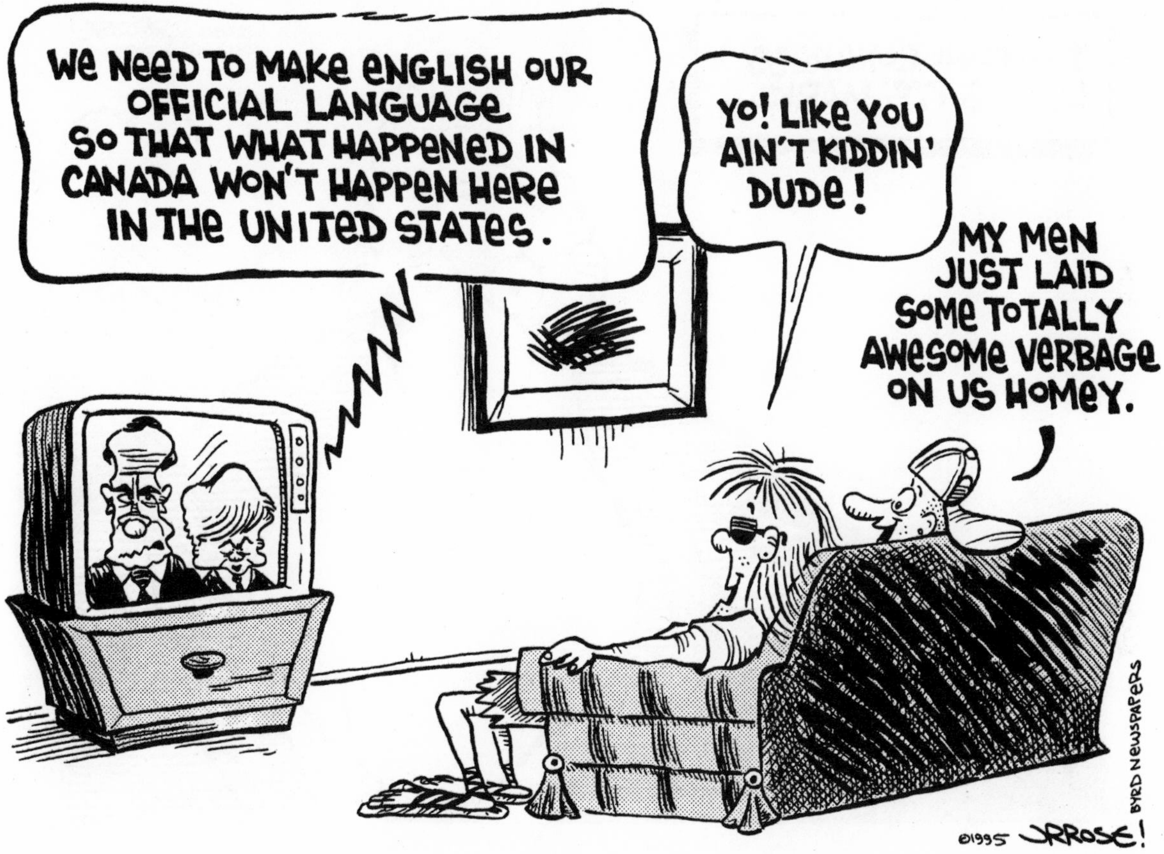
WE NEED TO MAKE ENGLISH OUR OFFICIAL LANGUAGE SO THAT WHAT HAPPENED IN CANADA WON'T HAPPEN HERE IN THE UNITED STATES.
YO! LIKE YOU AIN'T KIDDIN' DUDE!
MY MEN JUST LAID SOME TOTALLY AWESOME VERBAGE ON US HOMEY.
BYRD NEWSPAPERS
©1995 JRROSE!

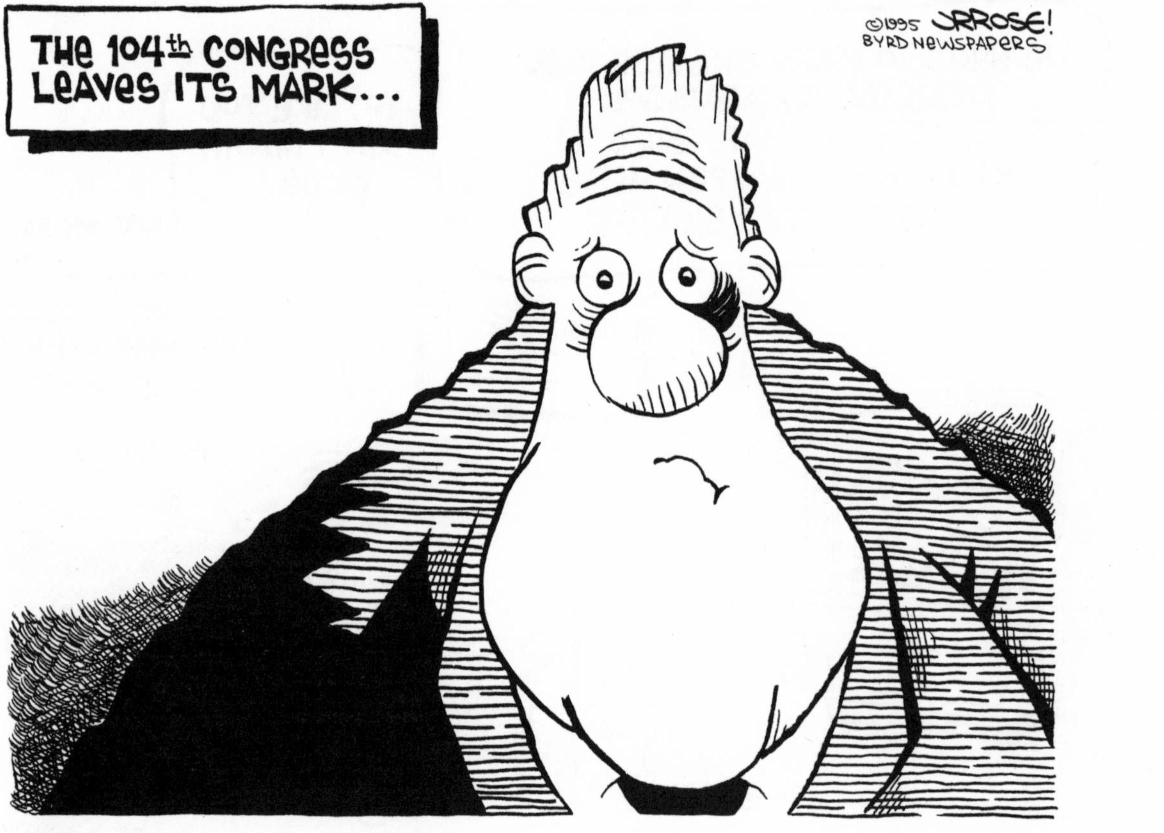
THE 104th CONGRESS LEAVES ITS MARK....
©1995 JRROSE!
BYRD NEWSPAPERS

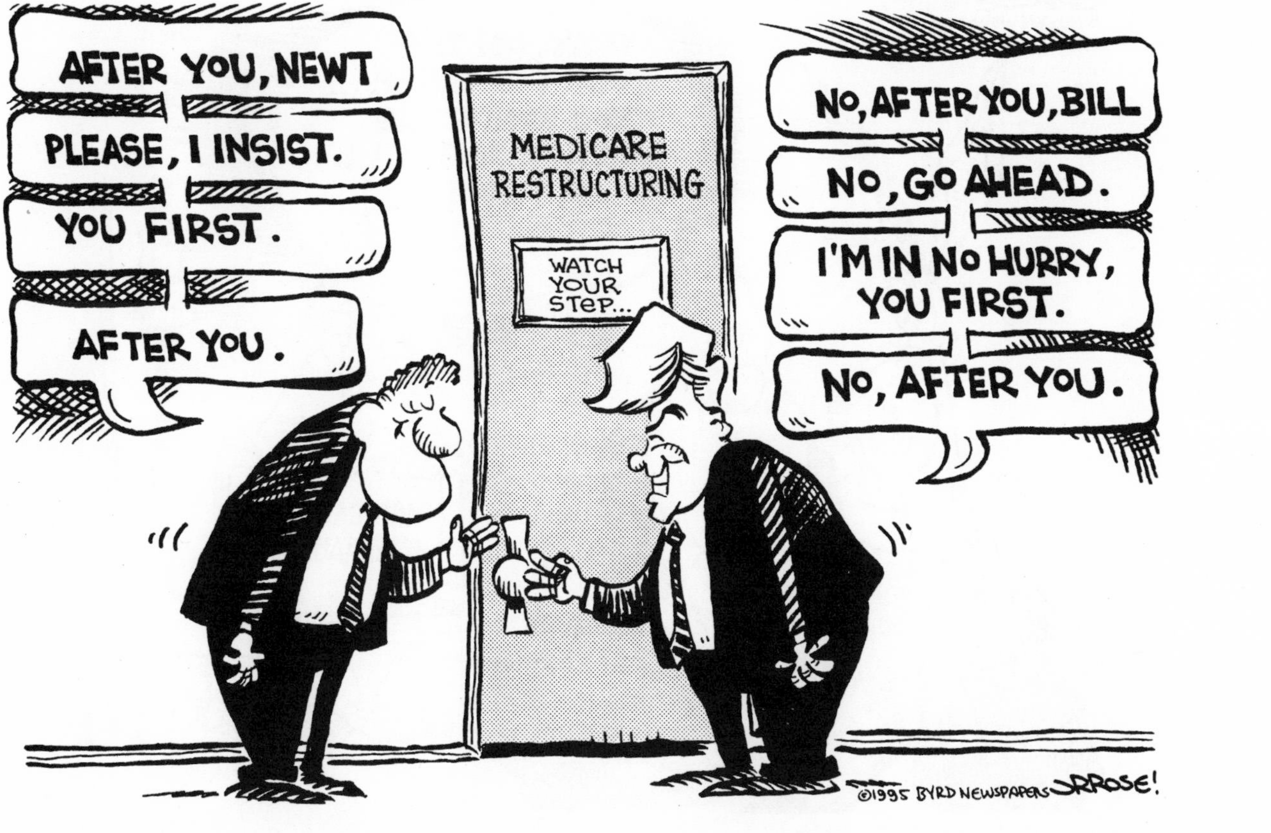
AFTER YOU, NEWT
PLEASE, I INSIST.
YOU FIRST.
AFTER YOU.
NO, AFTER YOU, BILL
NO, GO AHEAD.
I'M IN NO HURRY, YOU FIRST.
NO, AFTER YOU.
MEDICARE RESTRUCTURING
WATCH YOUR STEP...
©1995 BYRD NEWSPAPERS JRROSE!

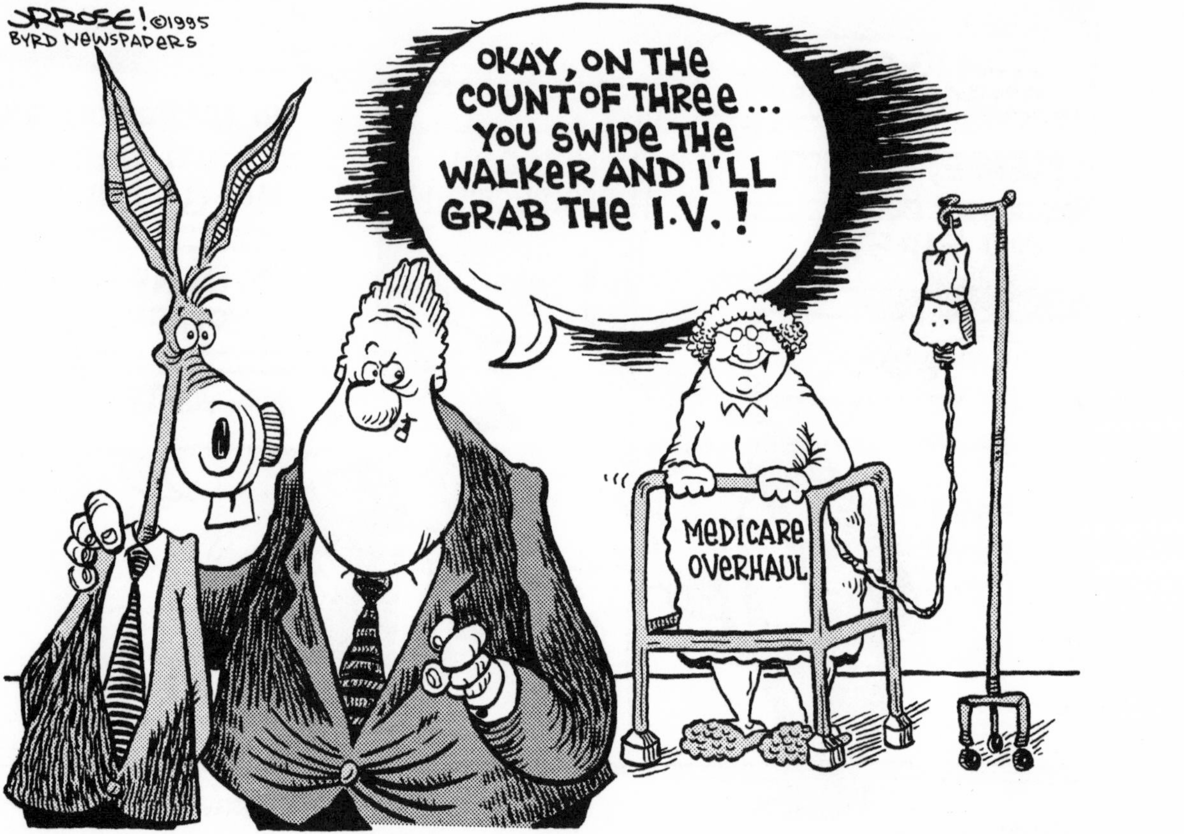
JRROSE! ©1995
BYRD NEWSPAPERS
OKAY, ON THE COUNT OF THREE ... YOU SWIPE THE WALKER AND I'LL GRAB THE I.V. !
MEDICARE OVERHAUL

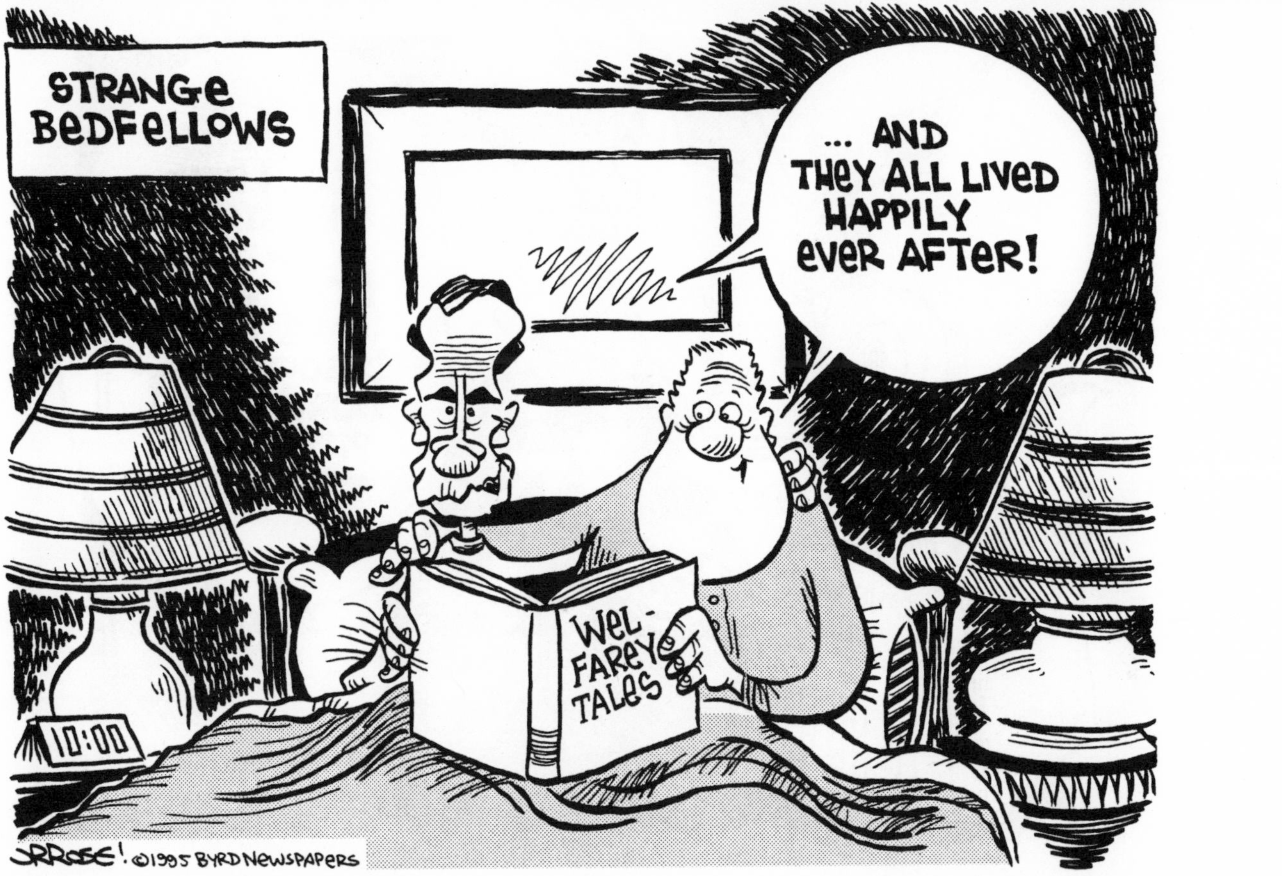
STRANGE BEDFELLOWS
... AND THEY ALL LIVED HAPPILY EVER AFTER!
WEL-FAREY TALES
10:00
JRROSE! ©1995 BYRD NEWSPAPERS

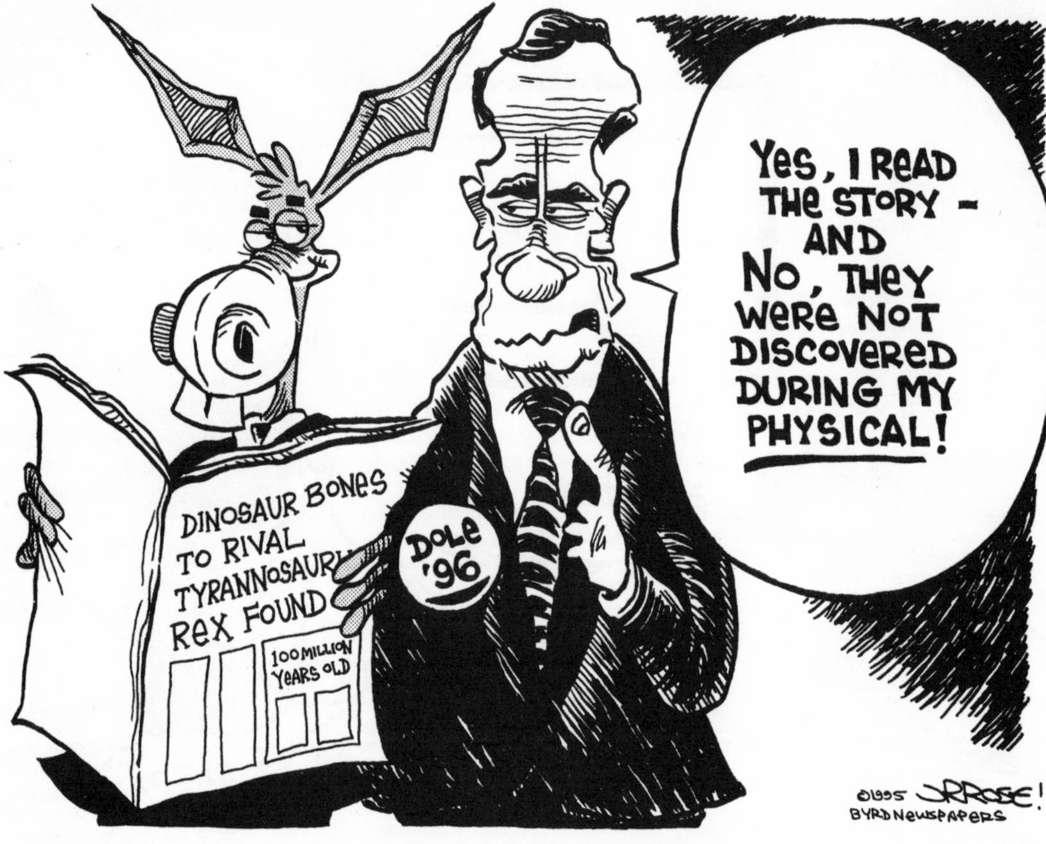
DINOSAUR BONES TO RIVAL TYRANNOSAURU REX FOUND
100 MILLION YEARS OLD
DOLE '96
YES, I READ THE STORY - AND NO, THEY WERE NOT DISCOVERED DURING MY PHYSICAL!
©1995 JRROSE!
BYRD NEWSPAPERS

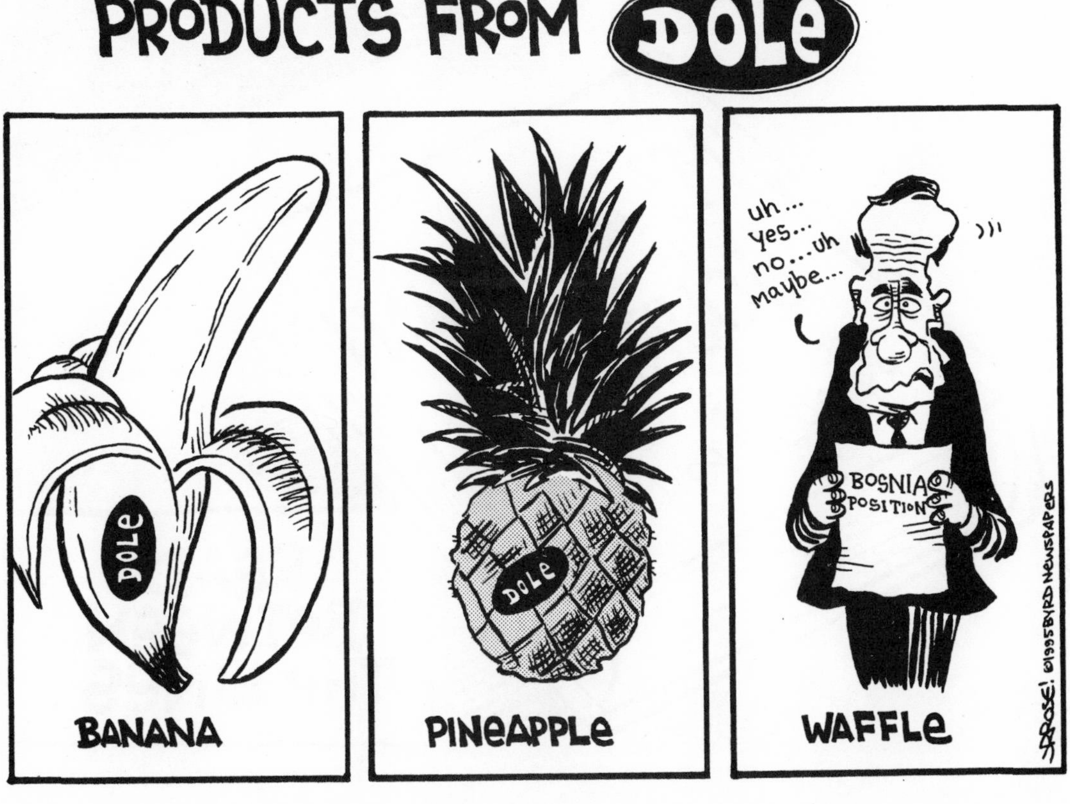
PRODUCTS FROM DOLE
DOLE
BANANA
DOLE
PINEAPPLE
uh... yes... no....uh maybe...
BOSNIA POSITION
WAFFLE
SDROSE! ©1995 BYRD NEWSPAPERS

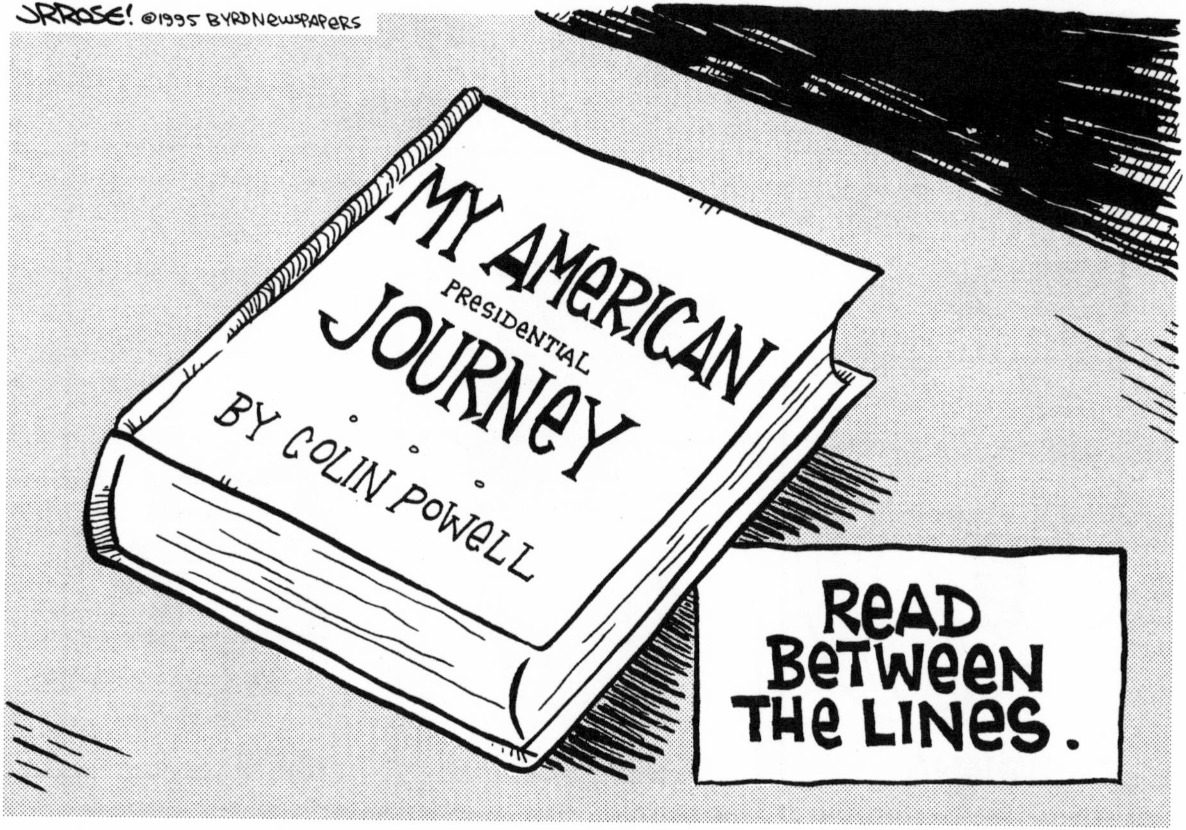
JRROSE! ©1995 BYRD NEWSPAPERS
MY AMERICAN
PRESIDENTIAL
JOURNEY
BY COLIN POWELL
READ BETWEEN THE LINES.

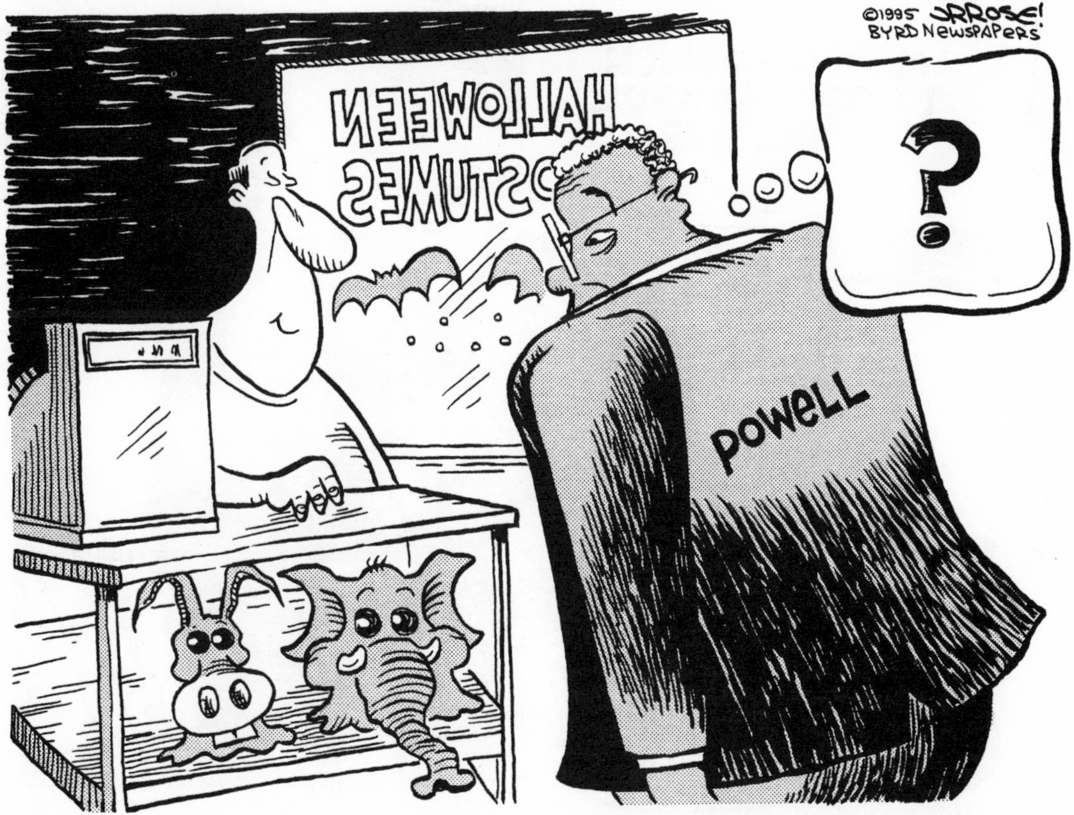
©1995 JRROSE!
BYRD NewsPAPers
HALLOWEEN
OSTUMES
?
POWELL

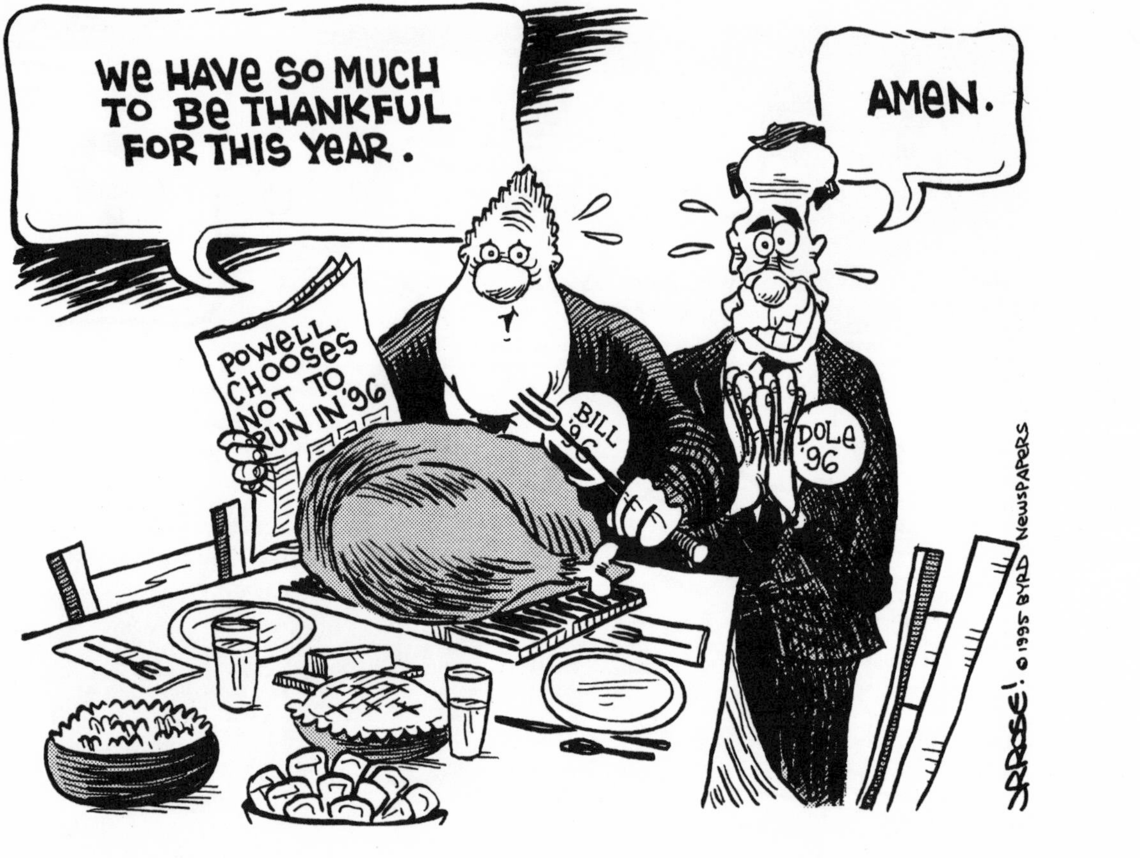
WE HAVE SO MUCH TO BE THANKFUL FOR THIS YEAR.
AMEN.
POWELL CHOOSES NOT TO RUN IN '96
BILL '96
DOLE '96
© 1995 BYRD NEWSPAPERS

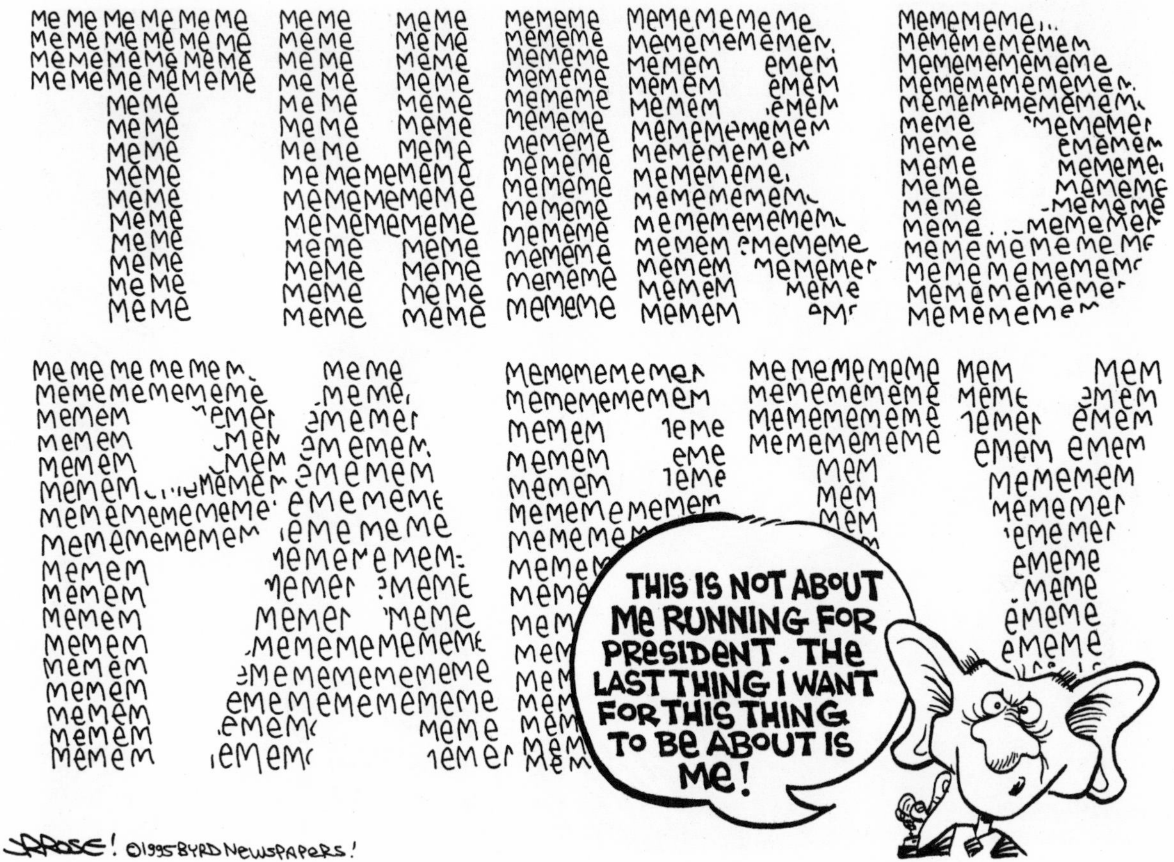
THIRD PARTY
THIS IS NOT ABOUT ME RUNNING FOR PRESIDENT. THE LAST THING I WANT FOR THIS THING TO BE ABOUT IS ME!
J.ROSE! ©1995 BYRD NEWSPAPERS!

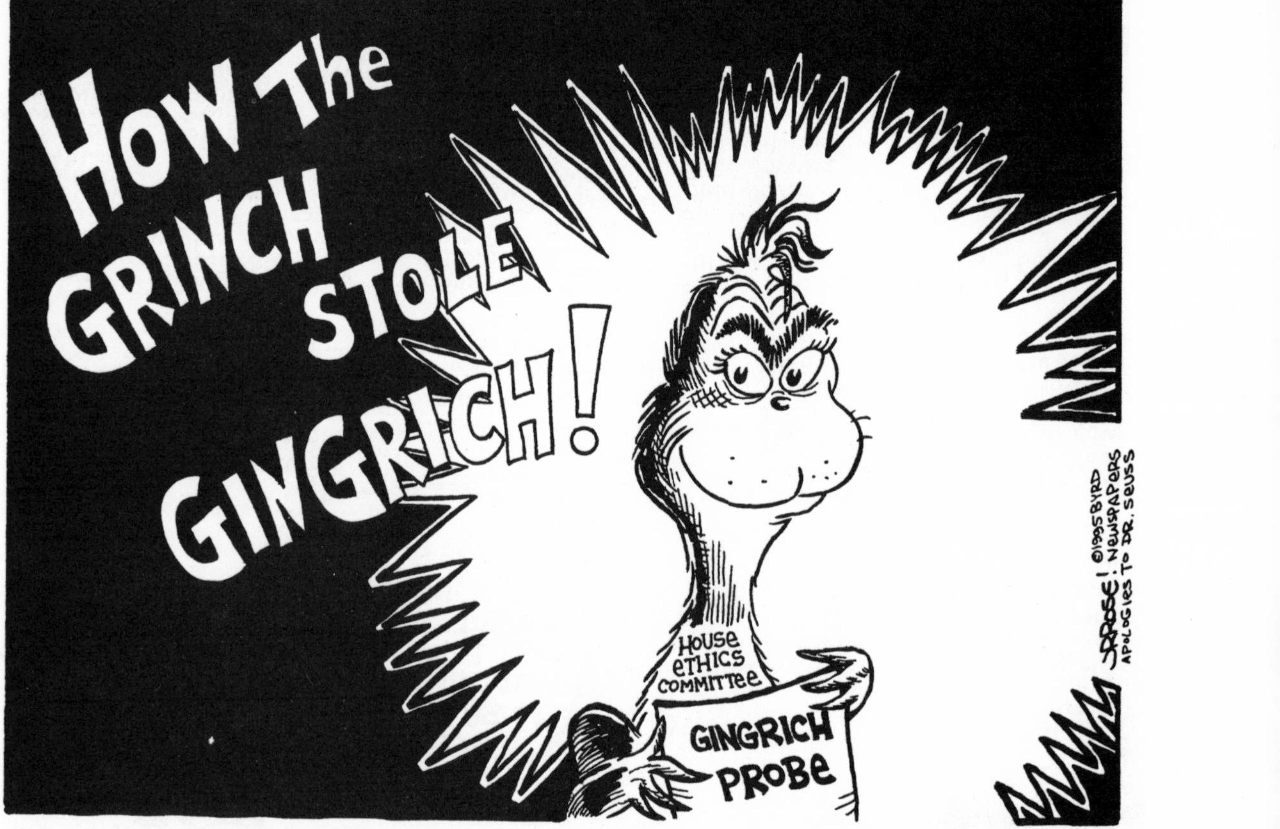

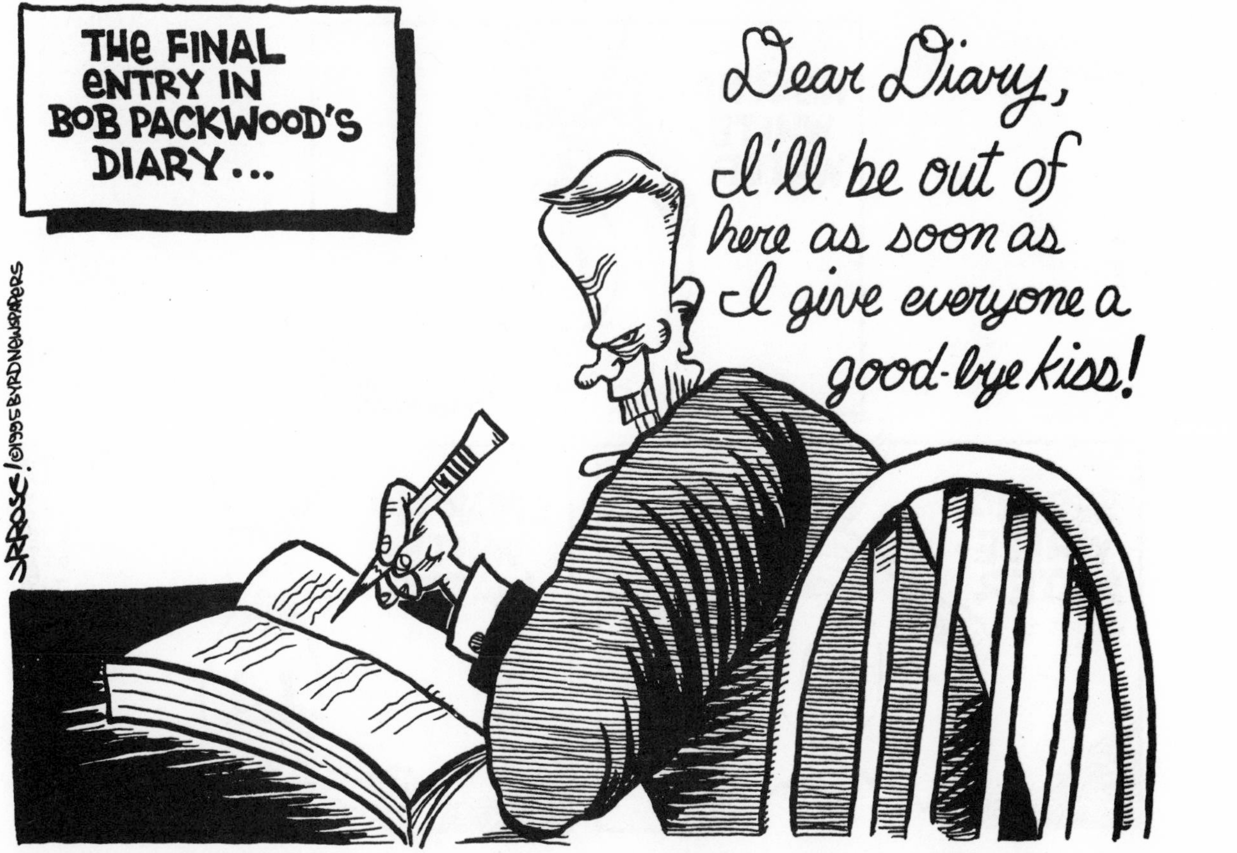
THE FINAL ENTRY IN BOB PACKWOOD'S DIARY...
Dear Diary, I'll be out of here as soon as I give everyone a good-bye kiss!
©1995 BYRD NEWSPAPERS

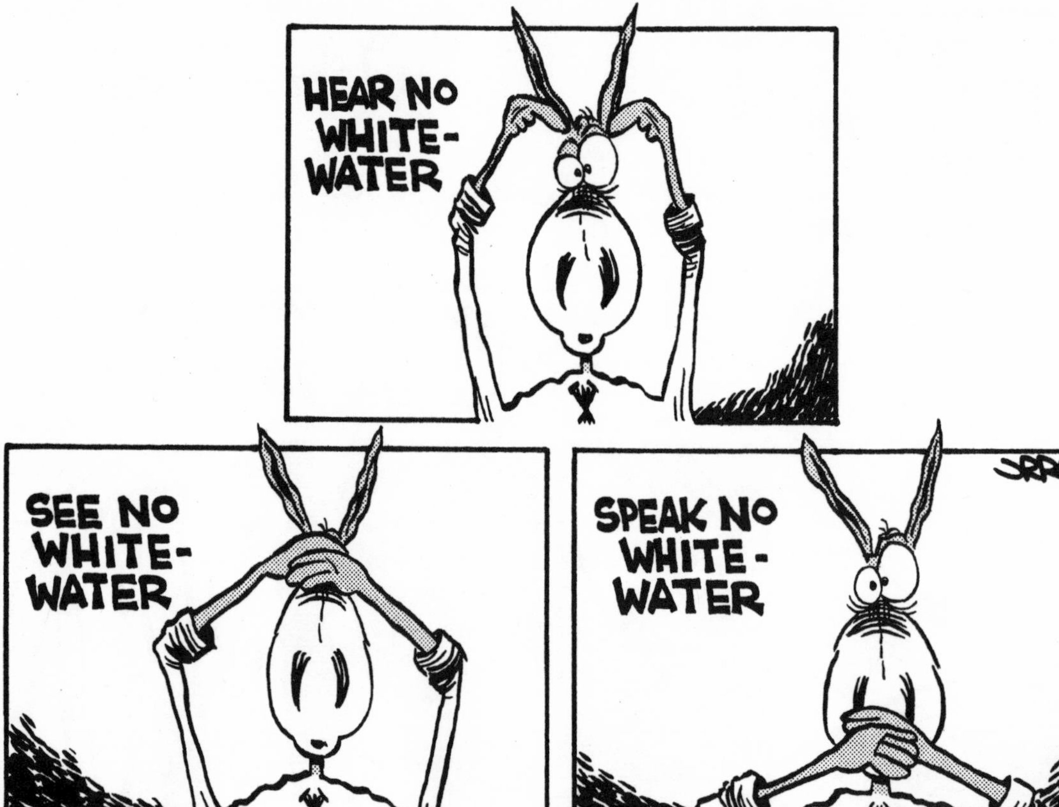
HEAR NO WHITE-WATER
SEE NO WHITE-WATER
SPEAK NO WHITE-WATER
JRROSE!
© 1994 BYRD NEWSPAPERS

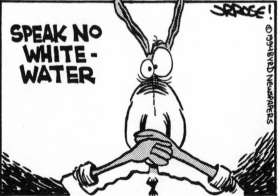

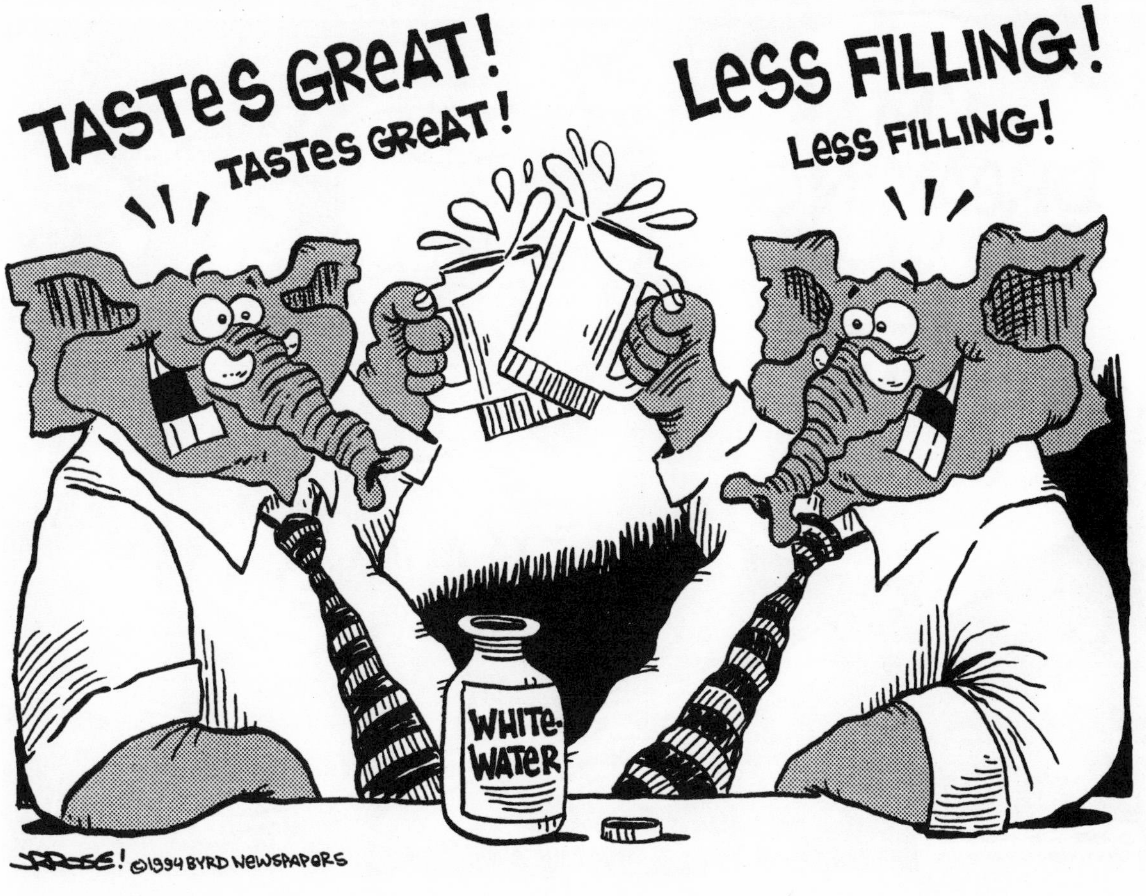
TASTES GREAT!
TASTES GREAT!
LESS FILLING!
LESS FILLING!
WHITE-WATER
JRROSE!
©1994 BYRD NEWSPAPERS

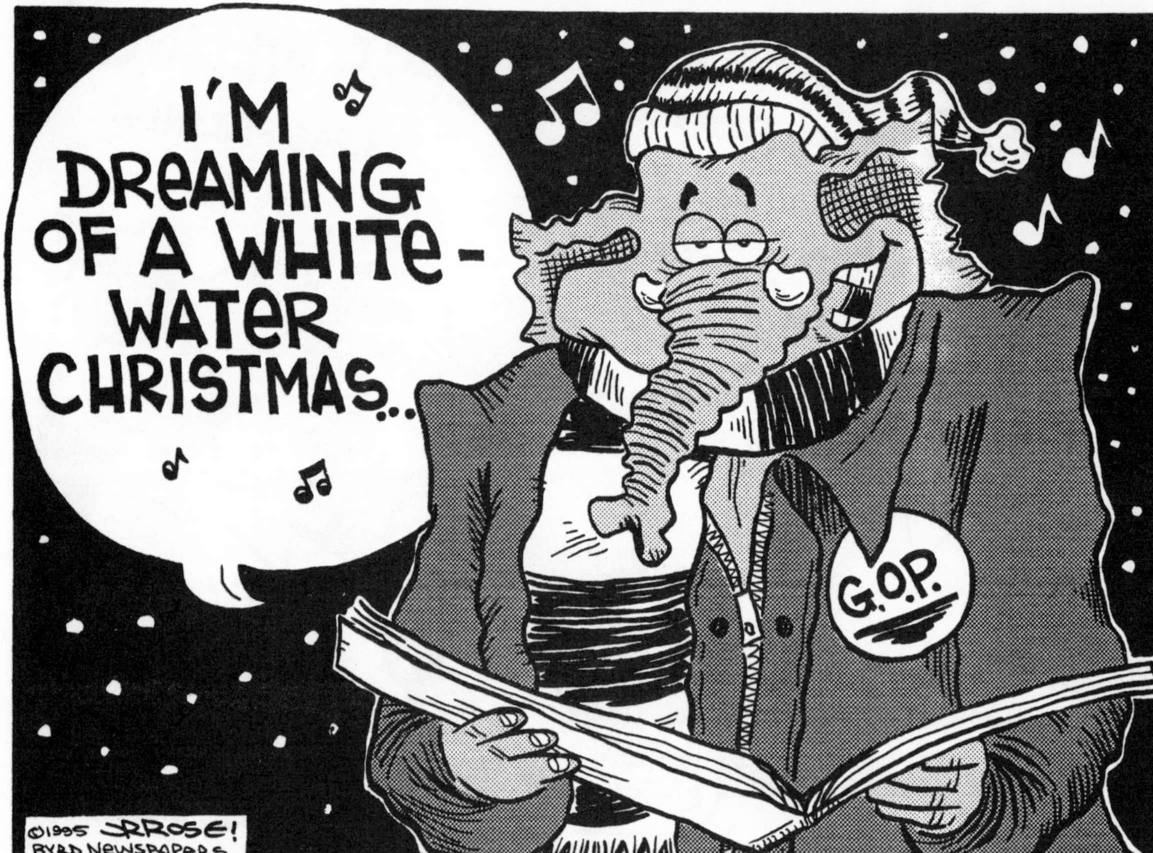
I'M DREAMING OF A WHITE-WATER CHRISTMAS...
G.O.P.
©1995 JRROSE!
BYRD NEWSPAPERS

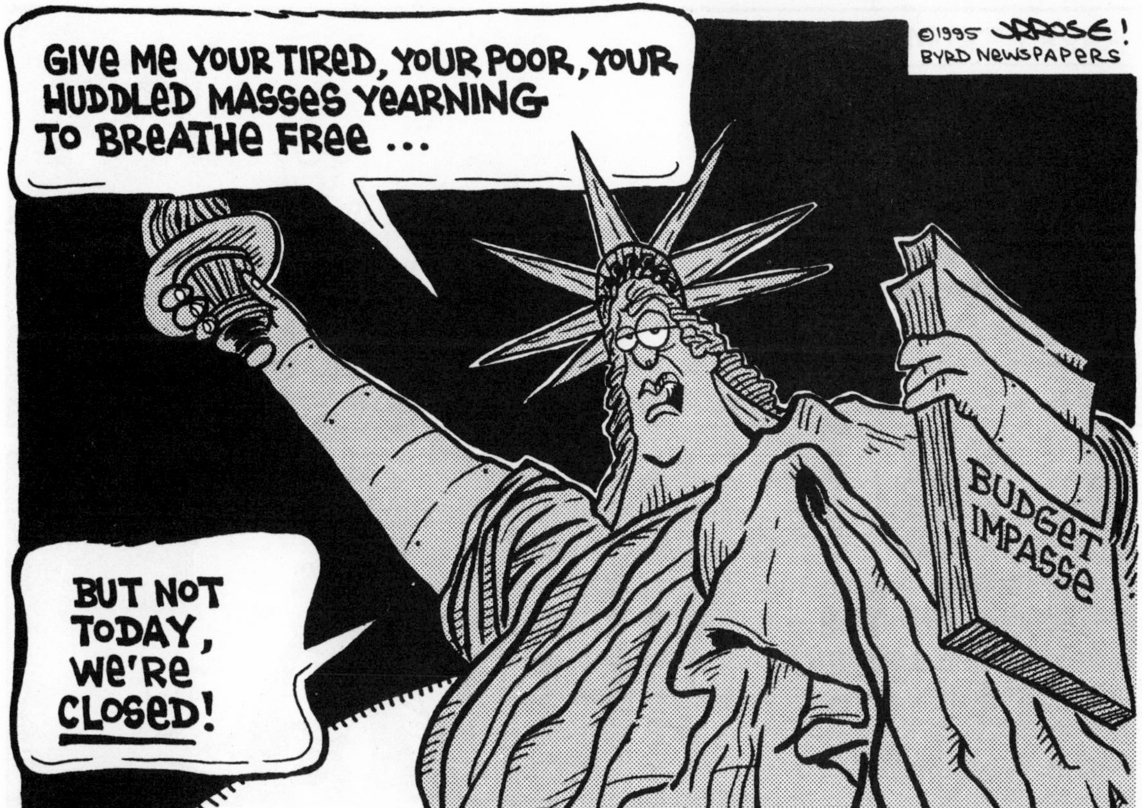

GIVE ME YOUR TIRED, YOUR POOR, YOUR HUDDLED MASSES YEARNING TO BREATHE FREE ...
BUT NOT TODAY, WE'RE CLOSED!
BUDGET IMPASSE
©1995 J.R.ROSE! BYRD NEWSPAPERS

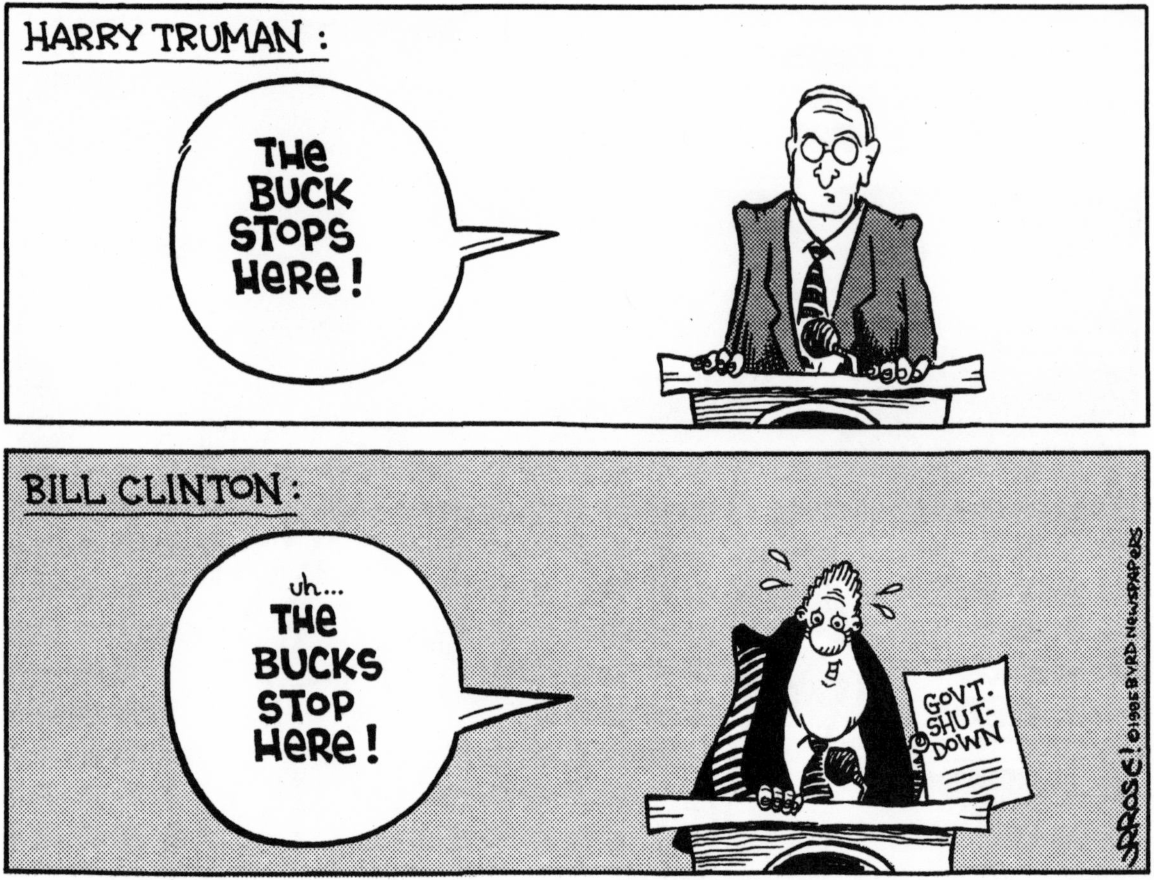
HARRY TRUMAN :
THE BUCK STOPS HERE !
BILL CLINTON :
uh...
THE BUCKS STOP HERE !
GOVT. SHUT-DOWN
©1995 BYRD NEWSPAPERS

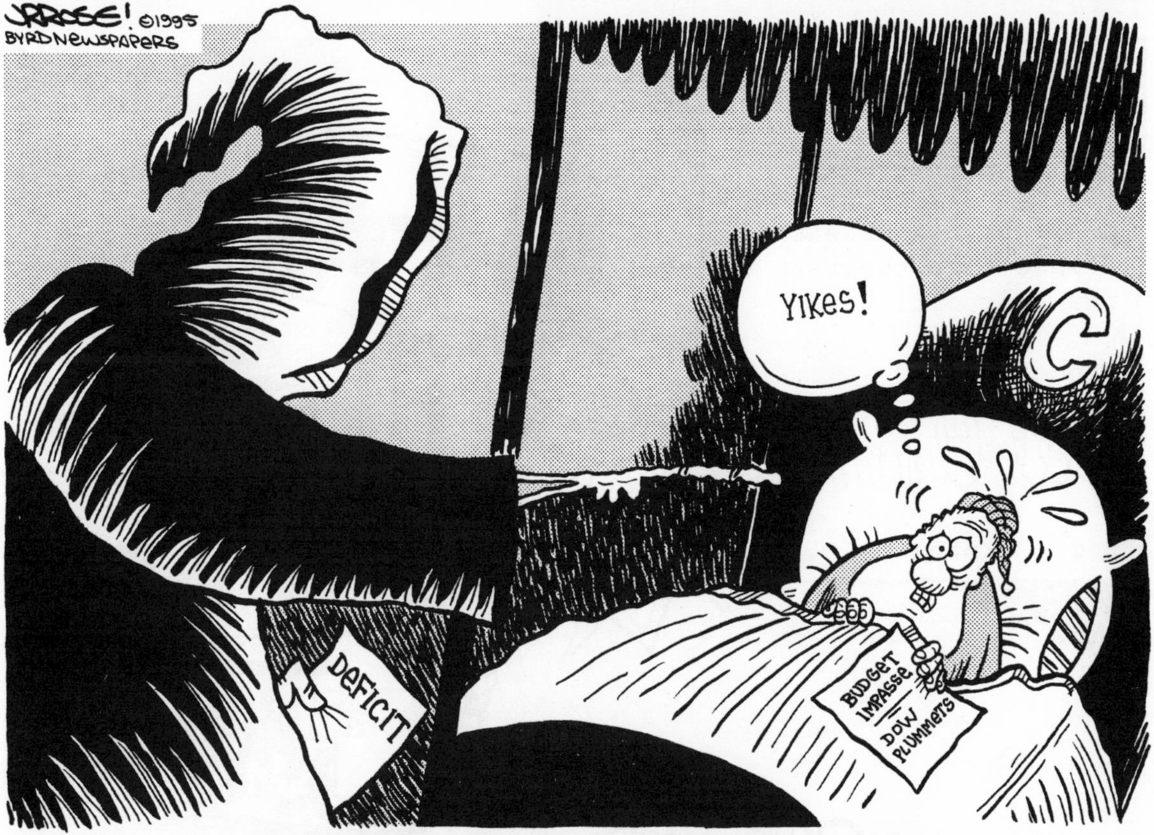
JRROSE! ©1995
BYRD NEWSPAPERS
YIKES!
DEFICIT
BUDGET IMPASSE
DOW PLUMMETS

THE GHOST OF STOCK MARKET FUTURE

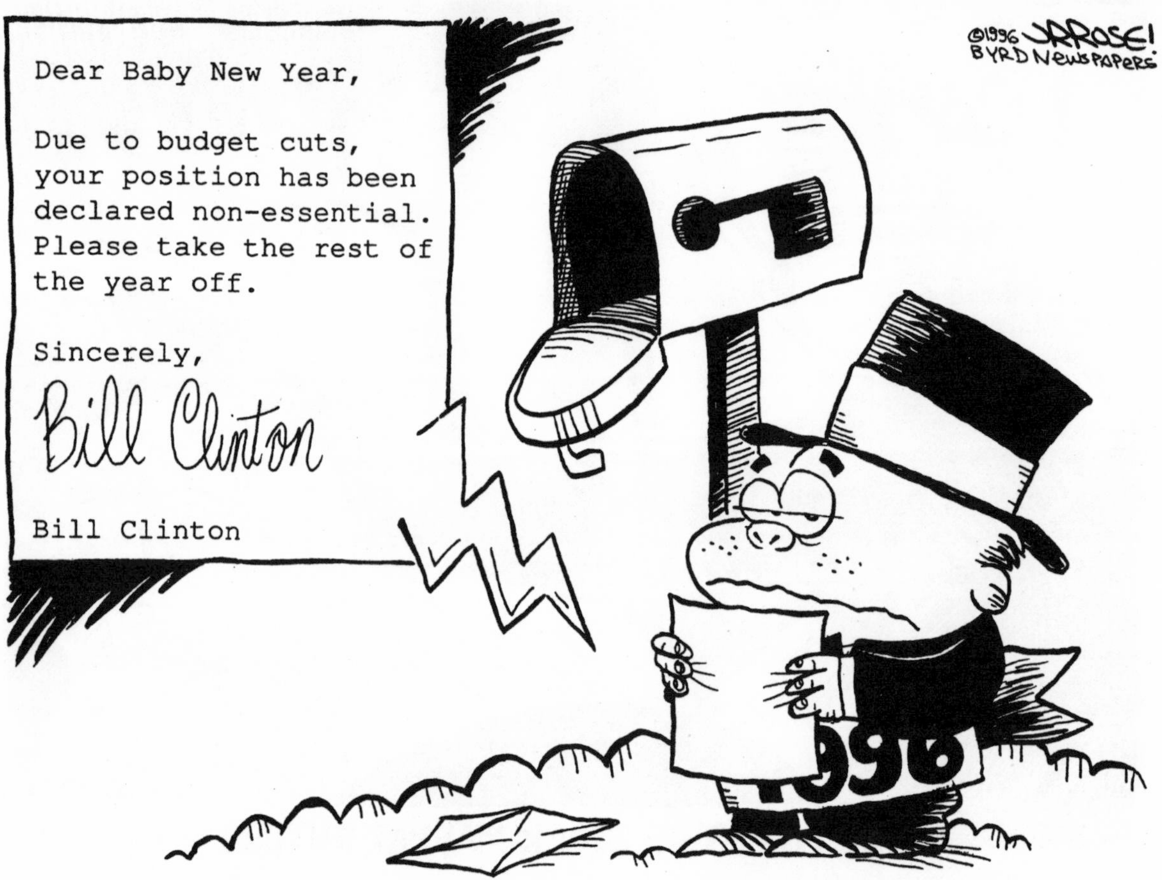
Dear Baby New Year,

Due to budget cuts, your position has been declared non-essential. Please take the rest of the year off.

Sincerely,
Bill Clinton

Bill Clinton
©1996 JRROSE!
BYRD Newspapers
1996

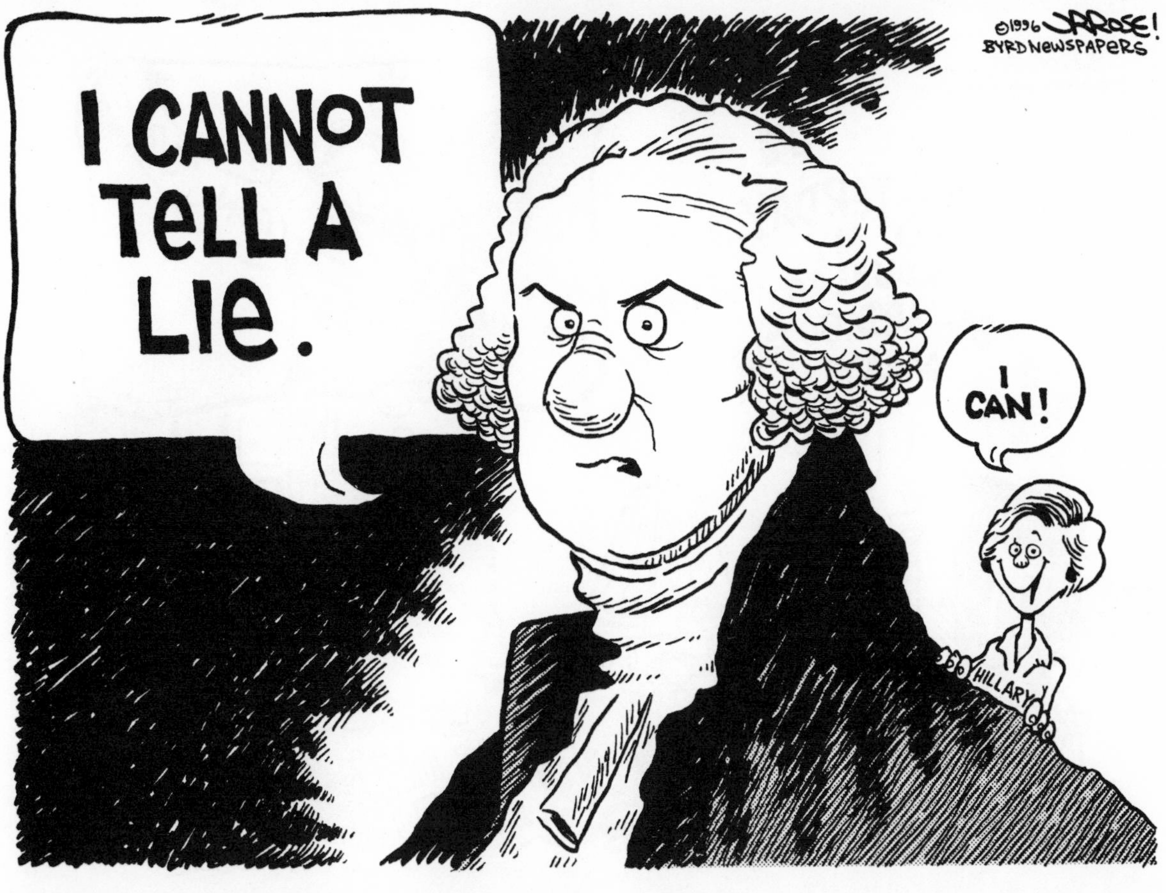
©1996 JRROSE!
BYRD NEWSPAPERS
I CANNOT TELL A LIE.
I CAN!
HILLARY

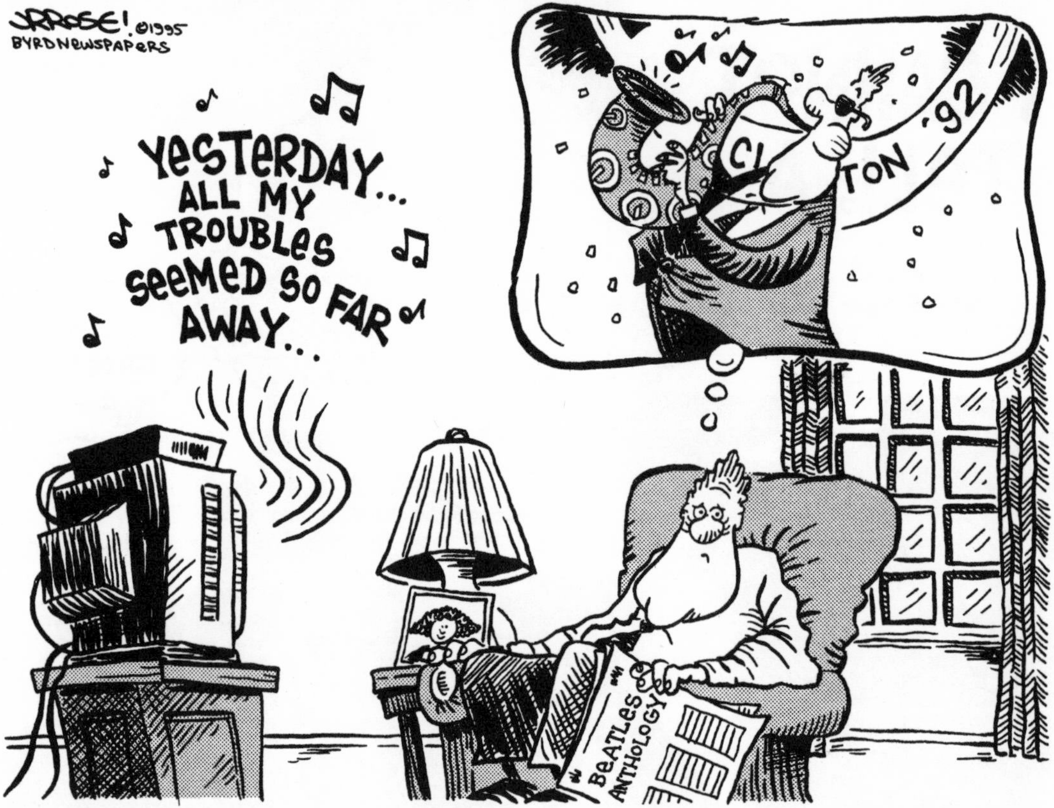
JRROSE! ©1995
BYRDNEWSPAPERS
YESTERDAY... ALL MY TROUBLES SEEMED SO FAR AWAY...
CL TON '92
BEATLES ANTHOLOGY

# Domestic Concerns

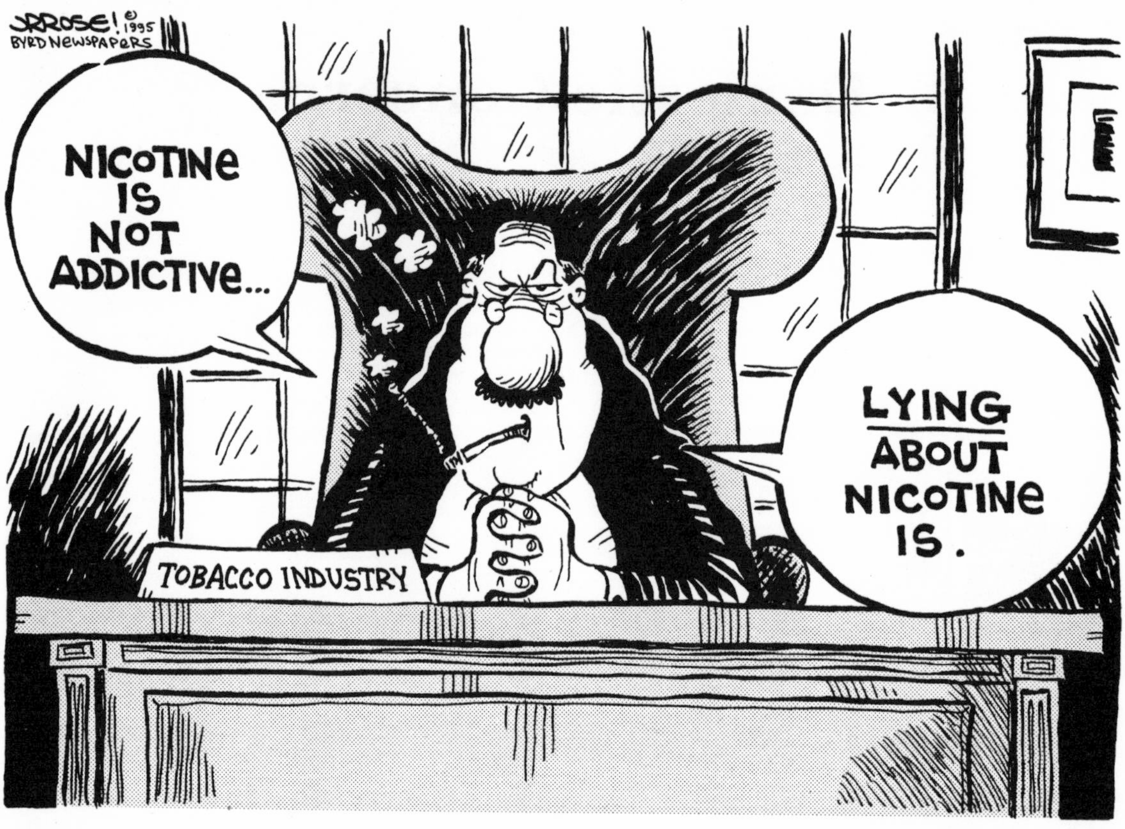
JRROSE! © 1995
BYRD NEWSPAPERS
NICOTINE IS NOT ADDICTIVE...
TOBACCO INDUSTRY
LYING ABOUT NICOTINE IS.

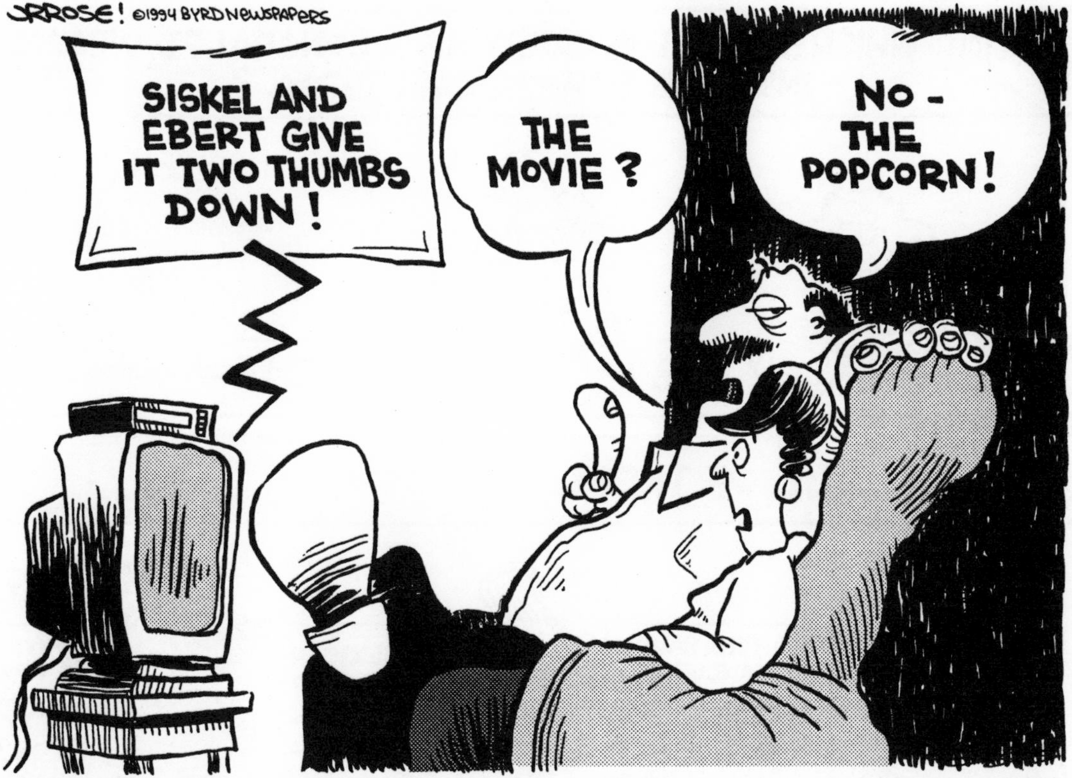
JRROSE! ©1994 BYRD NEWSPAPERS
SISKEL AND EBERT GIVE IT TWO THUMBS DOWN!
THE MOVIE?
NO - THE POPCORN!

**NEWS ITEM: Movie Theater Popcorn Contains More Fat Than Most Junk Food.**

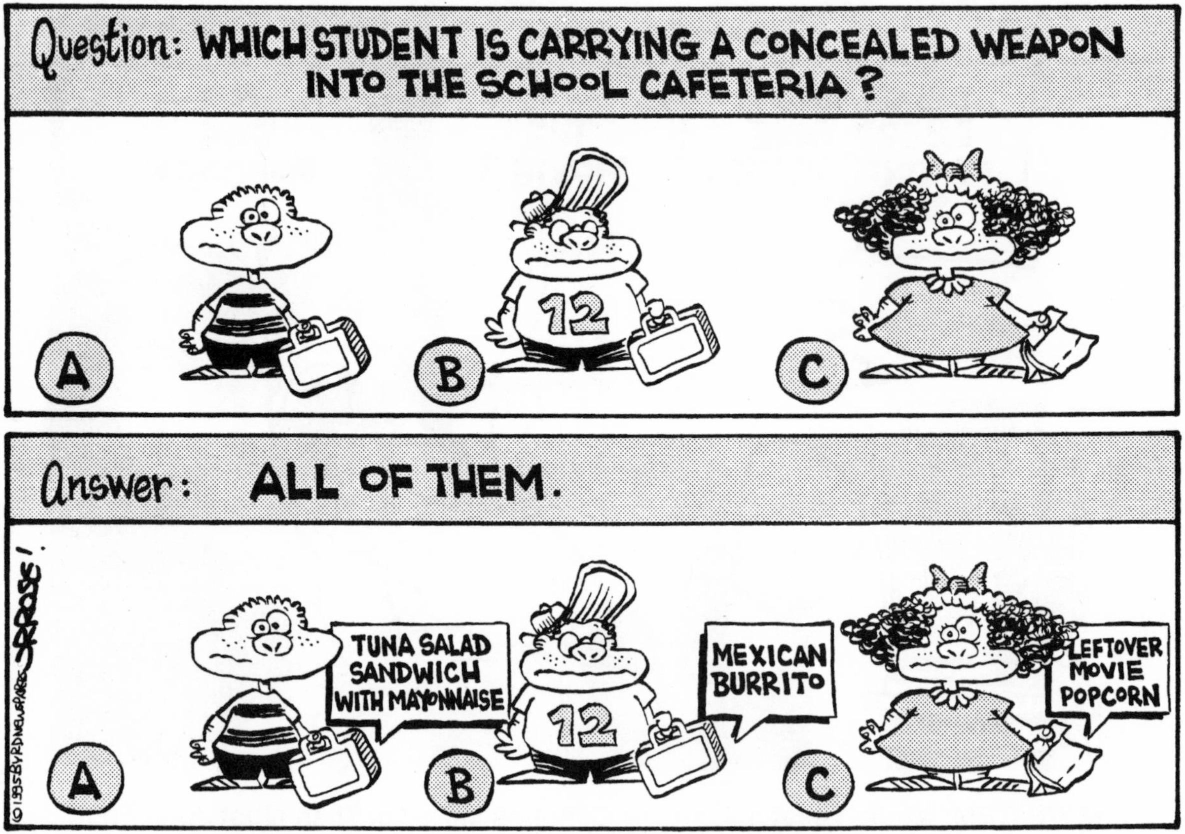

Question: WHICH STUDENT IS CARRYING A CONCEALED WEAPON INTO THE SCHOOL CAFETERIA?
A
12
B
C
Answer: ALL OF THEM.
©1995 BY RD NEWSPAPERS
A
TUNA SALAD SANDWICH WITH MAYONNAISE
12
B
MEXICAN BURRITO
C
LEFTOVER MOVIE POPCORN

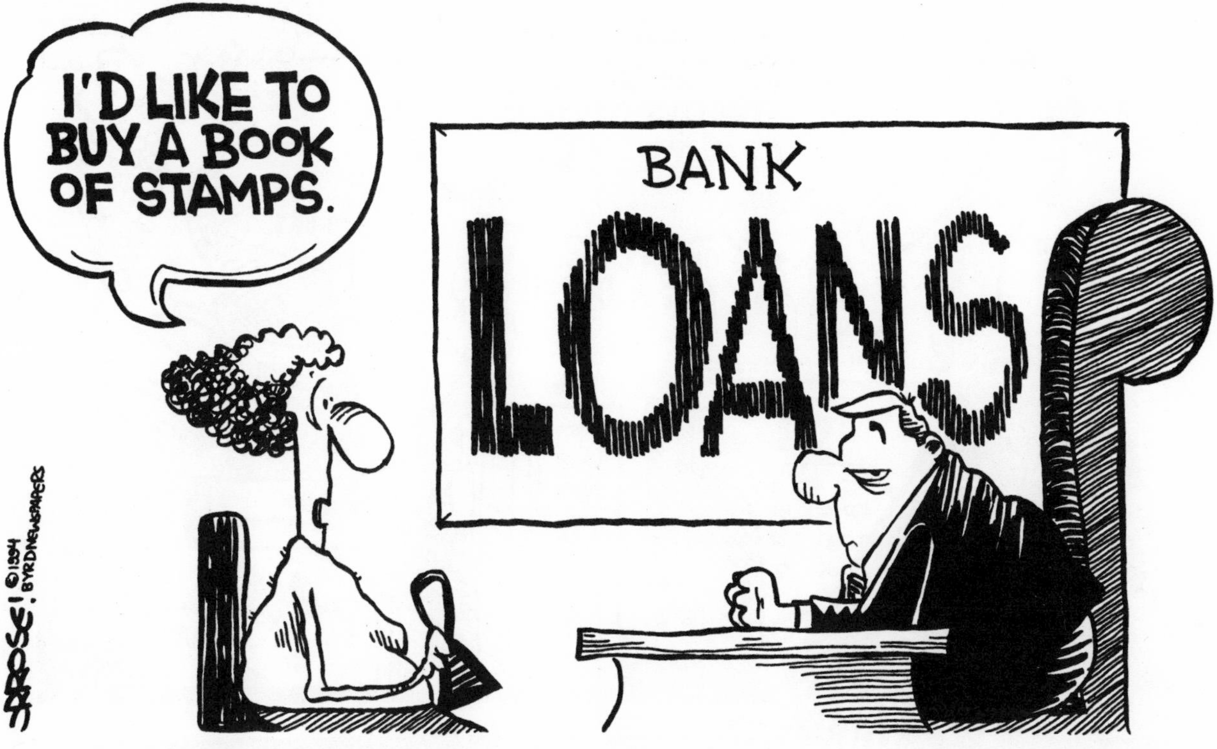
I'D LIKE TO BUY A BOOK OF STAMPS.
BANK
LOANS
©1994 BYRD NEWSPAPERS

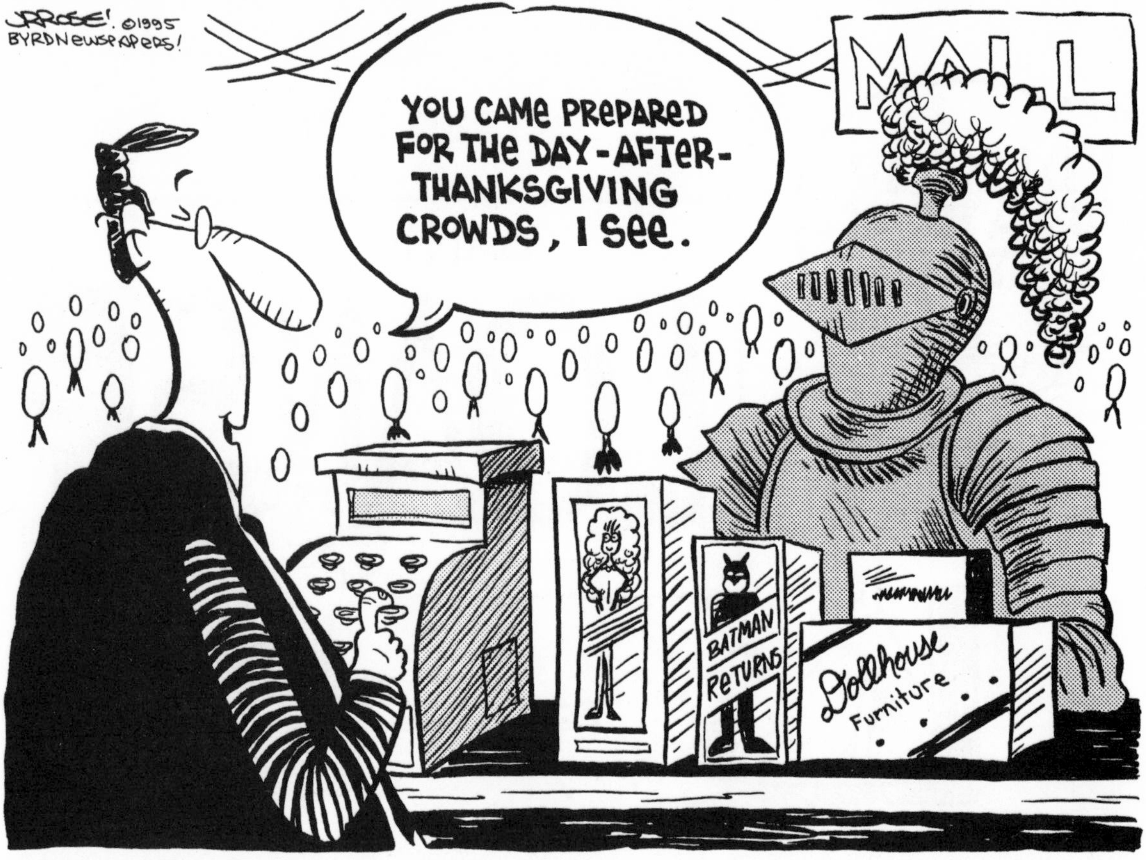
JRROSE! ©1995
BYRDNEWSPAPERS!
MALL
YOU CAME PREPARED FOR THE DAY-AFTER-THANKSGIVING CROWDS, I SEE.
BATMAN RETURNS
Dollhouse Furniture

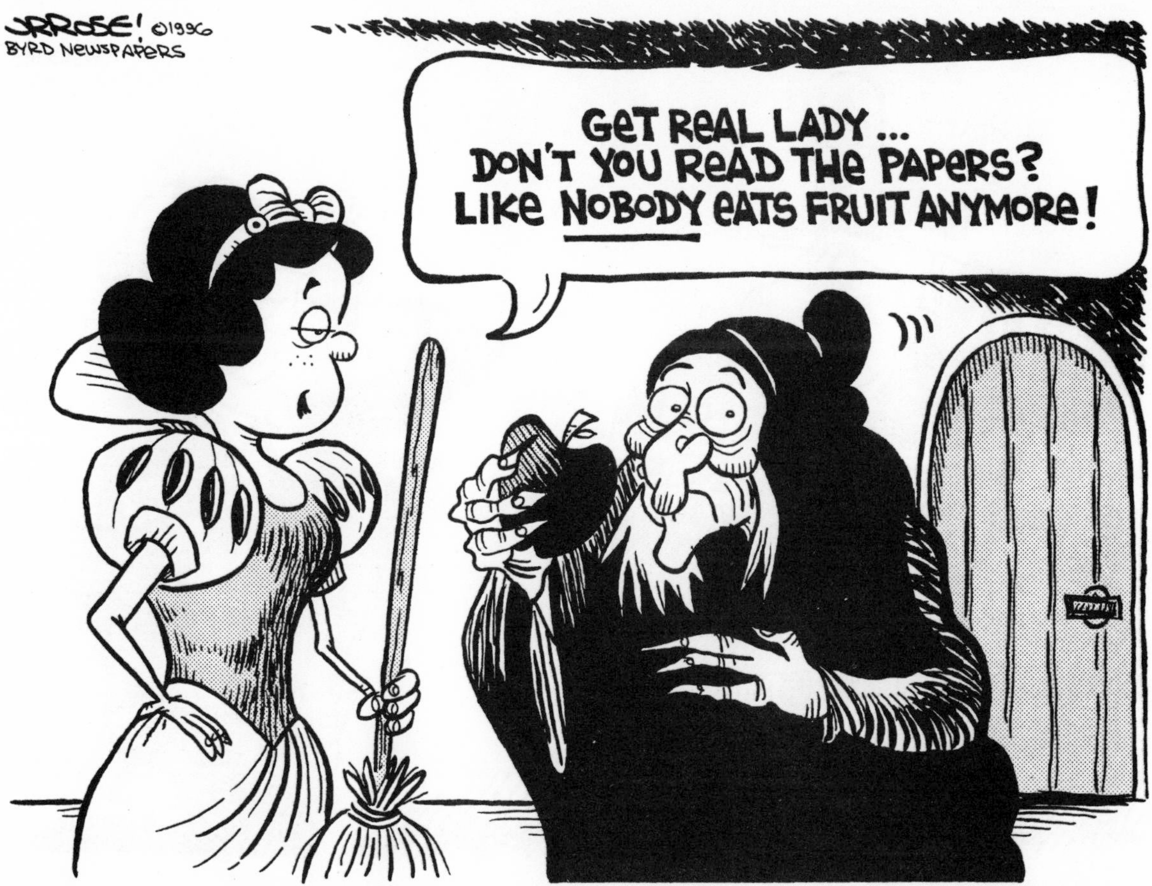
JRROSE! ©1996
BYRD NEWSPAPERS
GET REAL LADY ...
DON'T YOU READ THE PAPERS?
LIKE NOBODY EATS FRUIT ANYMORE!

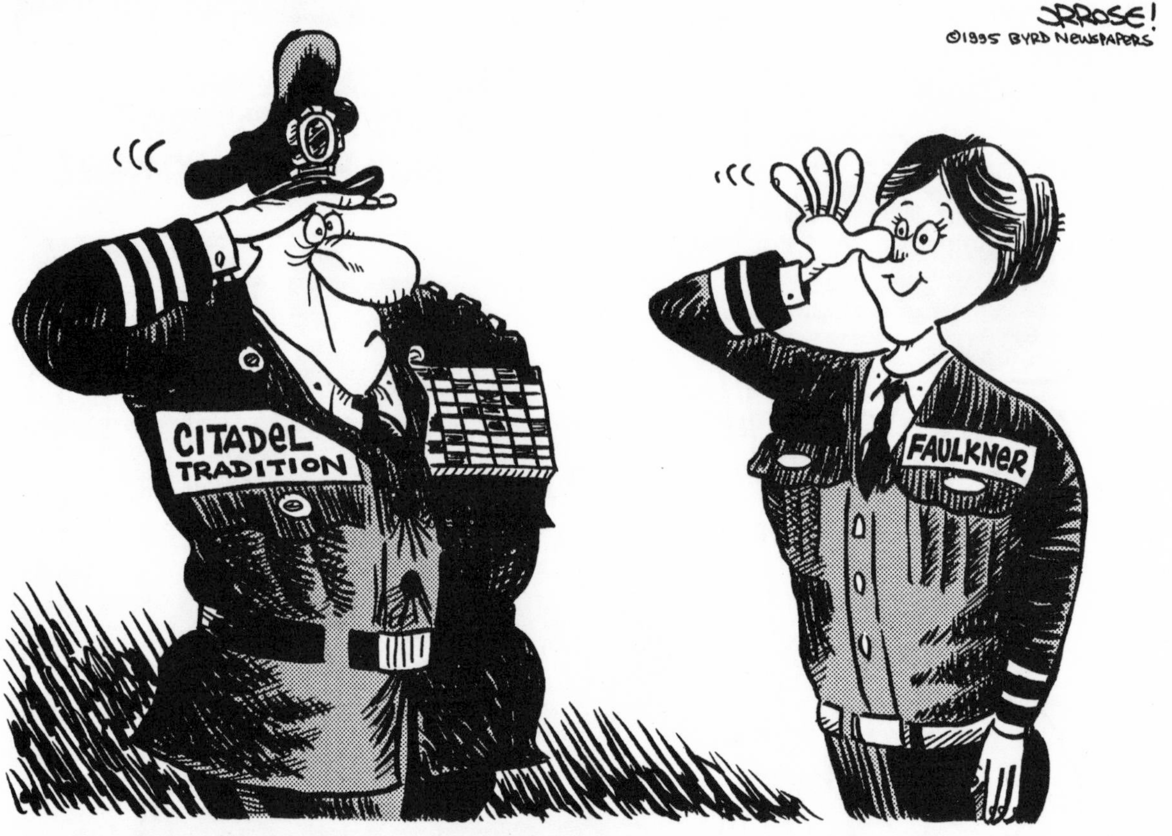
JRROSE!
©1995 BYRD NEWSPAPERS
CITADEL TRADITION
FAULKNER

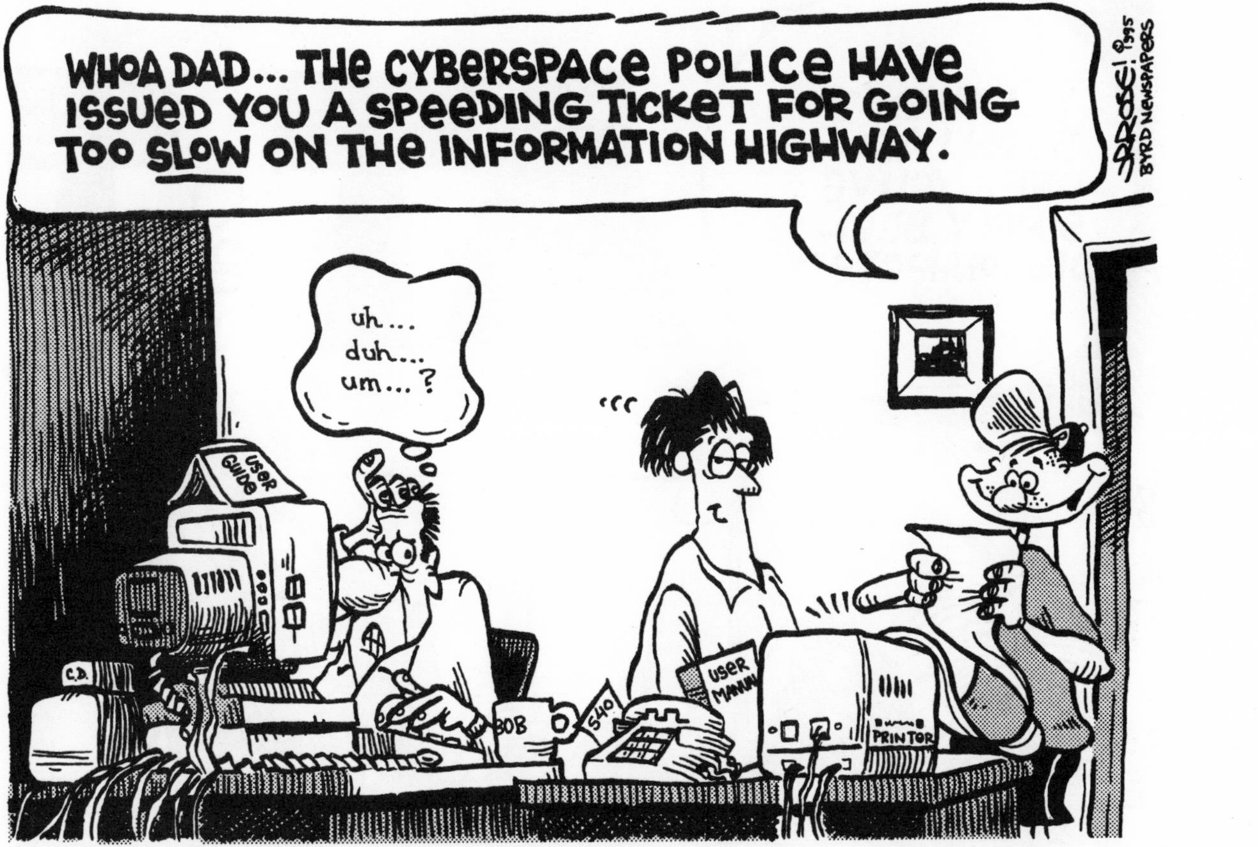
WHOA DAD... THE CYBERSPACE POLICE HAVE ISSUED YOU A SPEEDING TICKET FOR GOING TOO SLOW ON THE INFORMATION HIGHWAY.
uh... duh... um...?
USER GUIDE
C.D.
BOB
$40
USER MANUAL
PRINTER
©1995 BYRD NEWSPAPERS

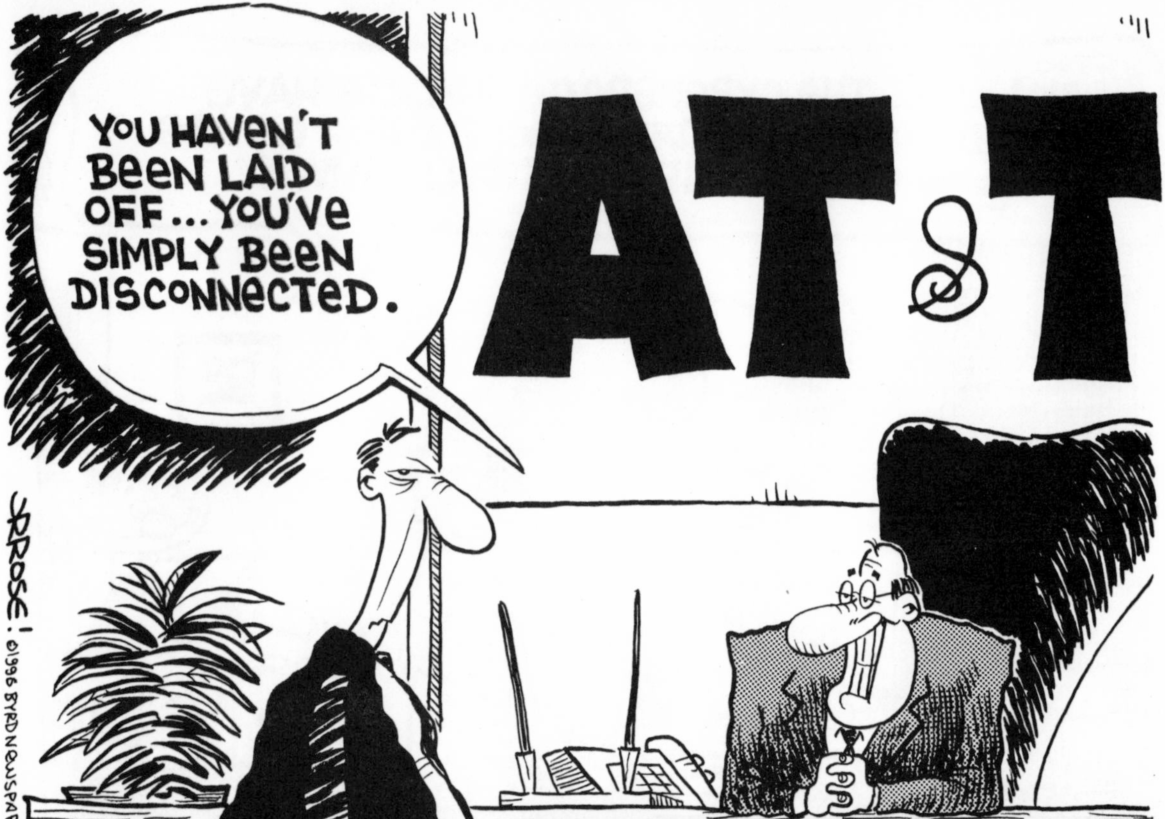
YOU HAVEN'T BEEN LAID OFF... YOU'VE SIMPLY BEEN DISCONNECTED.
©1996 BYRD NEWSPAPERS

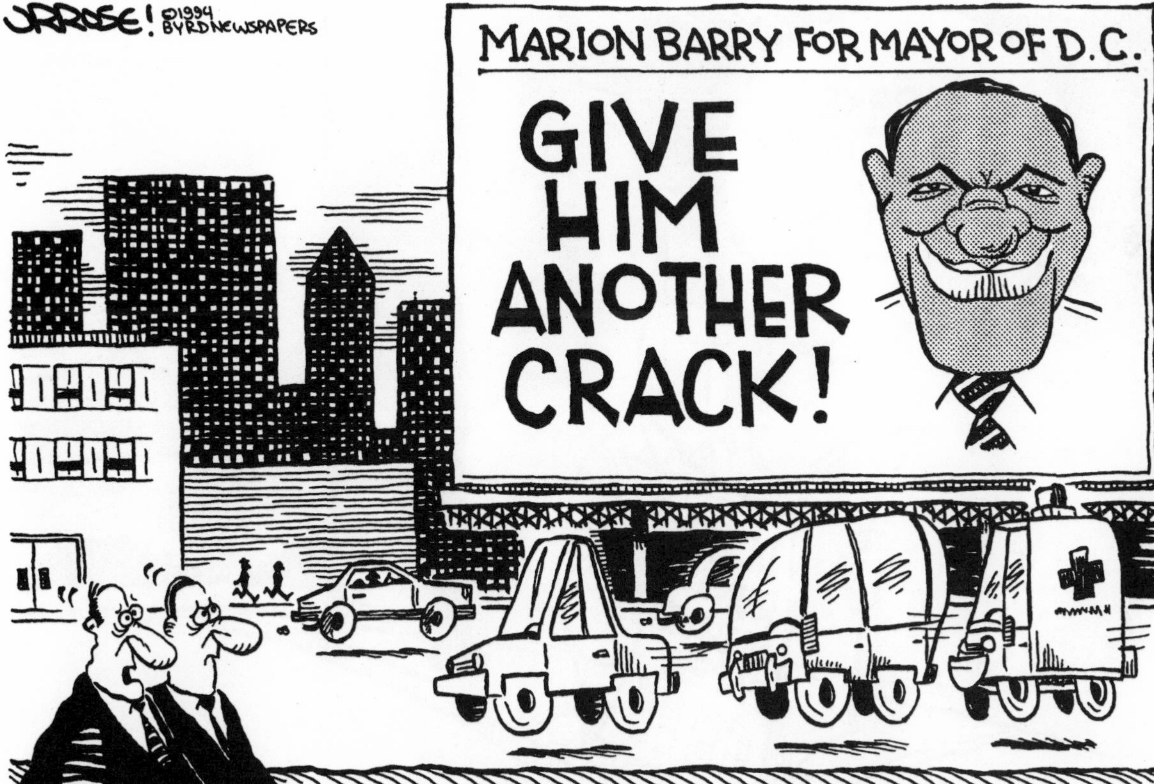
JRROSE! ©1994 BYRDNEWSPAPERS
MARION BARRY FOR MAYOR OF D.C.
GIVE HIM ANOTHER CRACK!

I CAN'T BELIEVE HIS CAMPAIGN SLOGAN IS ACTUALLY WORKING!

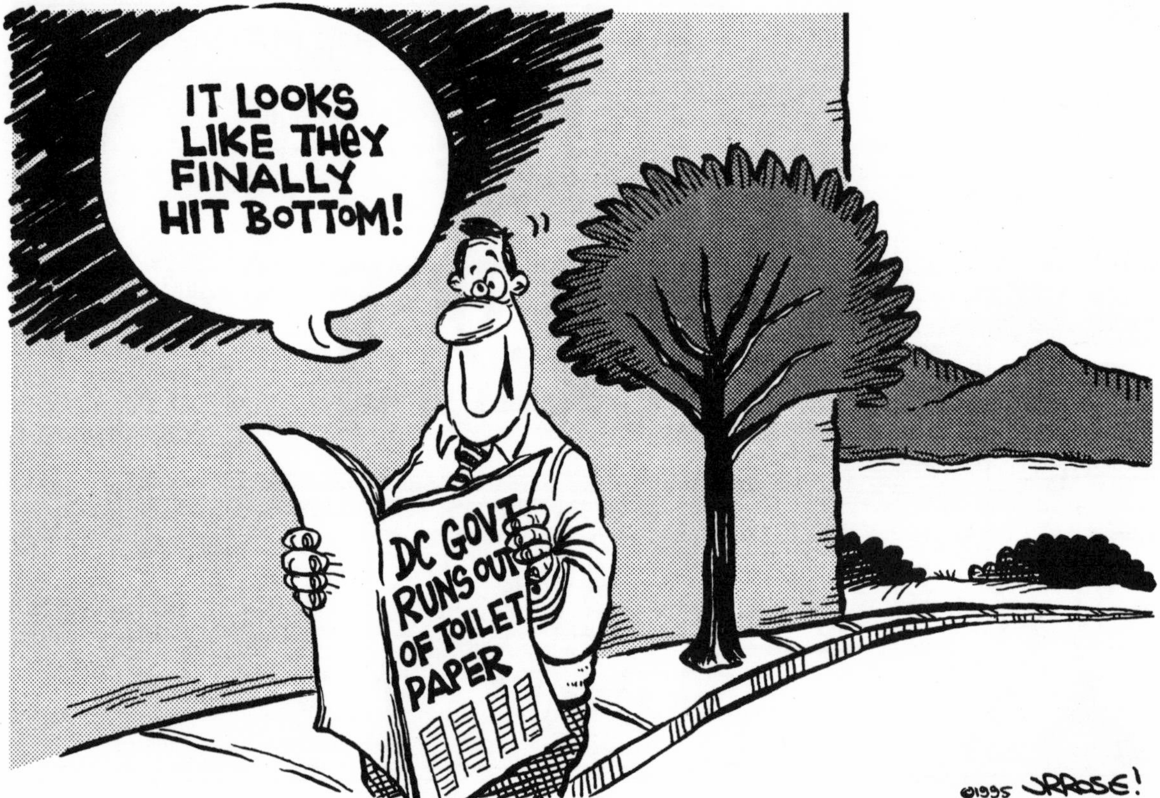
IT LOOKS LIKE THEY FINALLY HIT BOTTOM!
DC GOVT RUNS OUT OF TOILET PAPER
©1995 JRROSE!
BYRD NEWSPAPERS

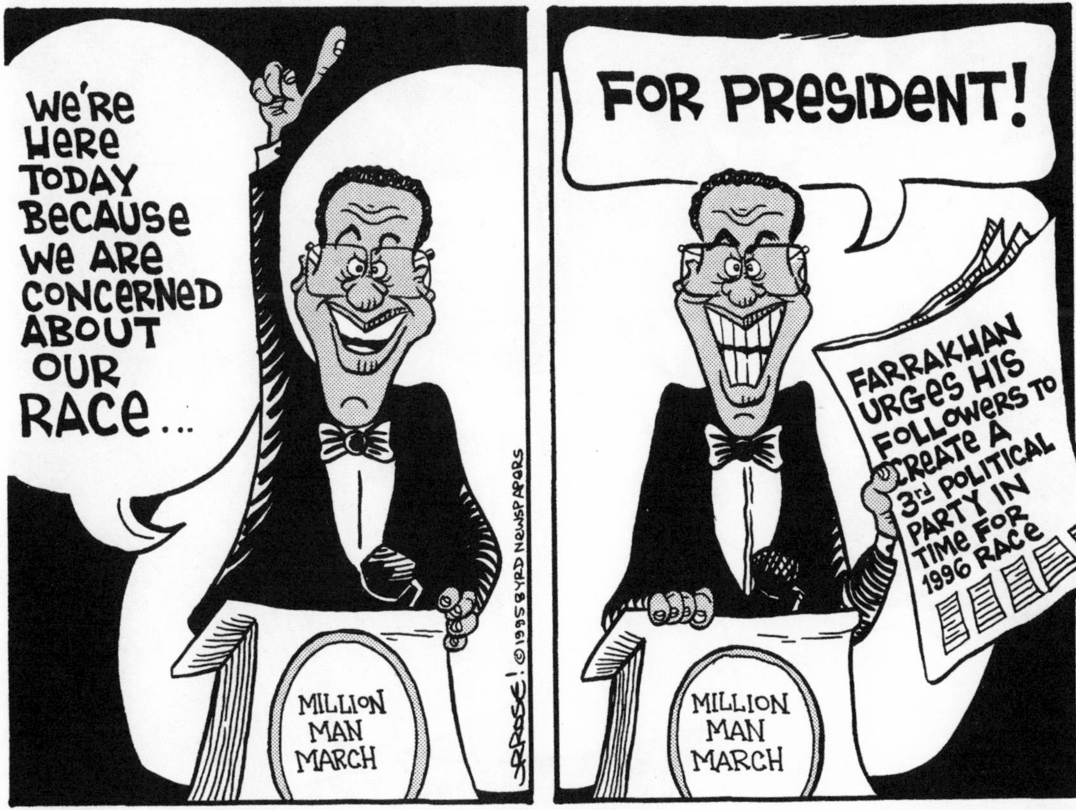
WE'RE HERE TODAY BECAUSE WE ARE CONCERNED ABOUT OUR RACE...
MILLION MAN MARCH
© 1995 BYRD NEWSPAPERS
FOR PRESIDENT!
FARRAKHAN URGES HIS FOLLOWERS TO CREATE A 3rd POLITICAL PARTY IN TIME FOR 1996 RACE
MILLION MAN MARCH

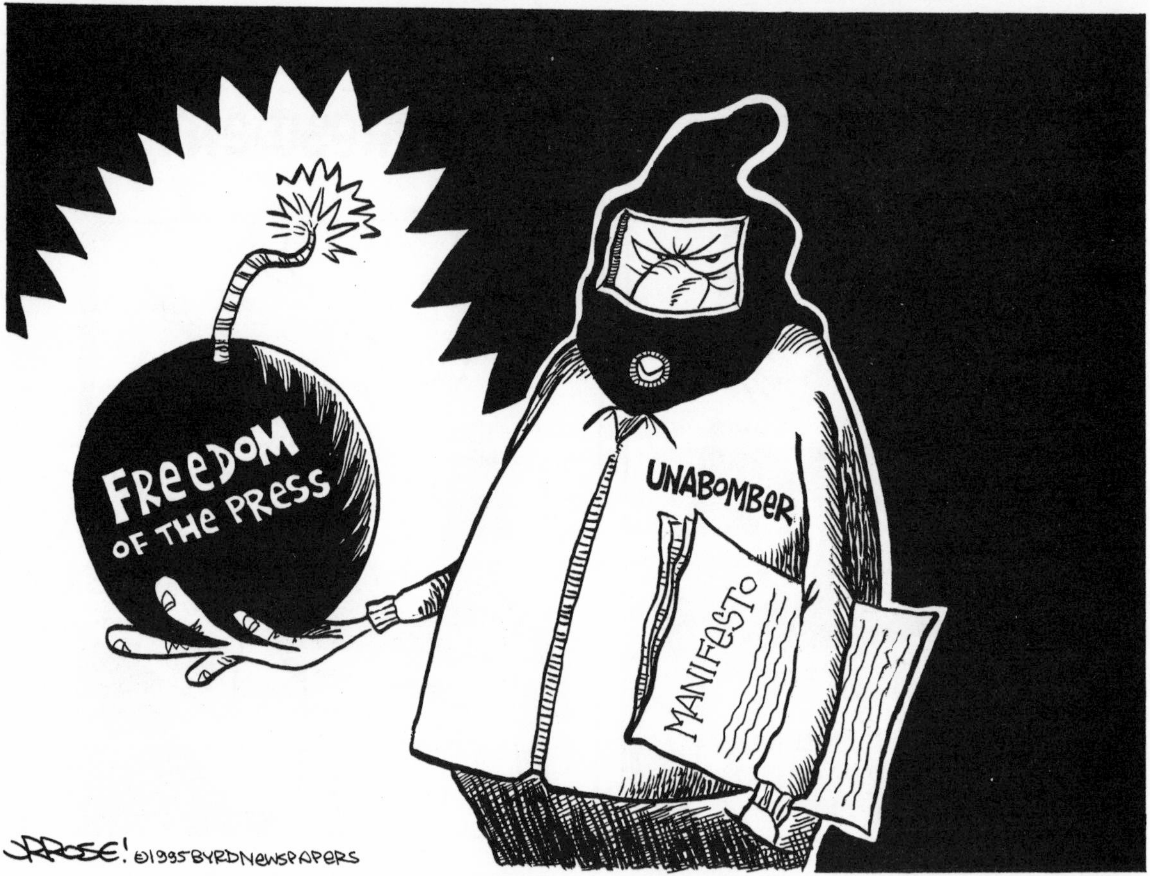
FREEDOM OF THE PRESS
UNABOMBER
MANIFESTO
JRROSE! ©1995 BYRD NEWSPAPERS

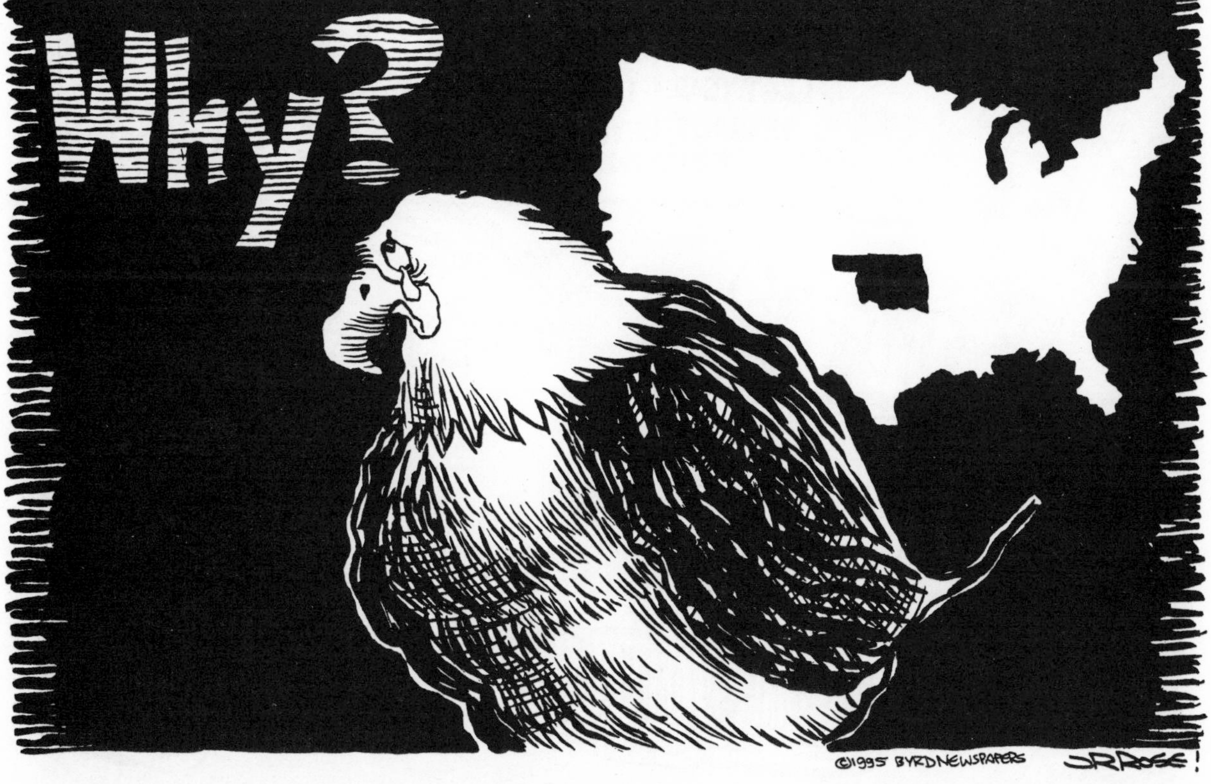

Why?
©1995 BYRD NEWSPAPERS
JR ROSE!

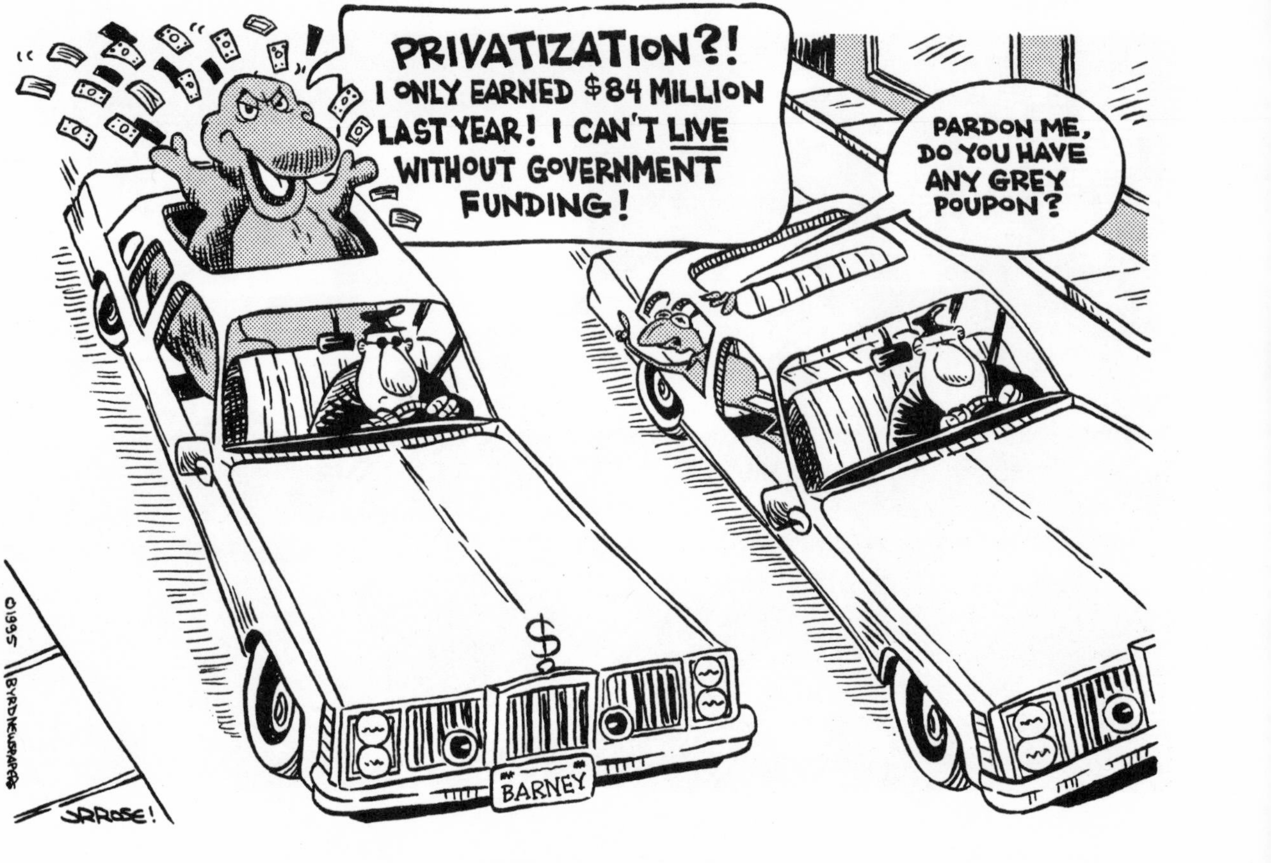
PRIVATIZATION?! I ONLY EARNED $84 MILLION LAST YEAR! I CAN'T LIVE WITHOUT GOVERNMENT FUNDING!
PARDON ME, DO YOU HAVE ANY GREY POUPON?
$
BARNEY
©1995 BYRDNEWSPAPERS
JRROSE!

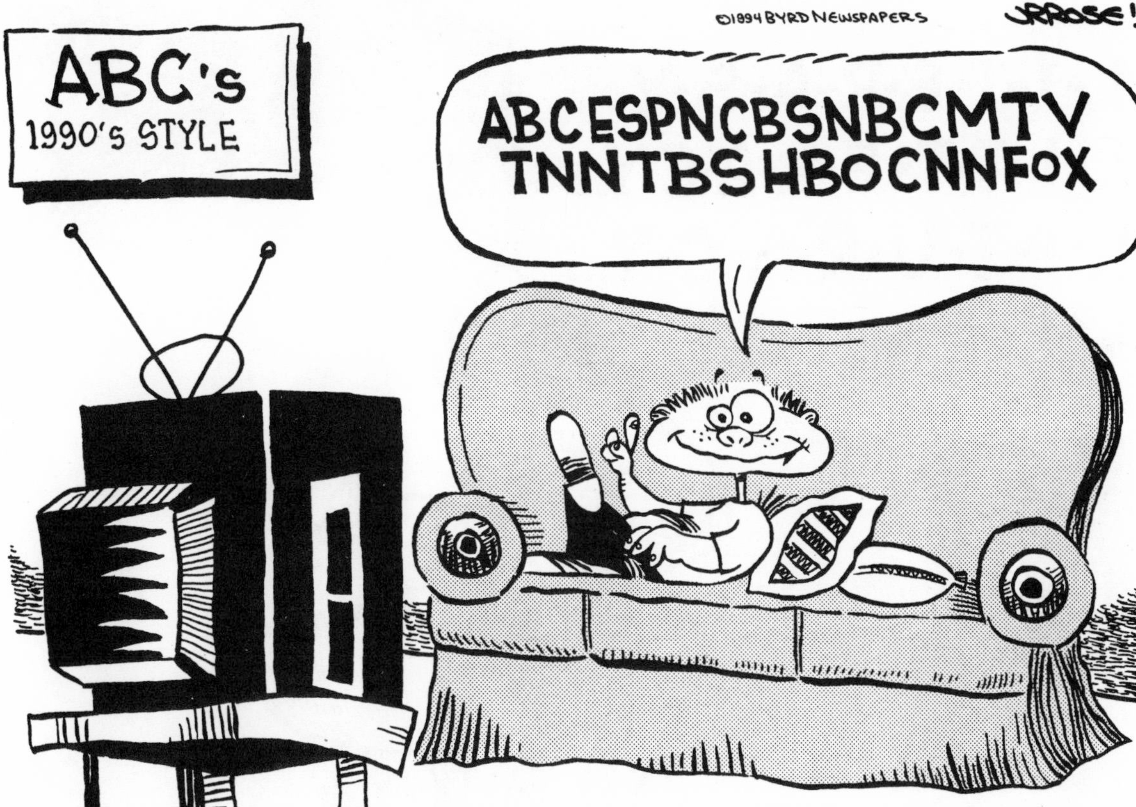
ABC's
1990's STYLE
ABCESPNCBSNBCMTV TNNTBSHBOCNNFOX
©1994 BYRD NEWSPAPERS
JRROSE!

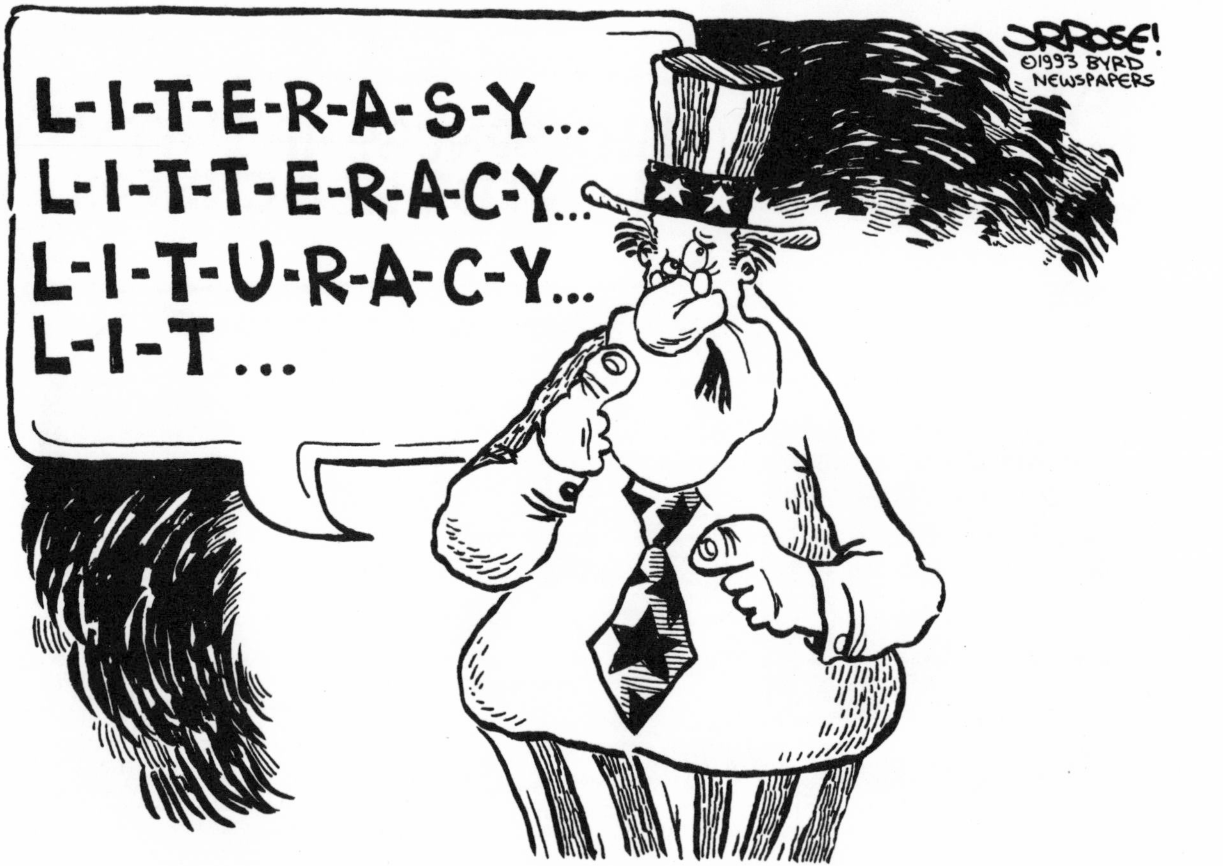
L-I-T-E-R-A-S-Y...
L-I-T-T-E-R-A-C-Y...
L-I-T-U-R-A-C-Y...
L-I-T ...
JRROSE!
©1993 BYRD NEWSPAPERS

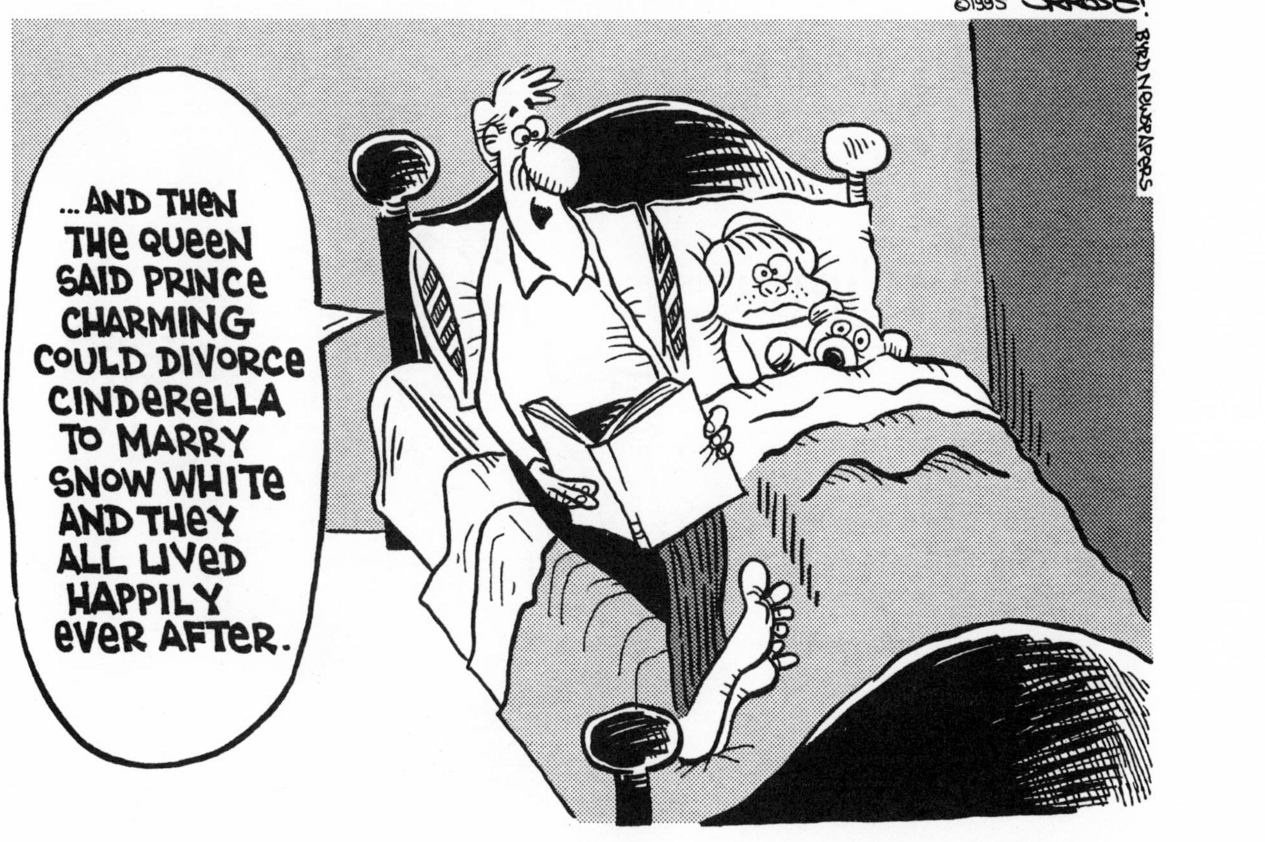
©1995 JRROSE!
BYRD NEWSPAPERS
...AND THEN THE QUEEN SAID PRINCE CHARMING COULD DIVORCE CINDERELLA TO MARRY SNOW WHITE AND THEY ALL LIVED HAPPILY EVER AFTER.

Yes Virginia,
there is a
Santa Claus...

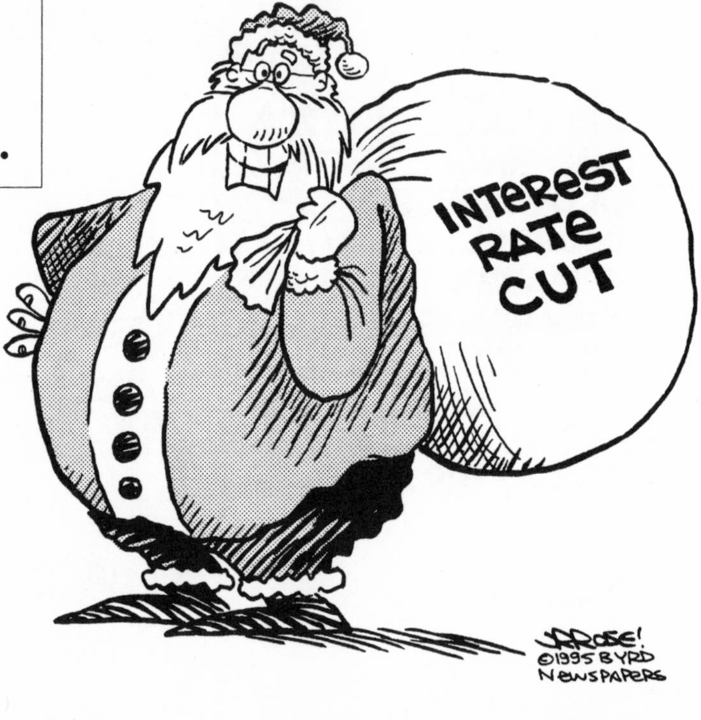
INTEREST
RATE
CUT
©1995 BYRD
NEWSPAPERS

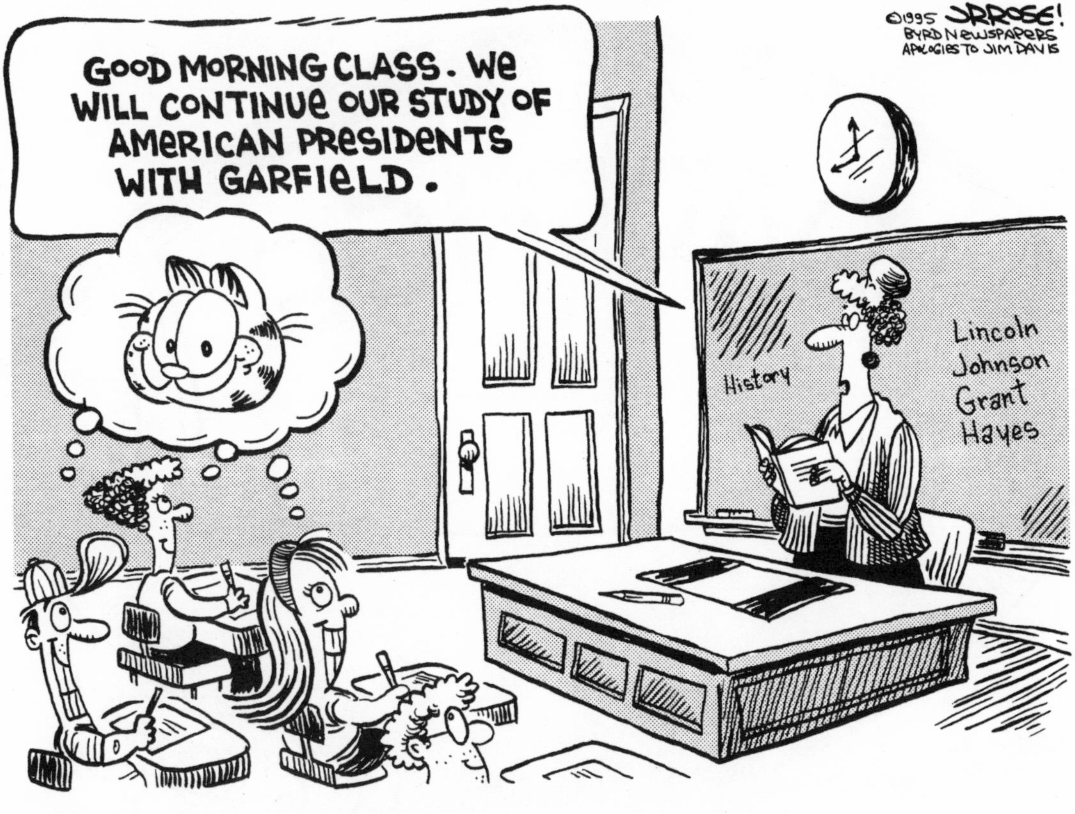

©1995 JRROSE!
BYRD NEWSPAPERS
APOLOGIES TO JIM DAVIS
GOOD MORNING CLASS. WE WILL CONTINUE OUR STUDY OF AMERICAN PRESIDENTS WITH GARFIELD.
History
Lincoln
Johnson
Grant
Hayes


News Item: More than half of America's high school seniors don't know basic facts about U.S. history.

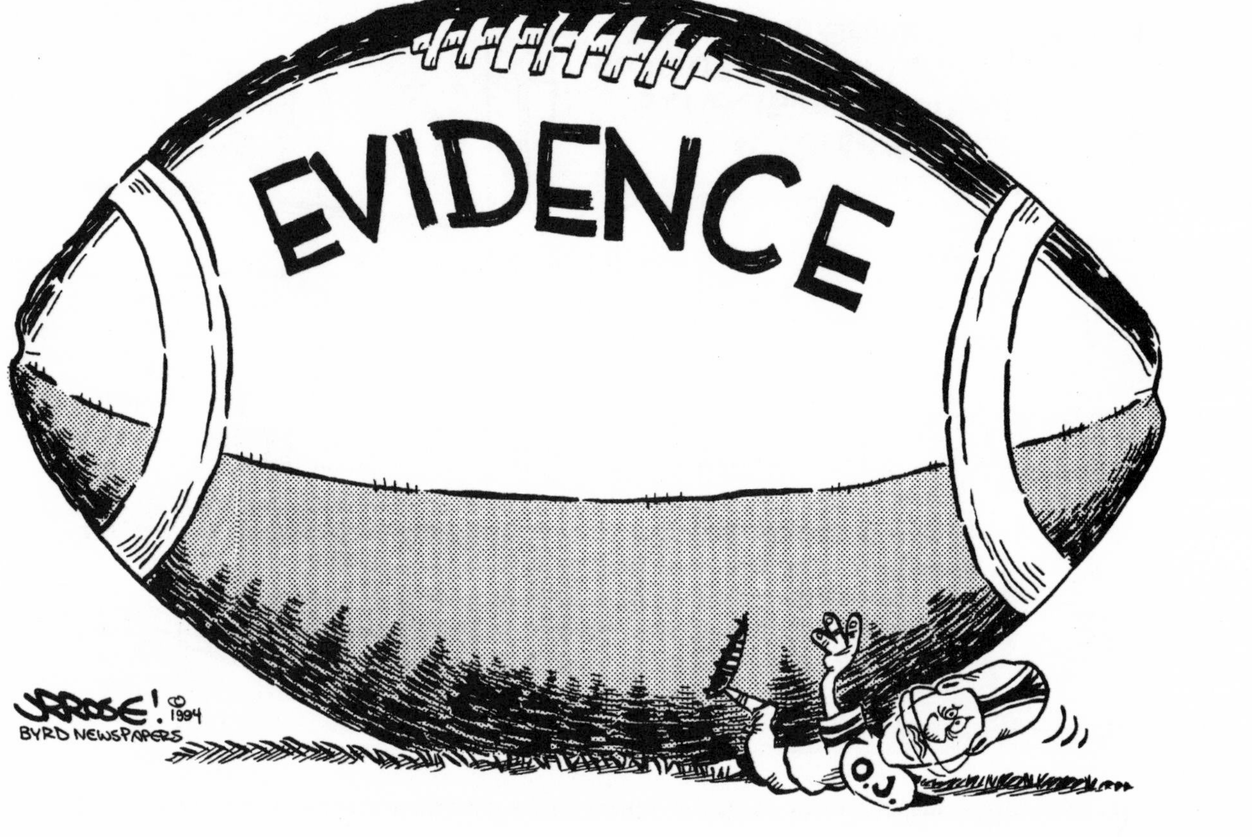
EVIDENCE
O.J.
JRROSE! © 1994
BYRD NEWSPAPERS

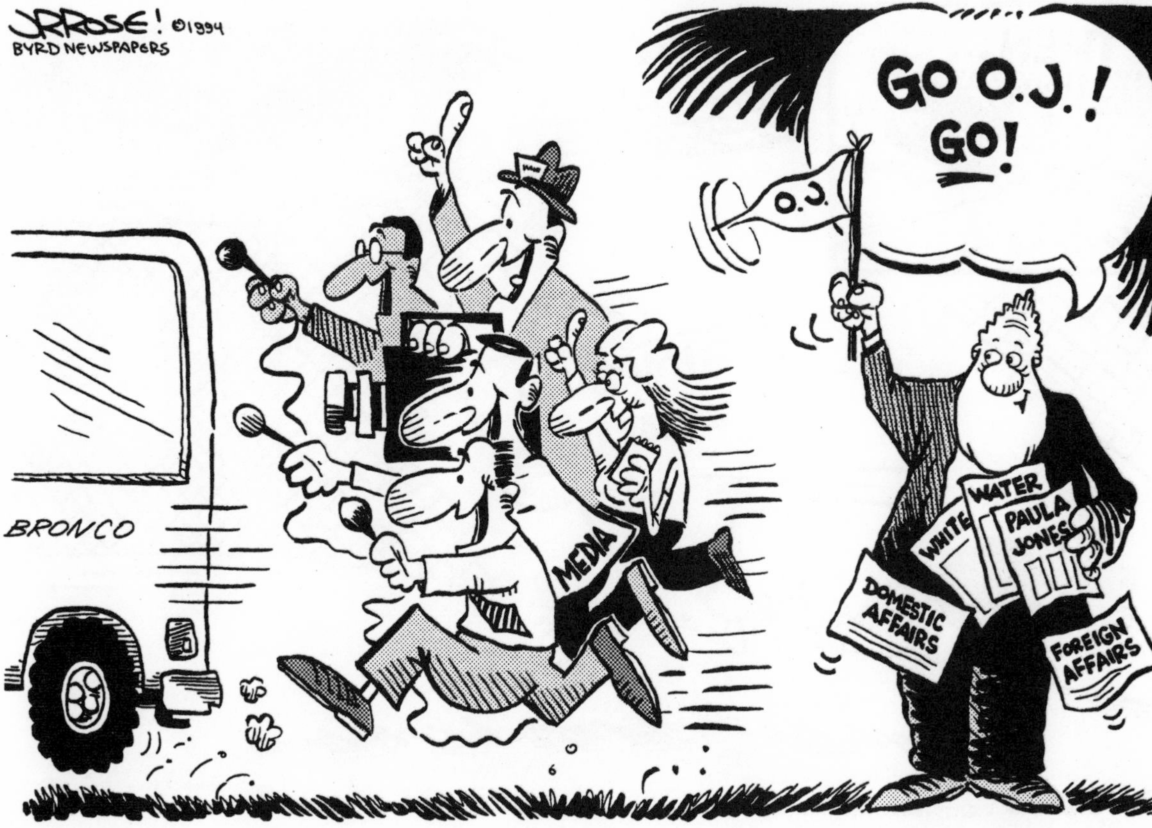
JRROSE! ©1994
BYRD NEWSPAPERS
GO O.J..! GO!
O.J.
BRONCO
MEDIA
WATER
WHITE
PAULA JONES
DOMESTIC AFFAIRS
FOREIGN AFFAIRS

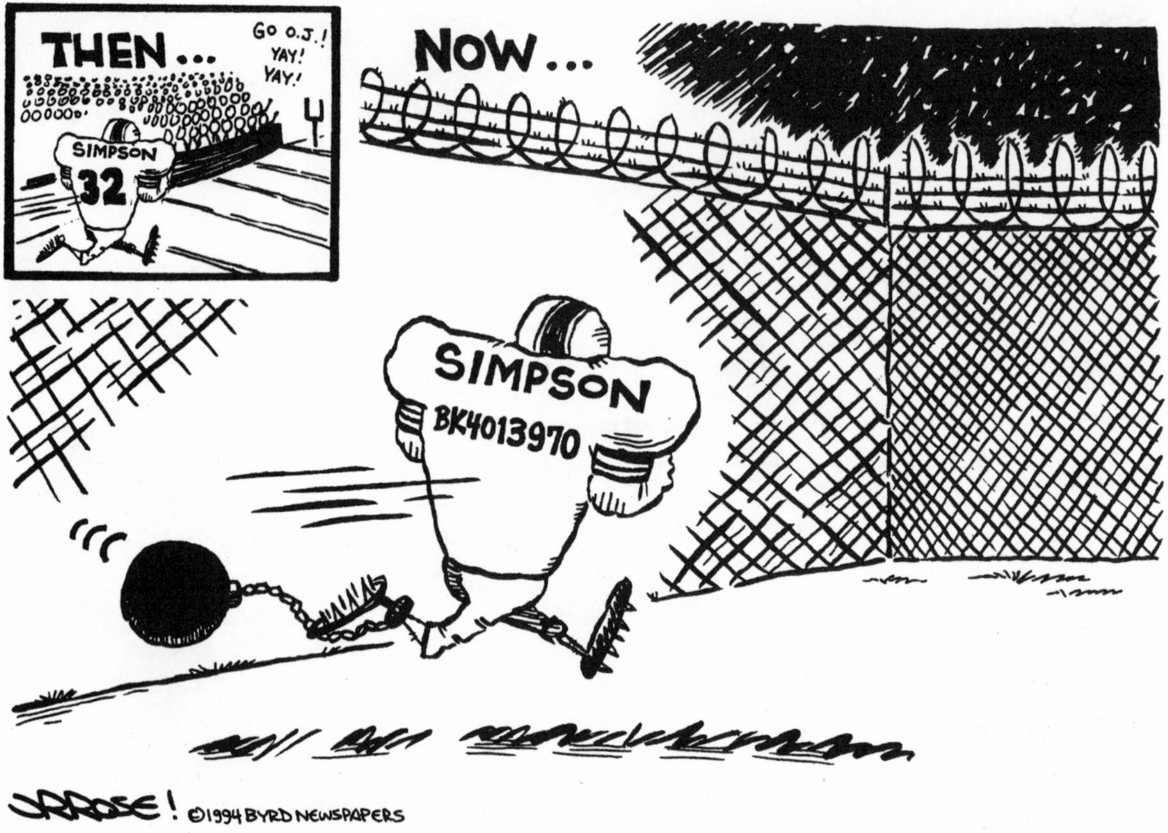
THEN...
GO O.J.! YAY! YAY!
SIMPSON
32
NOW...
SIMPSON
BK4013970
JRROSE!
©1994 BYRD NEWSPAPERS

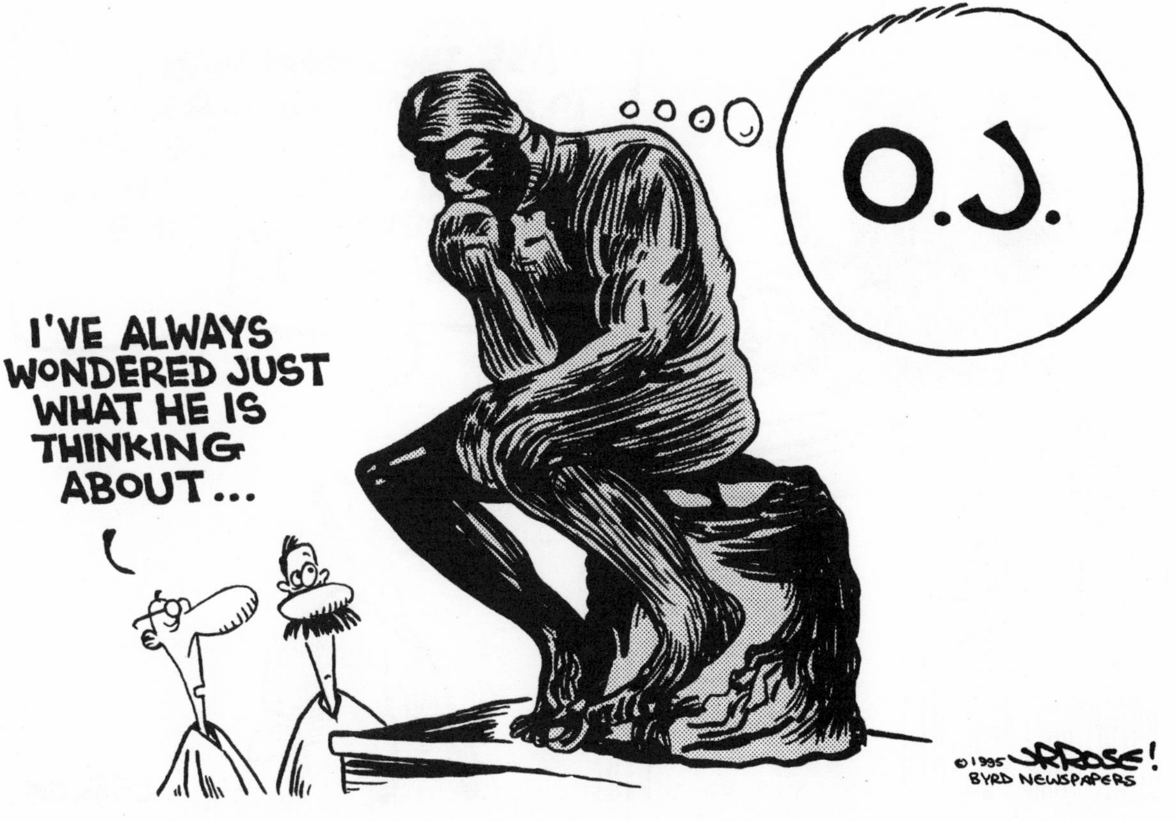
I'VE ALWAYS WONDERED JUST WHAT HE IS THINKING ABOUT...
O.J.
©1995 JRROSE!
BYRD NEWSPAPERS

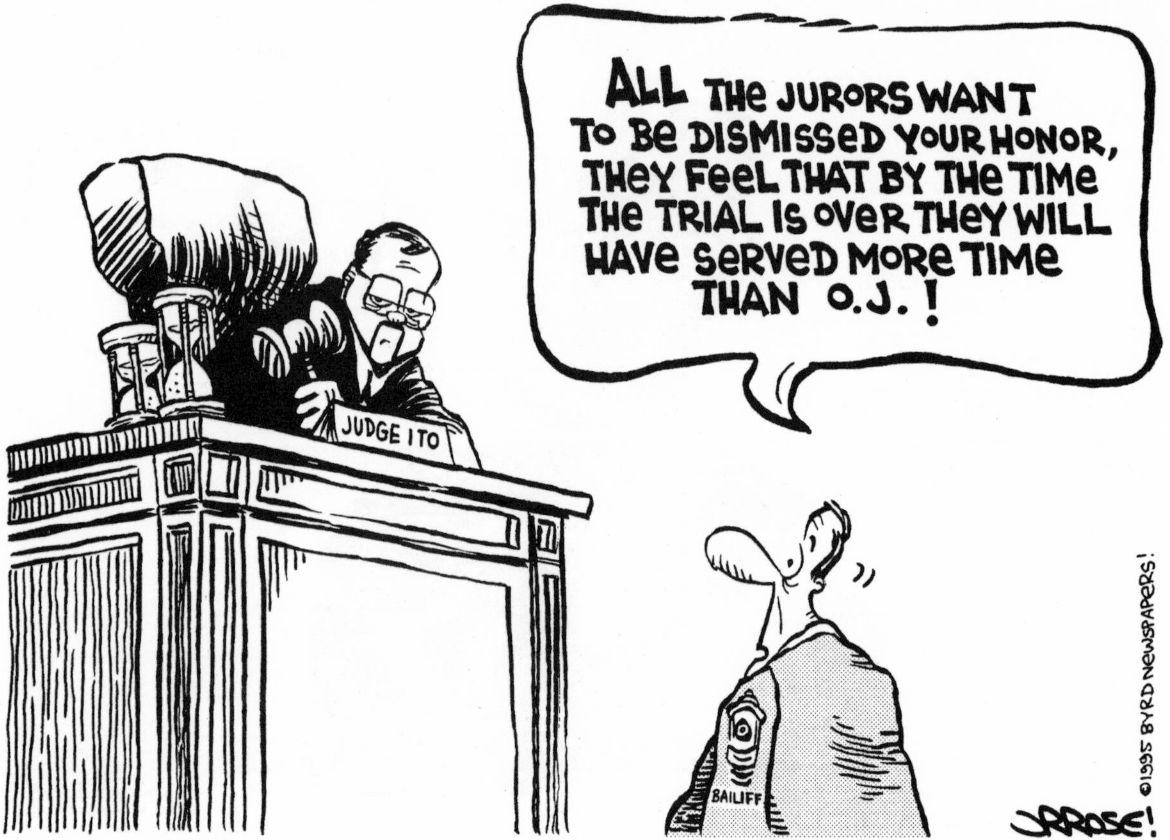

ALL THE JURORS WANT TO BE DISMISSED YOUR HONOR, THEY FEEL THAT BY THE TIME THE TRIAL IS OVER THEY WILL HAVE SERVED MORE TIME THAN O.J. !
JUDGE ITO
BAILIFF
©1995 BYRD NEWSPAPERS!
JRROSE!

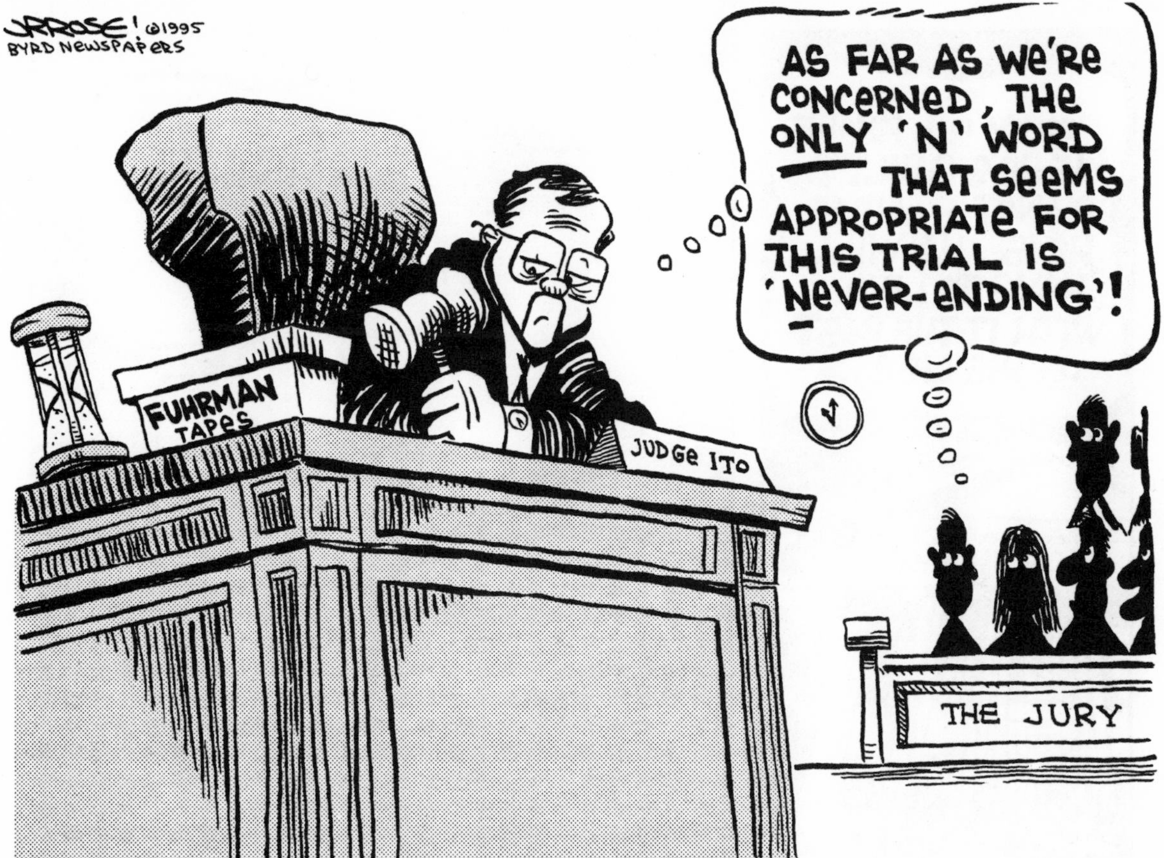
JRROSE! ©1995
BYRD NEWSPAPERS
AS FAR AS WE'RE CONCERNED, THE ONLY 'N' WORD THAT SEEMS APPROPRIATE FOR THIS TRIAL IS 'NEVER-ENDING'!
FUHRMAN TAPES
JUDGE ITO
THE JURY

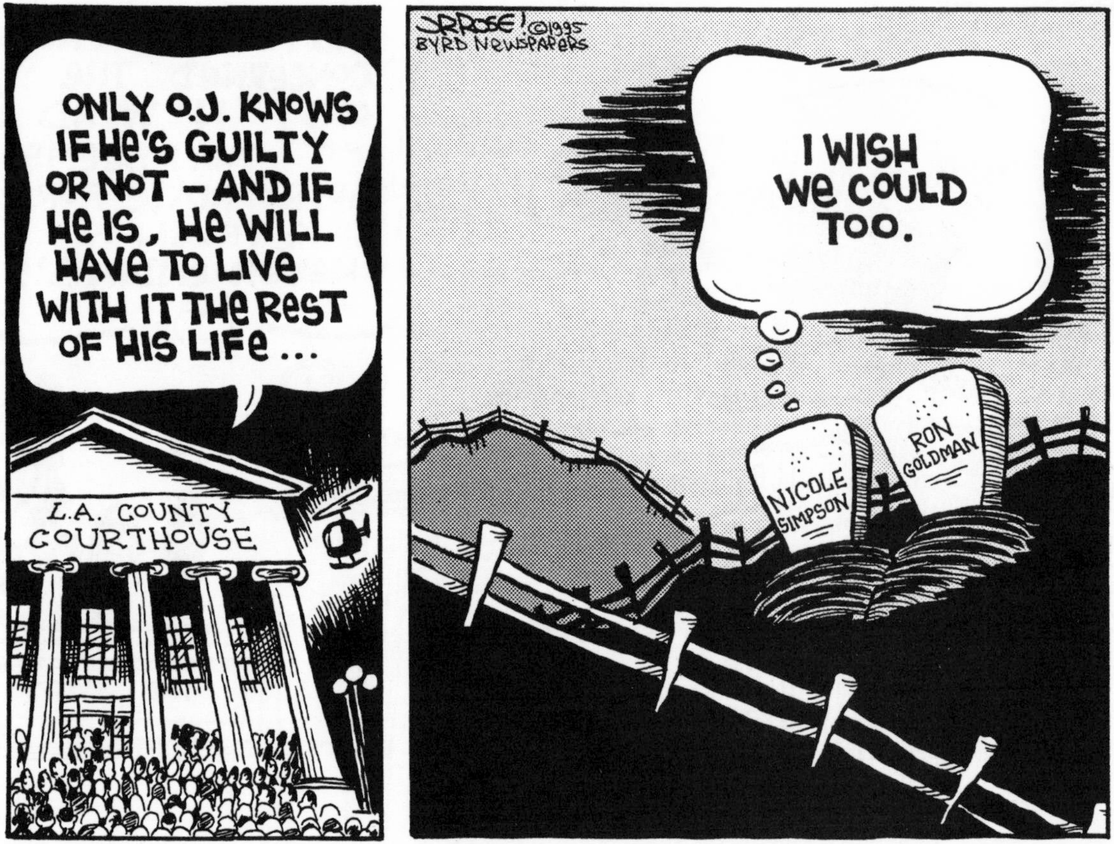
ONLY O.J. KNOWS IF HE'S GUILTY OR NOT - AND IF HE IS, HE WILL HAVE TO LIVE WITH IT THE REST OF HIS LIFE...
L.A. COUNTY COURTHOUSE
JRROSE! ©1995 BYRD NEWSPAPERS
I WISH WE COULD TOO.
NICOLE SIMPSON
RON GOLDMAN

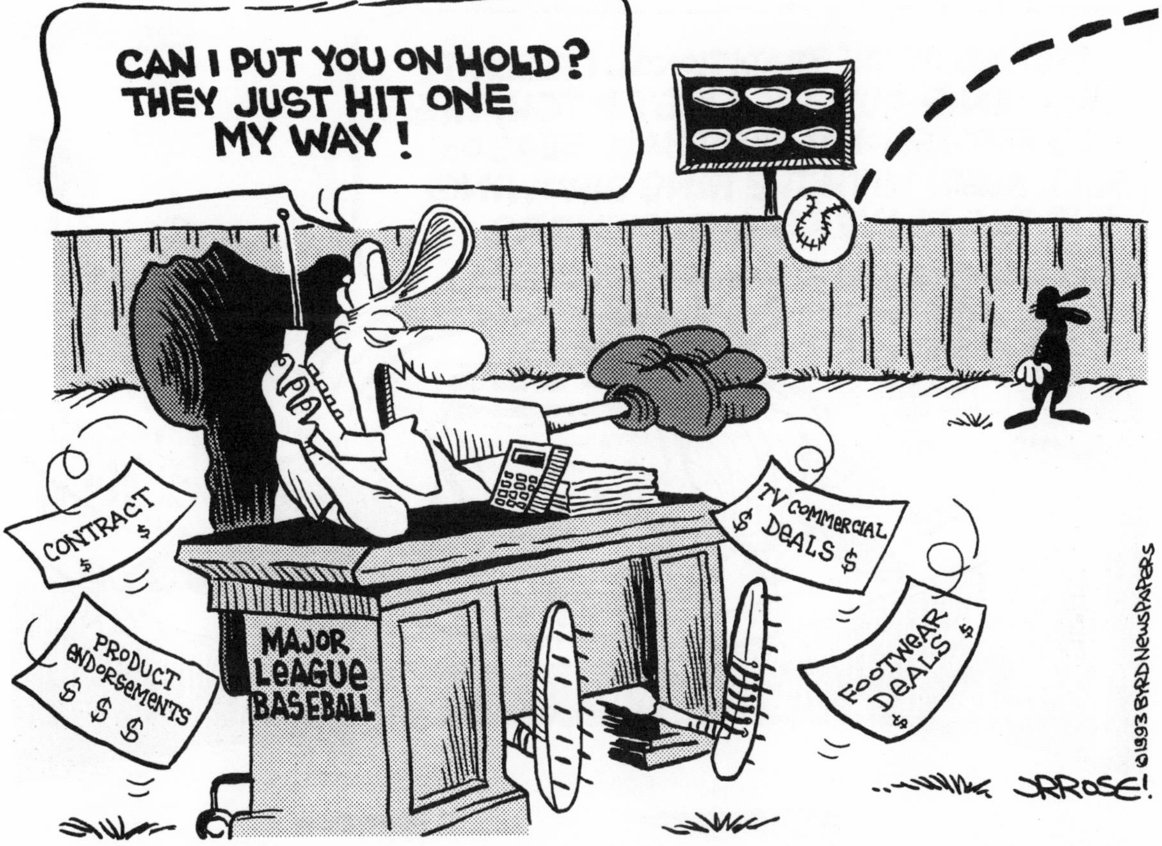
CAN I PUT YOU ON HOLD? THEY JUST HIT ONE MY WAY!
CONTRACT $ $
PRODUCT ENDORSEMENTS $ $ $
MAJOR LEAGUE BASEBALL
TV COMMERCIAL $ DEALS $
FOOTWEAR DEALS $ $
©1993 BYRD NEWSPAPERS
JRROSE!

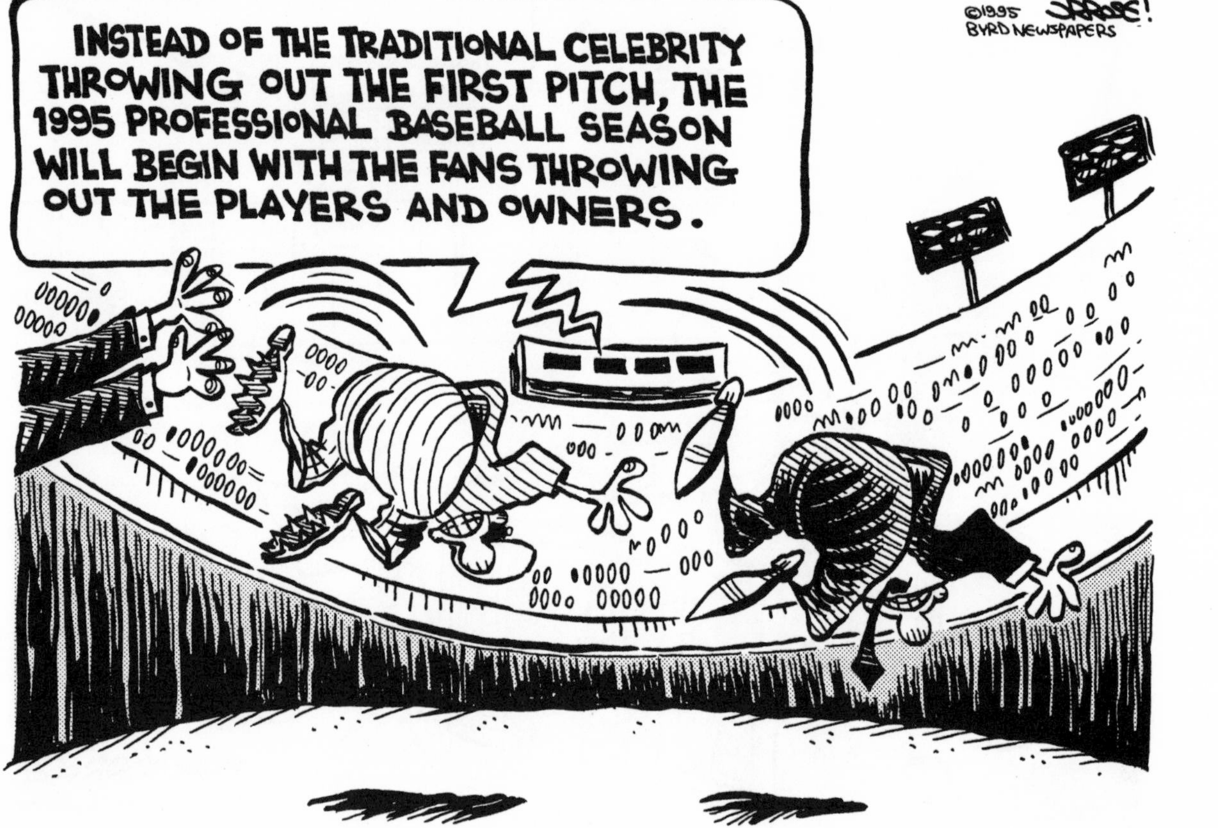
INSTEAD OF THE TRADITIONAL CELEBRITY THROWING OUT THE FIRST PITCH, THE 1995 PROFESSIONAL BASEBALL SEASON WILL BEGIN WITH THE FANS THROWING OUT THE PLAYERS AND OWNERS.
©1995 BYRD NEWSPAPERS

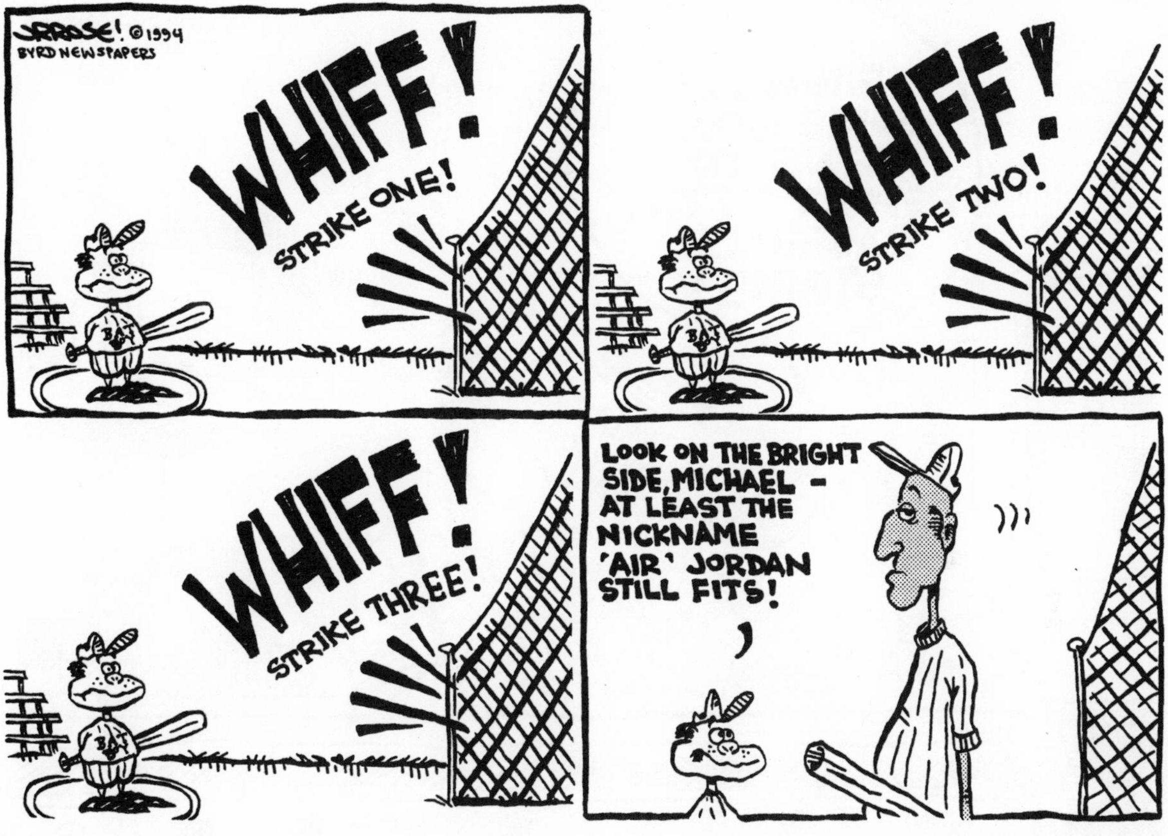
JRROSE! ©1994
BYRD NEWSPAPERS
WHIFF!
STRIKE ONE!
BAT
WHIFF!
STRIKE TWO!
BAT
WHIFF!
STRIKE THREE!
BAT
LOOK ON THE BRIGHT SIDE, MICHAEL - AT LEAST THE NICKNAME 'AIR' JORDAN STILL FITS!

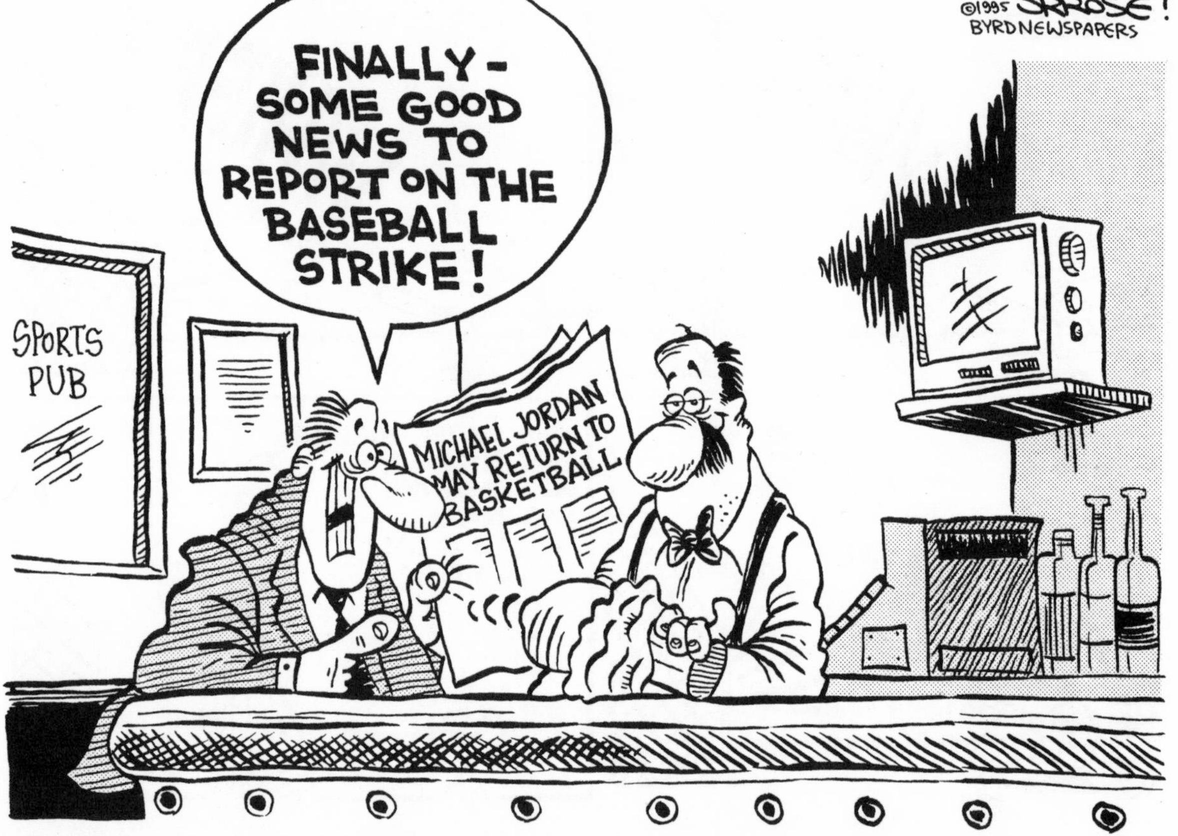
©1995 JRROSE!
BYRDNEWSPAPERS
FINALLY - SOME GOOD NEWS TO REPORT ON THE BASEBALL STRIKE!
SPORTS PUB
MICHAEL JORDAN MAY RETURN TO BASKETBALL

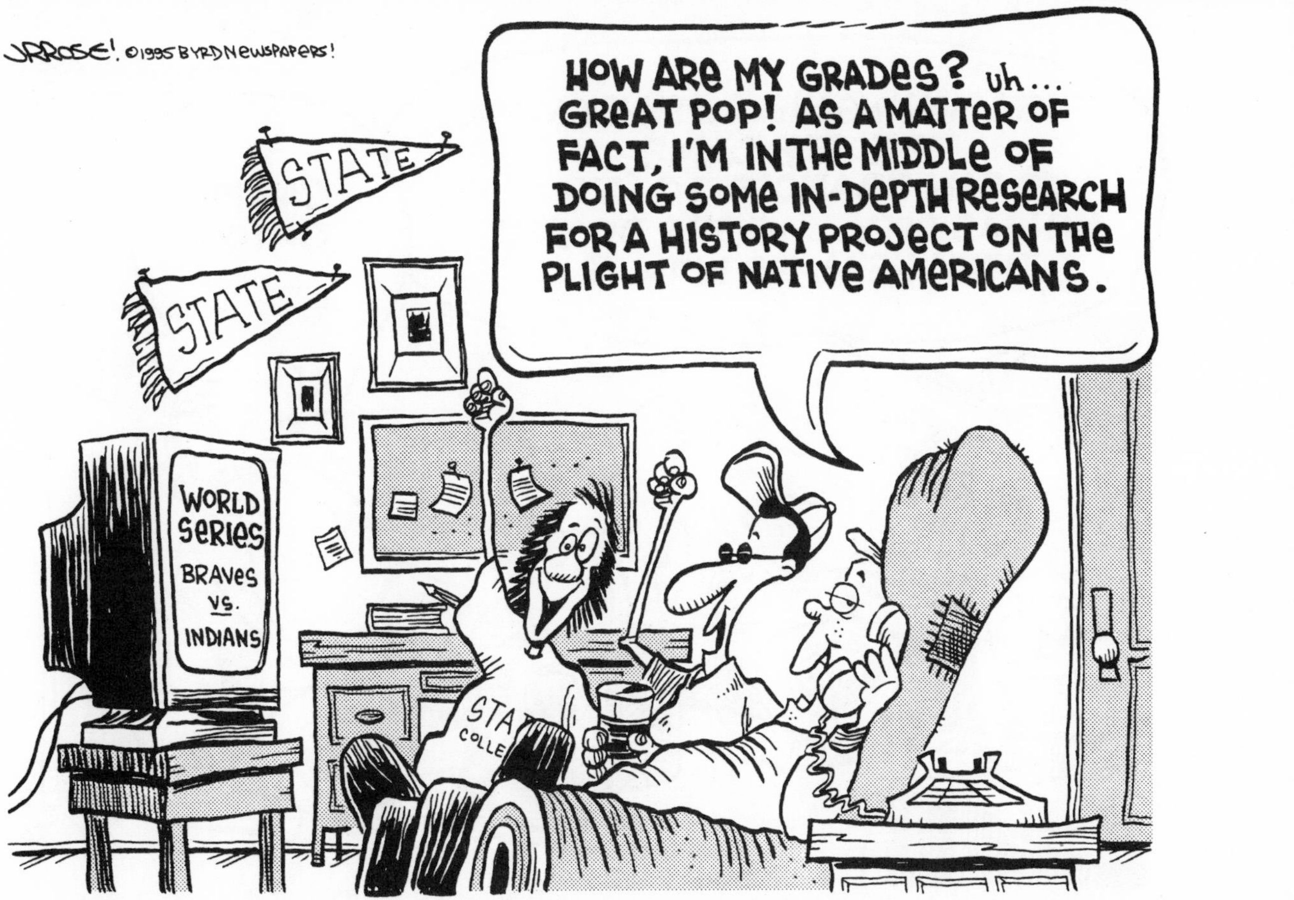
JRROSE! ©1995 BYRD NEWSPAPERS!
HOW ARE MY GRADES? uh... GREAT POP! AS A MATTER OF FACT, I'M IN THE MIDDLE OF DOING SOME IN-DEPTH RESEARCH FOR A HISTORY PROJECT ON THE PLIGHT OF NATIVE AMERICANS.
STATE
STATE
WORLD SERIES
BRAVES VS. INDIANS
STAT
COLLE

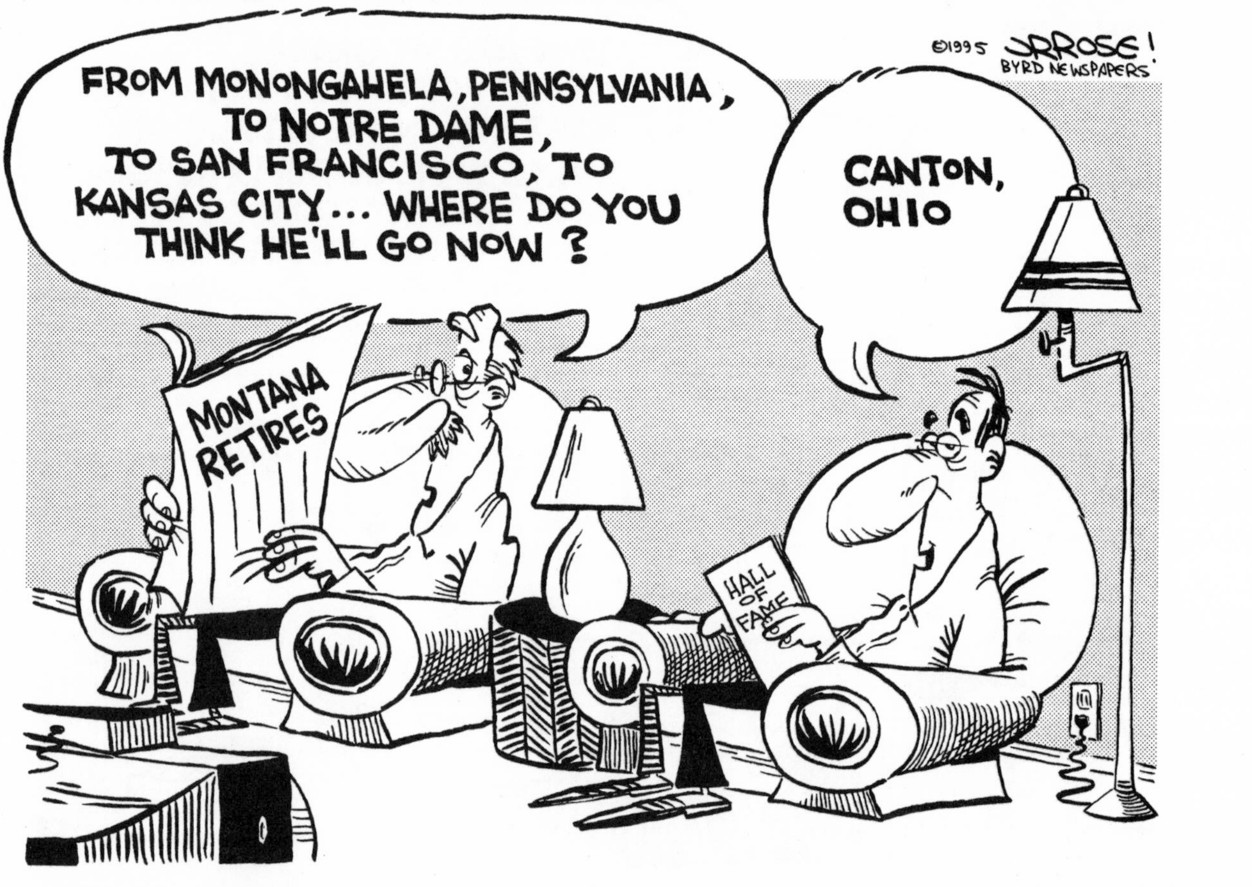
©1995 JRROSE! BYRD NEWSPAPERS
FROM MONONGAHELA, PENNSYLVANIA, TO NOTRE DAME, TO SAN FRANCISCO, TO KANSAS CITY... WHERE DO YOU THINK HE'LL GO NOW?
CANTON, OHIO
MONTANA RETIRES
HALL OF FAME

# Virginia
# and the
# Shenandoah Valley

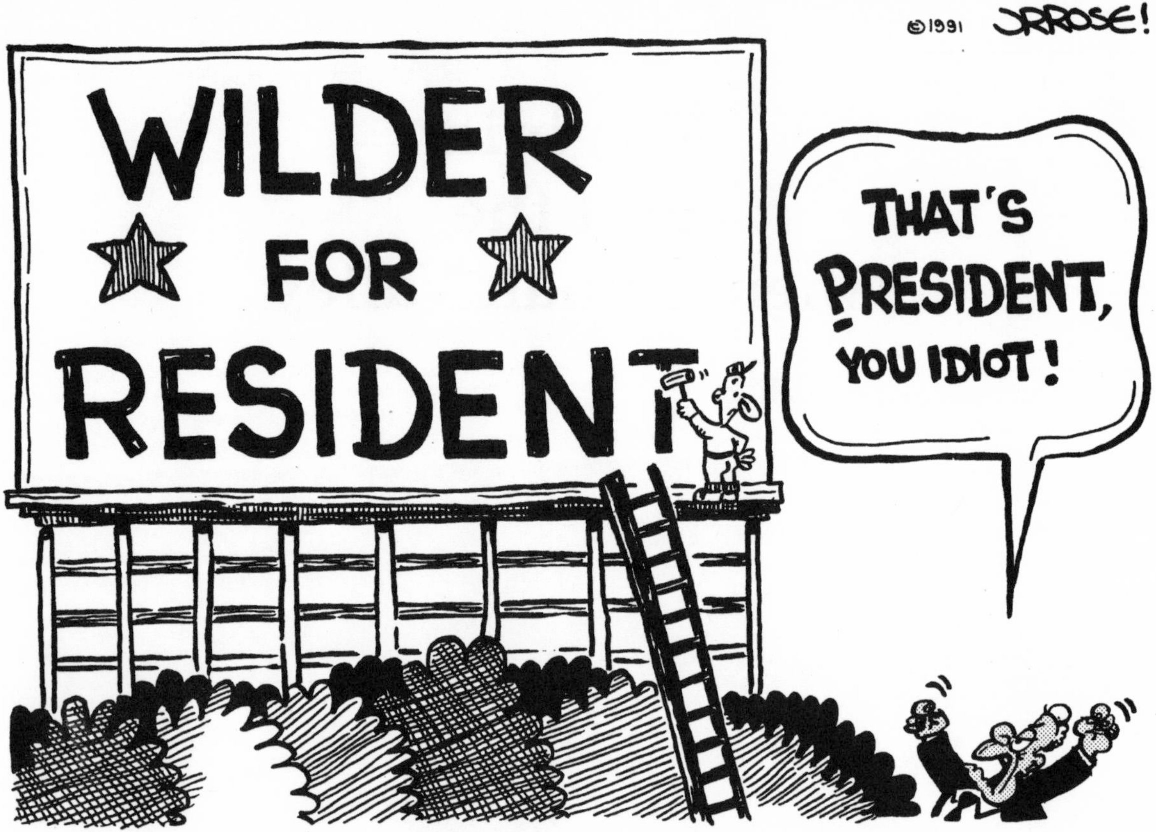

©1991 JRROSE!
WILDER FOR RESIDENT
THAT'S PRESIDENT, YOU IDIOT!


News Item: Governor Wilder spends a lot of time outside Virginia campaigning for President.

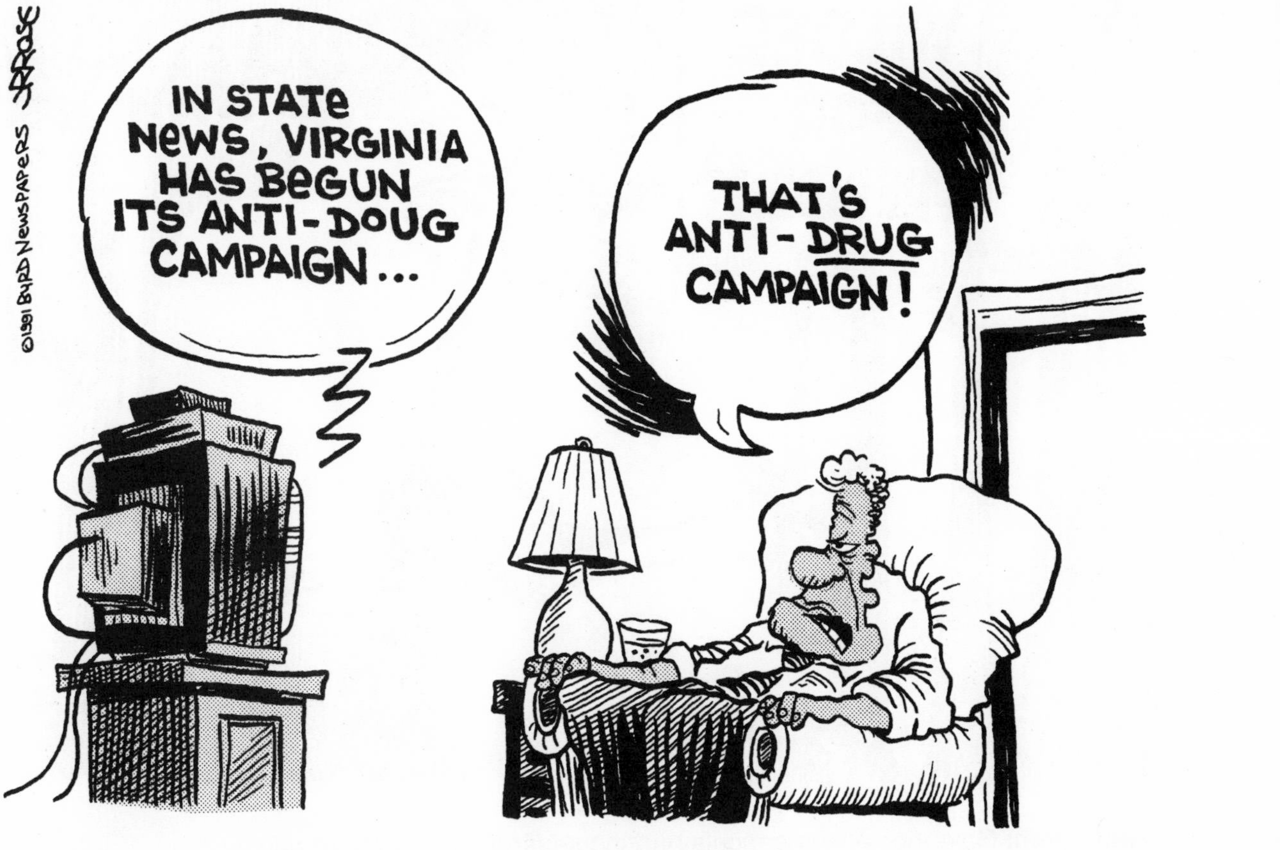
IN STATE NEWS, VIRGINIA HAS BEGUN ITS ANTI-DOUG CAMPAIGN...
THAT'S ANTI-DRUG CAMPAIGN!
©1991 BYRD NEWSPAPERS
JDROSE

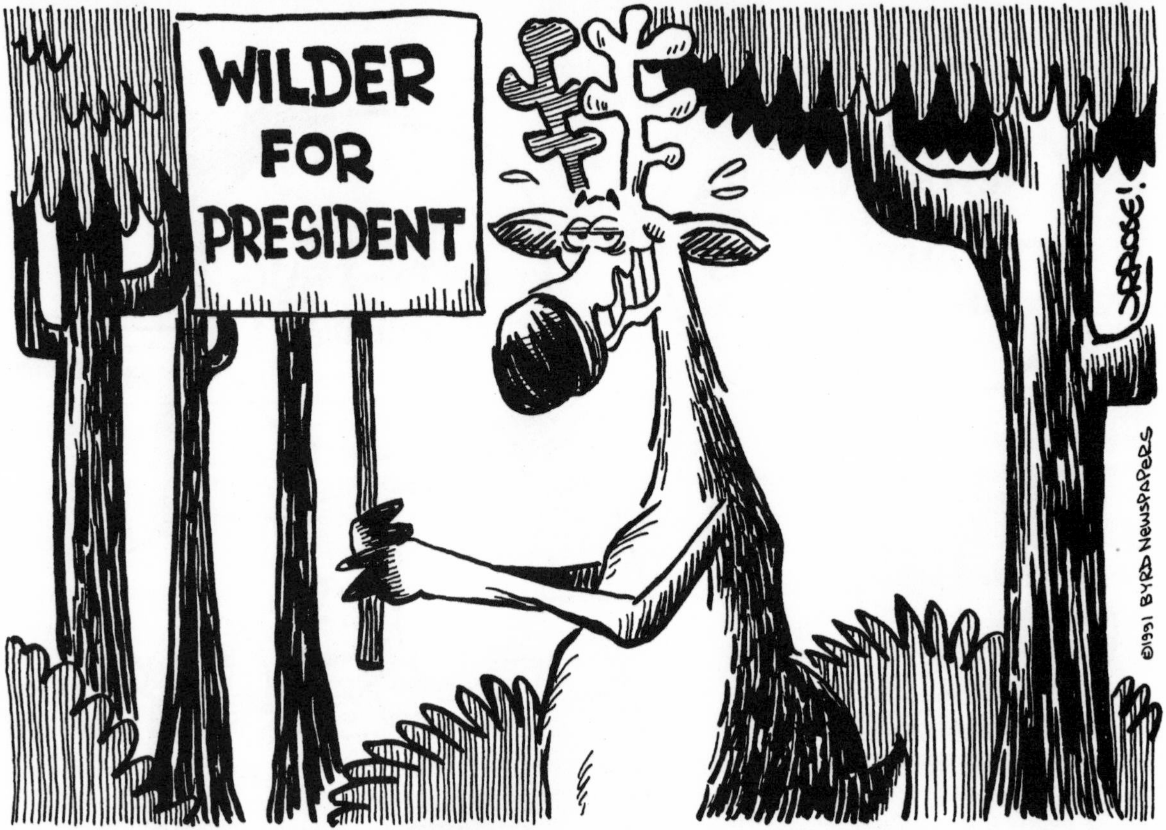
WILDER
FOR
PRESIDENT
©1991 BYRD NEWSPAPERS

News Item: Governor Wilder cancels hunting season due to lack of rain.

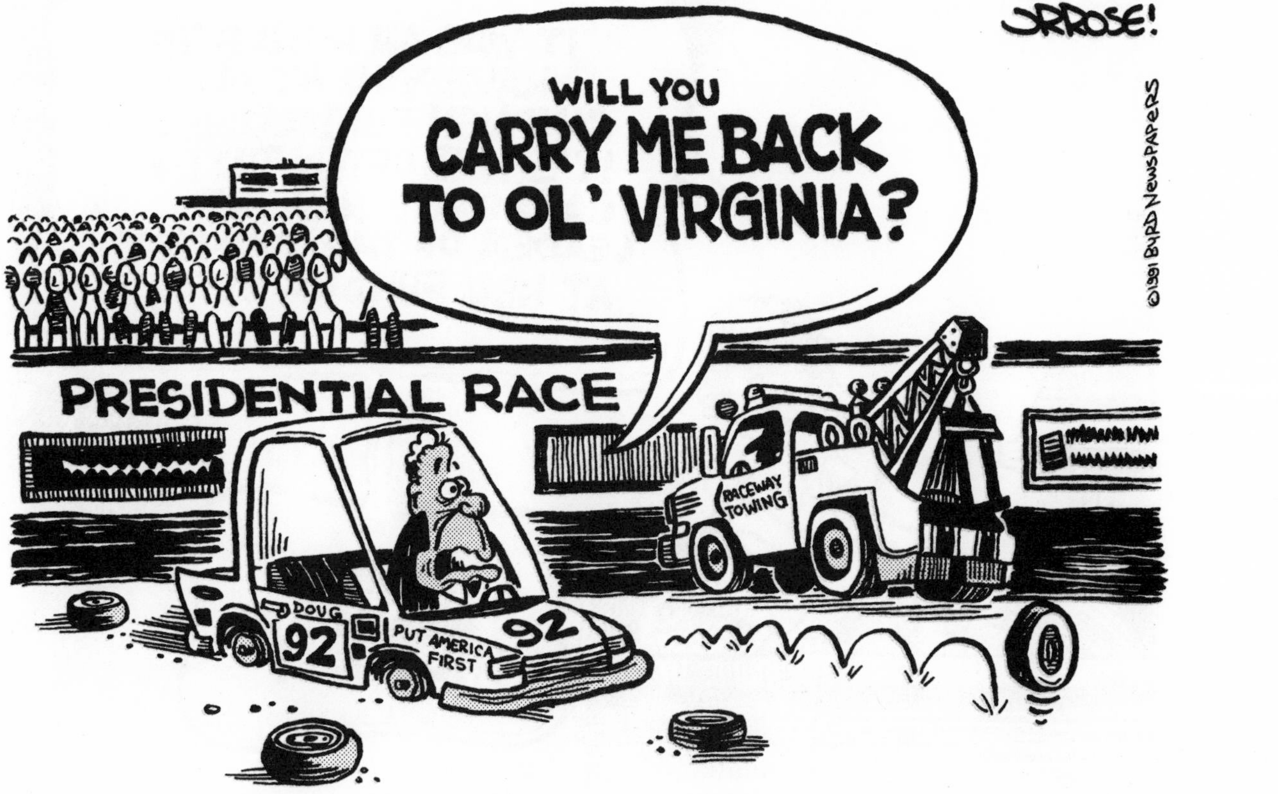

JRROSE!
©1991 BYRD NEWSPAPERS
WILL YOU
CARRY ME BACK
TO OL' VIRGINIA?
PRESIDENTIAL RACE
RACEWAY TOWING
DOUG
92
92
PUT AMERICA FIRST

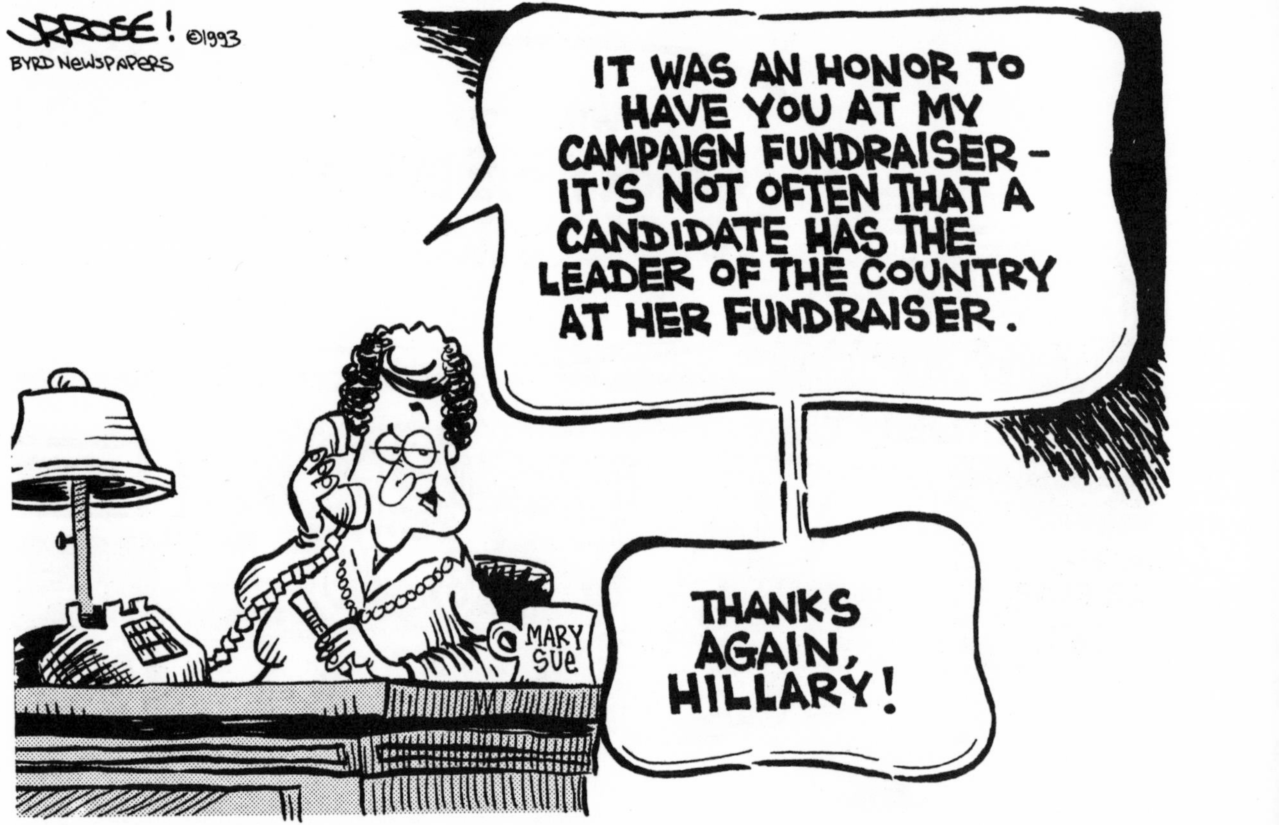
JRROSE! ©1993
BYRD NEWSPAPERS
IT WAS AN HONOR TO HAVE YOU AT MY CAMPAIGN FUNDRAISER - IT'S NOT OFTEN THAT A CANDIDATE HAS THE LEADER OF THE COUNTRY AT HER FUNDRAISER.
THANKS AGAIN, HILLARY!
MARY SUE

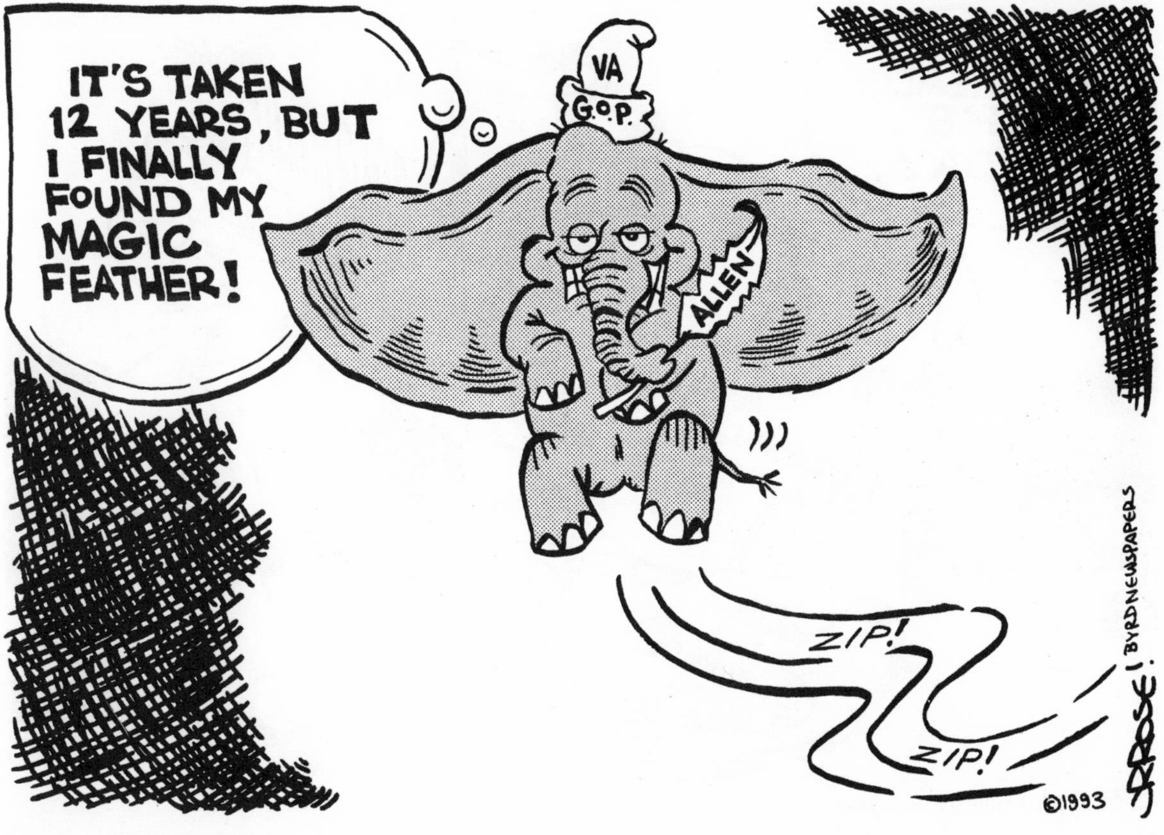
IT'S TAKEN 12 YEARS, BUT I FINALLY FOUND MY MAGIC FEATHER!
VA
G.O.P.
ALLEN
ZIP!
ZIP!
BYRDNEWSPAPERS
©1993

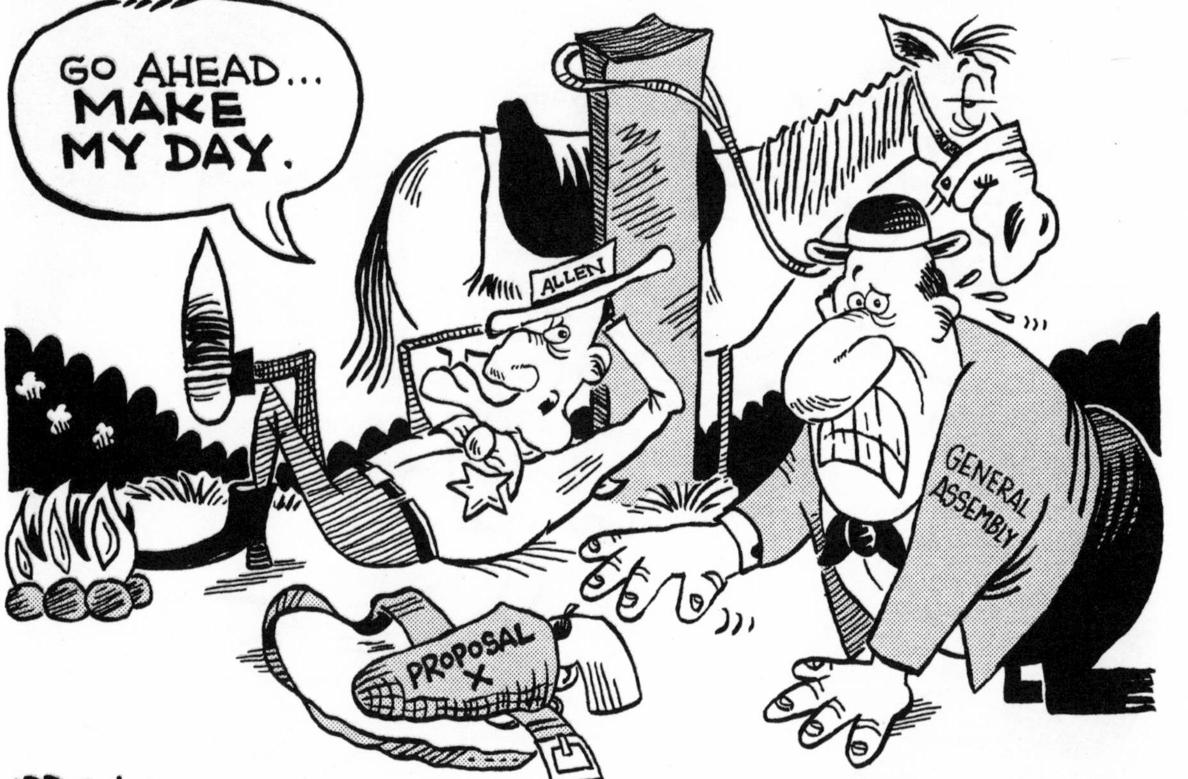
GO AHEAD... MAKE MY DAY.
ALLEN
GENERAL ASSEMBLY
PROPOSAL X
JRROSE! ©1994 BYRD NEWSPAPERS

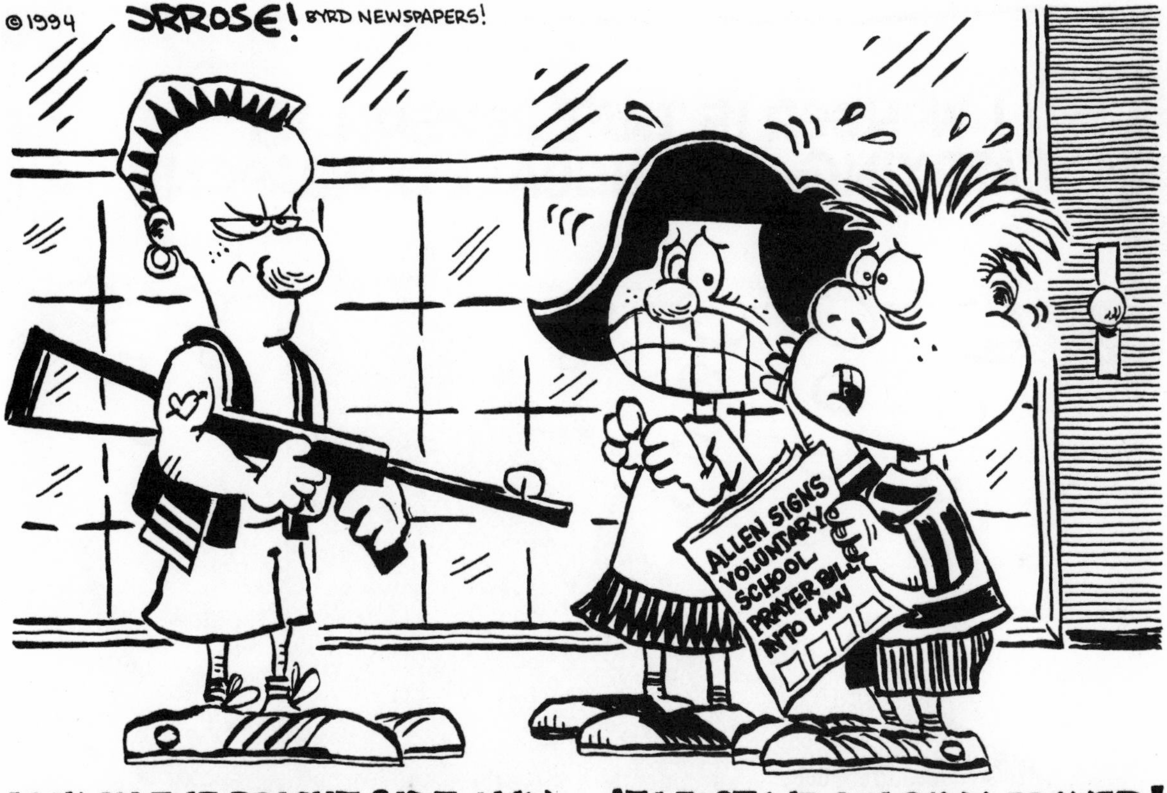
©1994
JRROSE! BYRD NEWSPAPERS!
ALLEN SIGNS VOLUNTARY SCHOOL PRAYER BILL INTO LAW

LOOK ON THE BRIGHT SIDE AMY...AT LEAST WE CAN SAY A PRAYER!

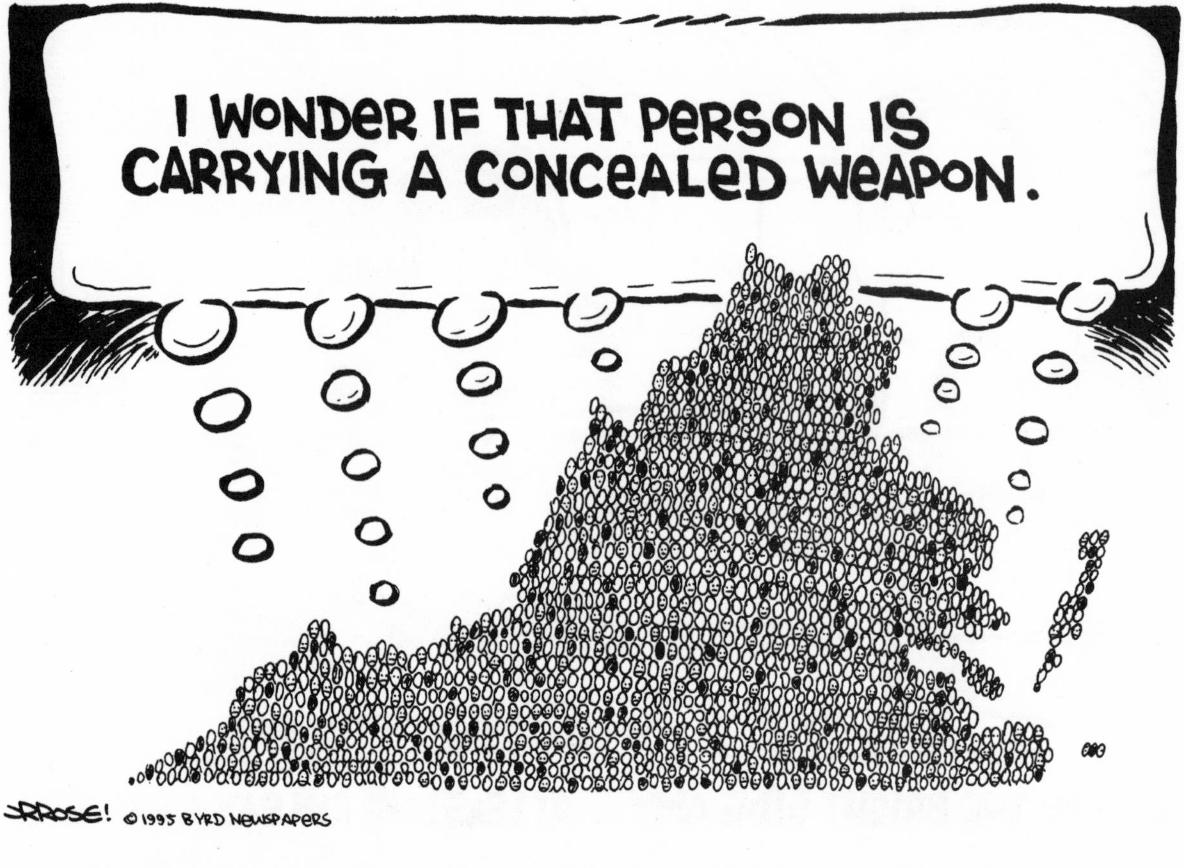
I WONDER IF THAT PERSON IS CARRYING A CONCEALED WEAPON.
JRROSE! © 1995 BYRD NEWSPAPERS

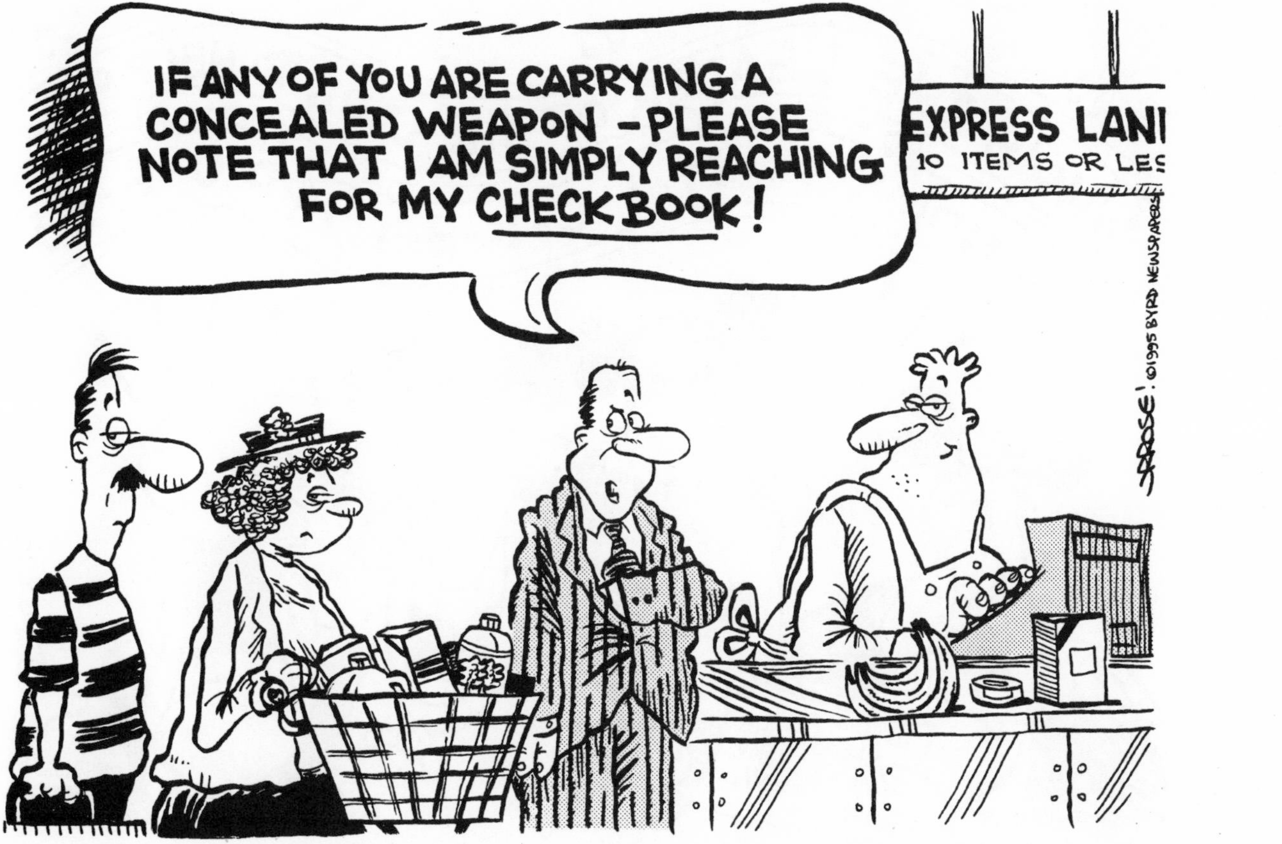
IF ANY OF YOU ARE CARRYING A CONCEALED WEAPON - PLEASE NOTE THAT I AM SIMPLY REACHING FOR MY CHECKBOOK!
EXPRESS LANE
10 ITEMS OR LESS
©1995 BYRD NEWSPAPERS

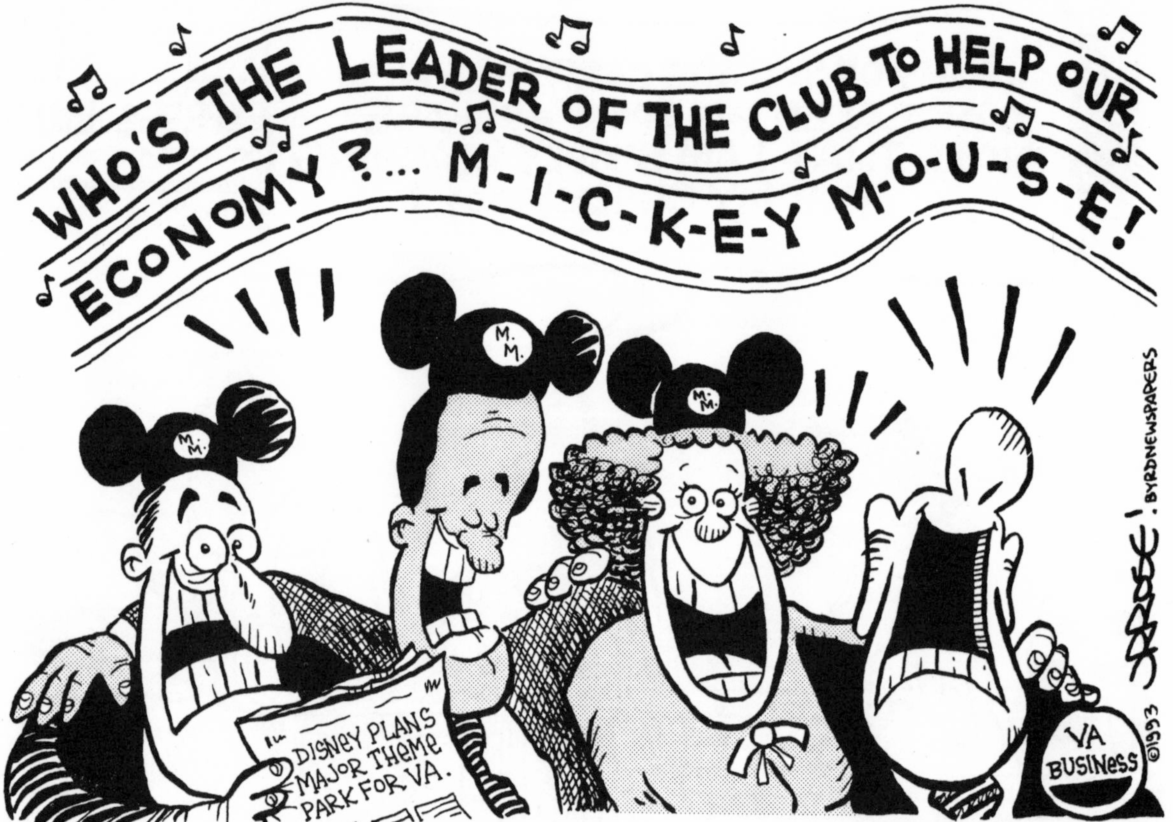
WHO'S THE LEADER OF THE CLUB TO HELP OUR ECONOMY?... M-I-C-K-E-Y M-O-U-S-E!
M. M.
DISNEY PLANS MAJOR THEME PARK FOR VA.
VA BUSINESS
©1993 . BYRDNEWSPAPERS

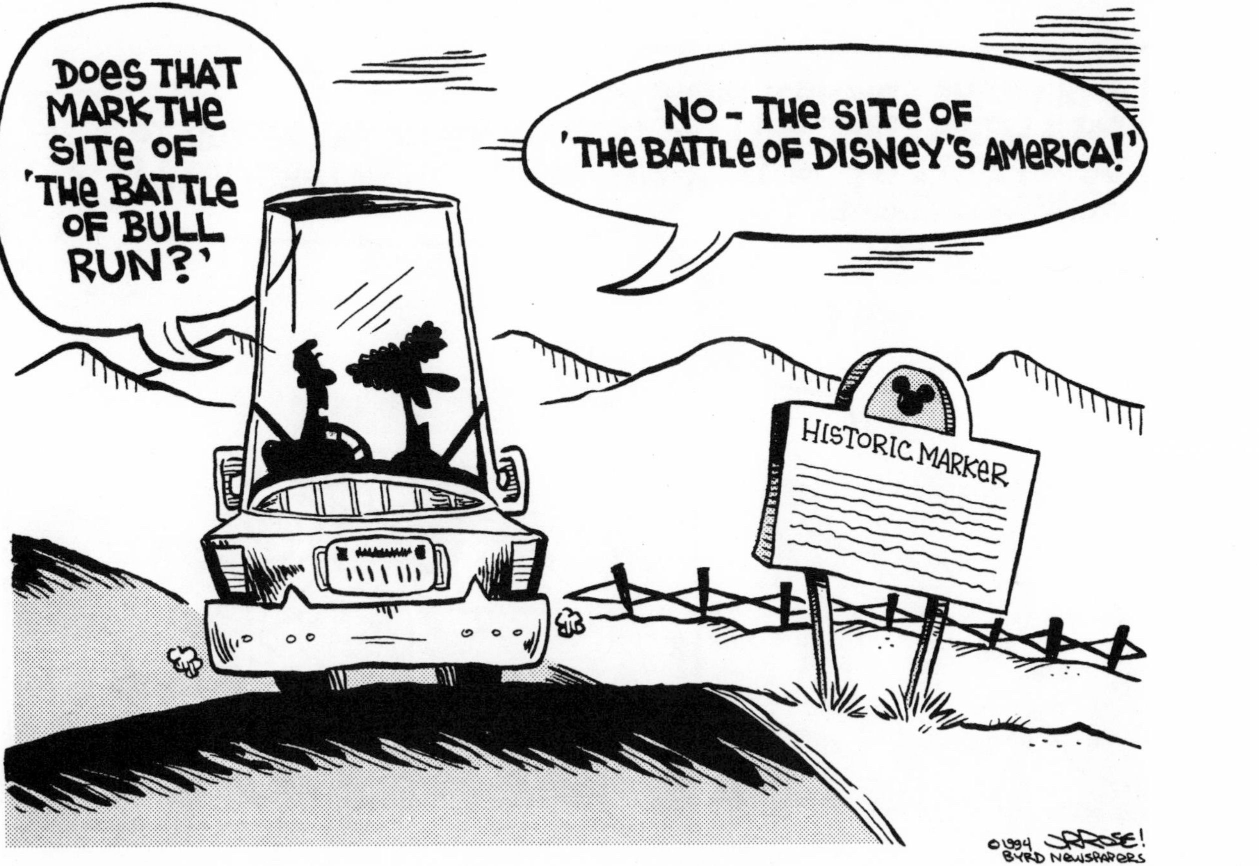
DOES THAT MARK THE SITE OF 'THE BATTLE OF BULL RUN?'
NO - THE SITE OF 'THE BATTLE OF DISNEY'S AMERICA!'
HISTORIC MARKER
©1994 JRROSE! BYRD NEWSPAPERS

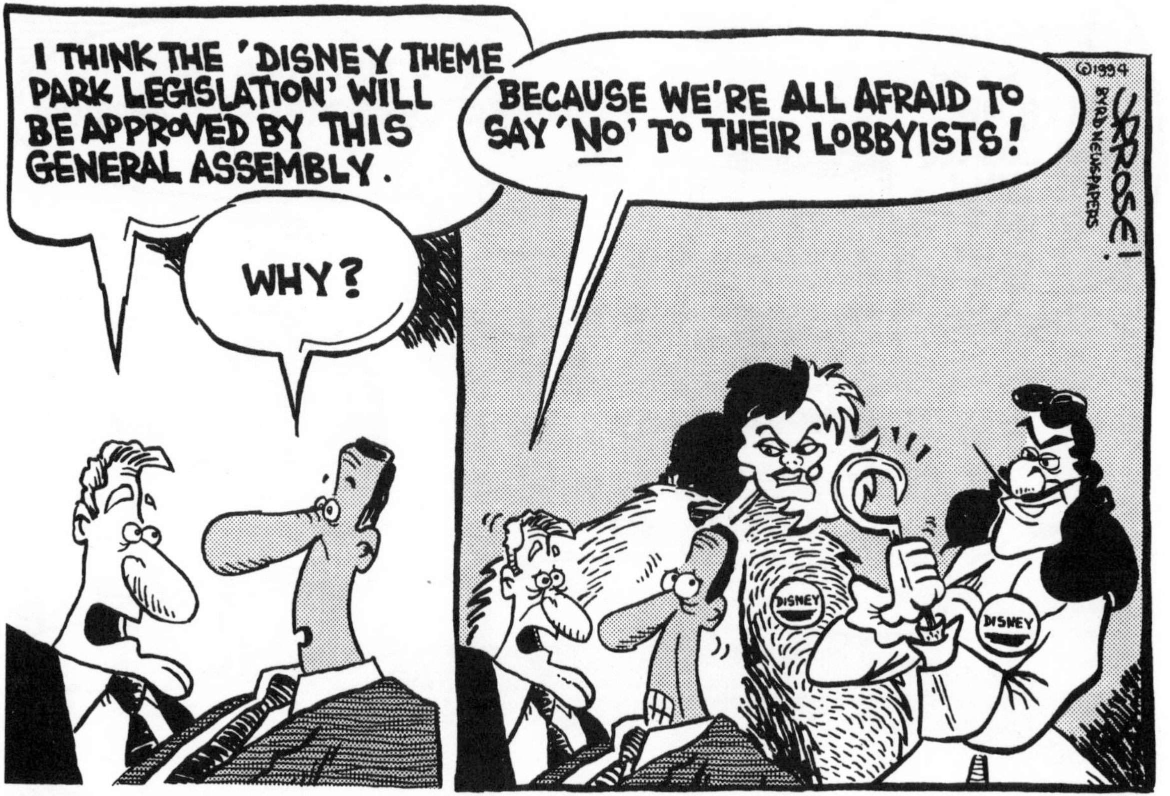
I THINK THE 'DISNEY THEME PARK LEGISLATION' WILL BE APPROVED BY THIS GENERAL ASSEMBLY.
WHY?
BECAUSE WE'RE ALL AFRAID TO SAY 'NO' TO THEIR LOBBYISTS!
DISNEY
DISNEY
©1994
ROSE
BYRD NEWSPAPERS

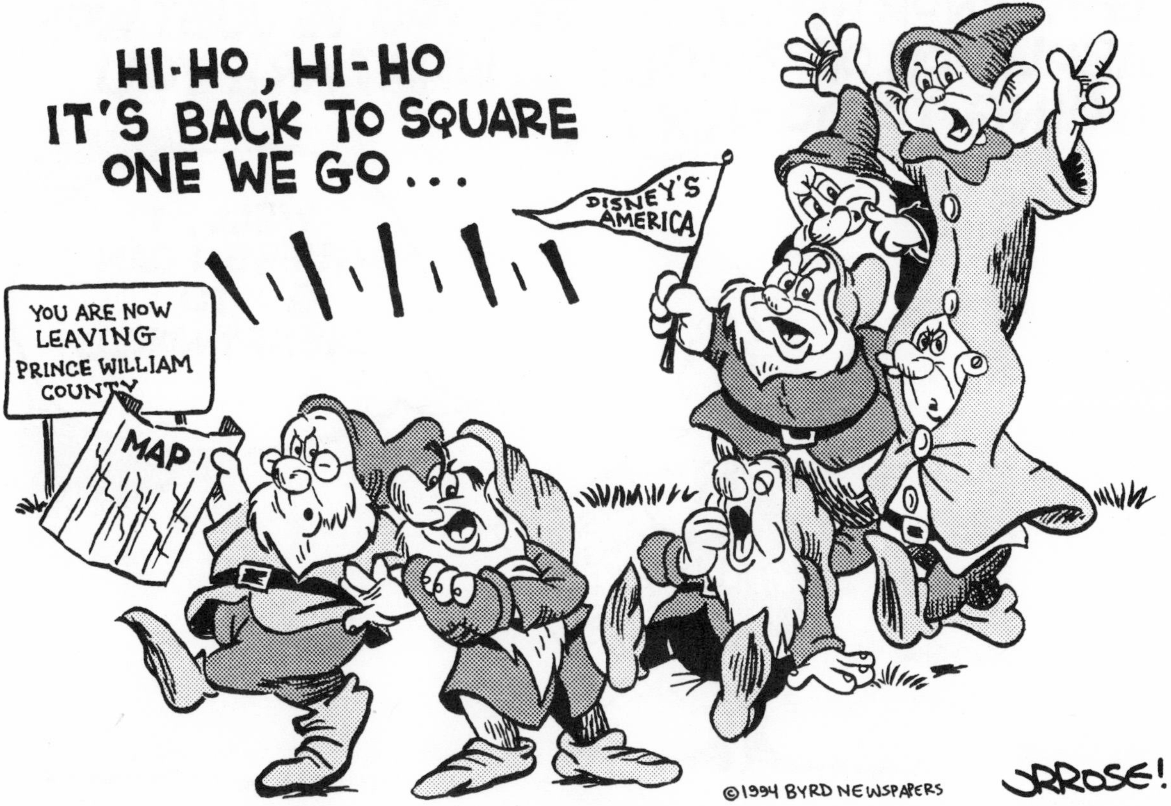
HI-HO, HI-HO
IT'S BACK TO SQUARE
ONE WE GO...
DISNEY'S AMERICA
YOU ARE NOW
LEAVING
PRINCE WILLIAM
COUNTY
MAP
©1994 BYRD NEWSPAPERS
JRROSE!

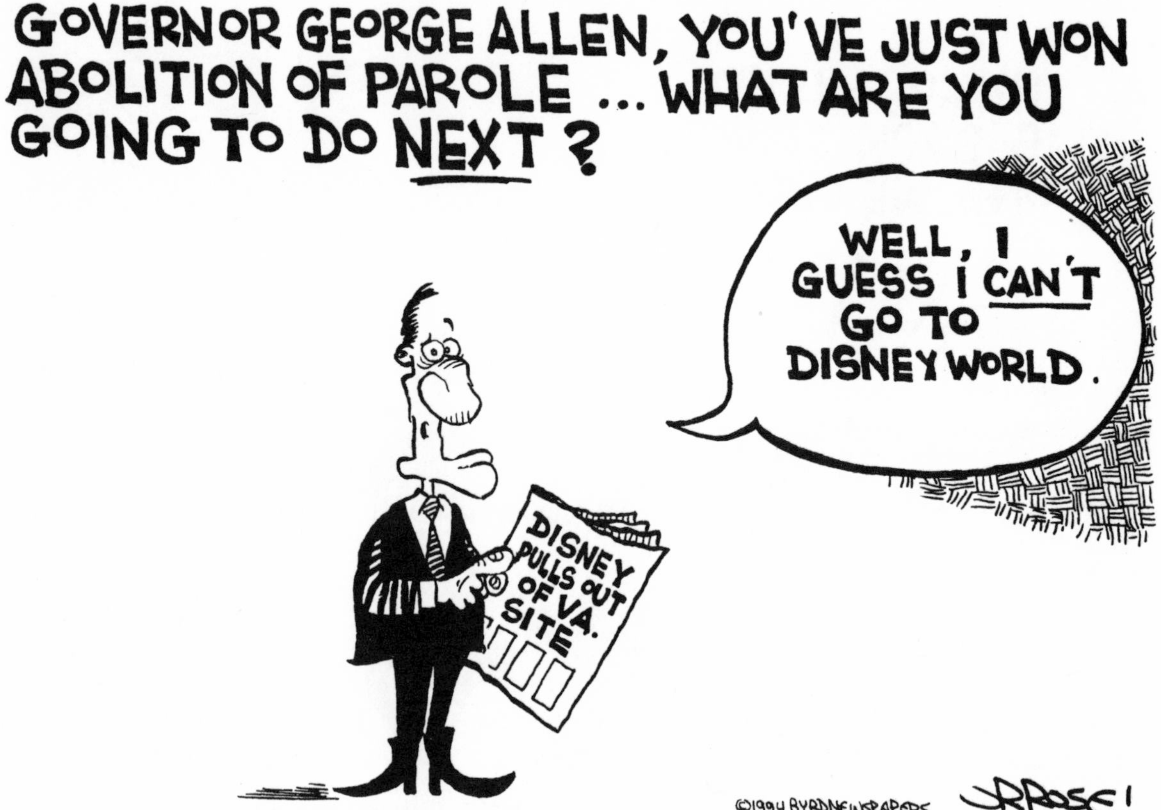
GOVERNOR GEORGE ALLEN, YOU'VE JUST WON ABOLITION OF PAROLE ... WHAT ARE YOU GOING TO DO NEXT ?
WELL, I GUESS I CAN'T GO TO DISNEY WORLD.
DISNEY PULLS OUT OF VA. SITE
©1994 BYRD NEWSPAPERS
JRROSE!

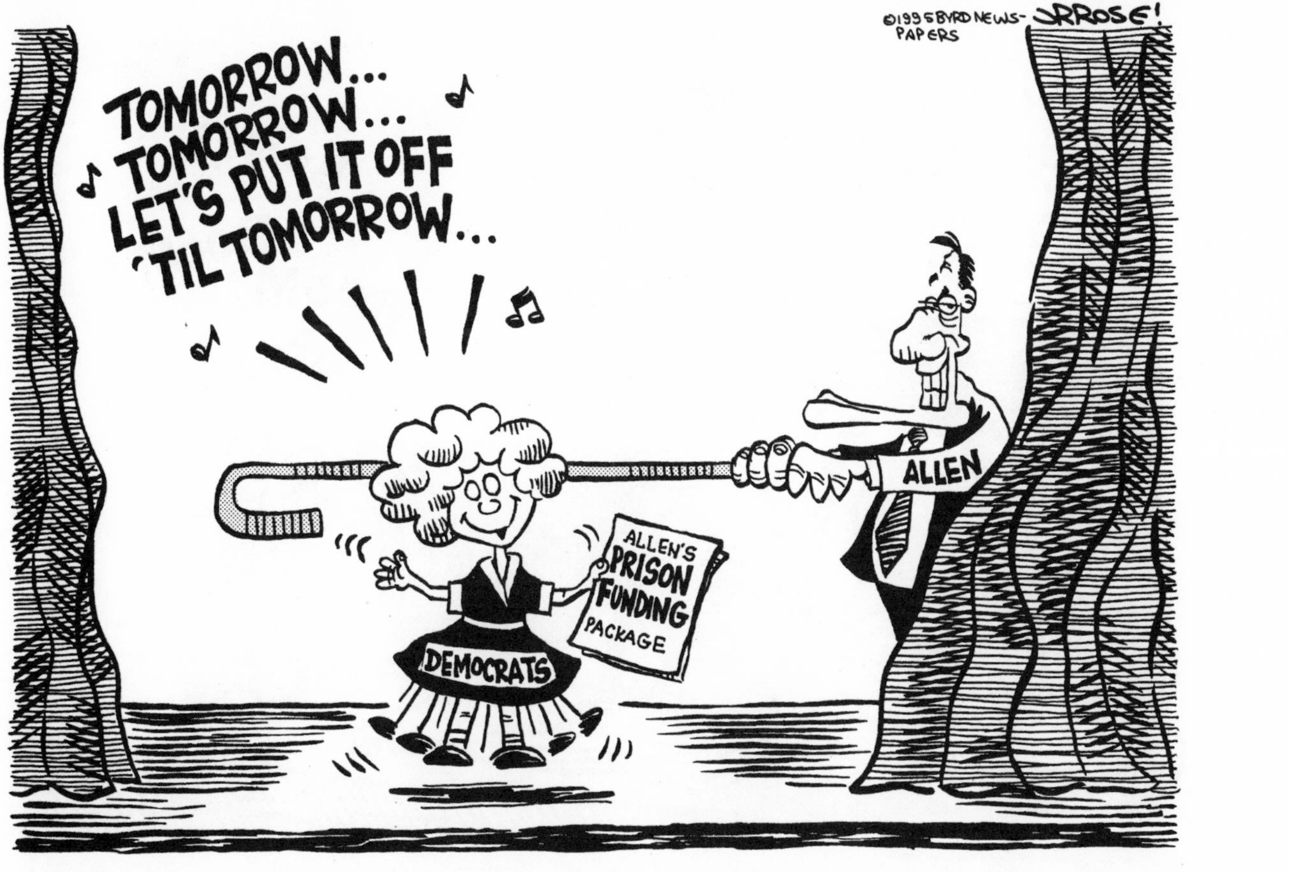

©1995 BYRD NEWS-PAPERS
JRROSE!
TOMORROW... TOMORROW... LET'S PUT IT OFF 'TIL TOMORROW...
ALLEN
ALLEN'S PRISON FUNDING PACKAGE
DEMOCRATS

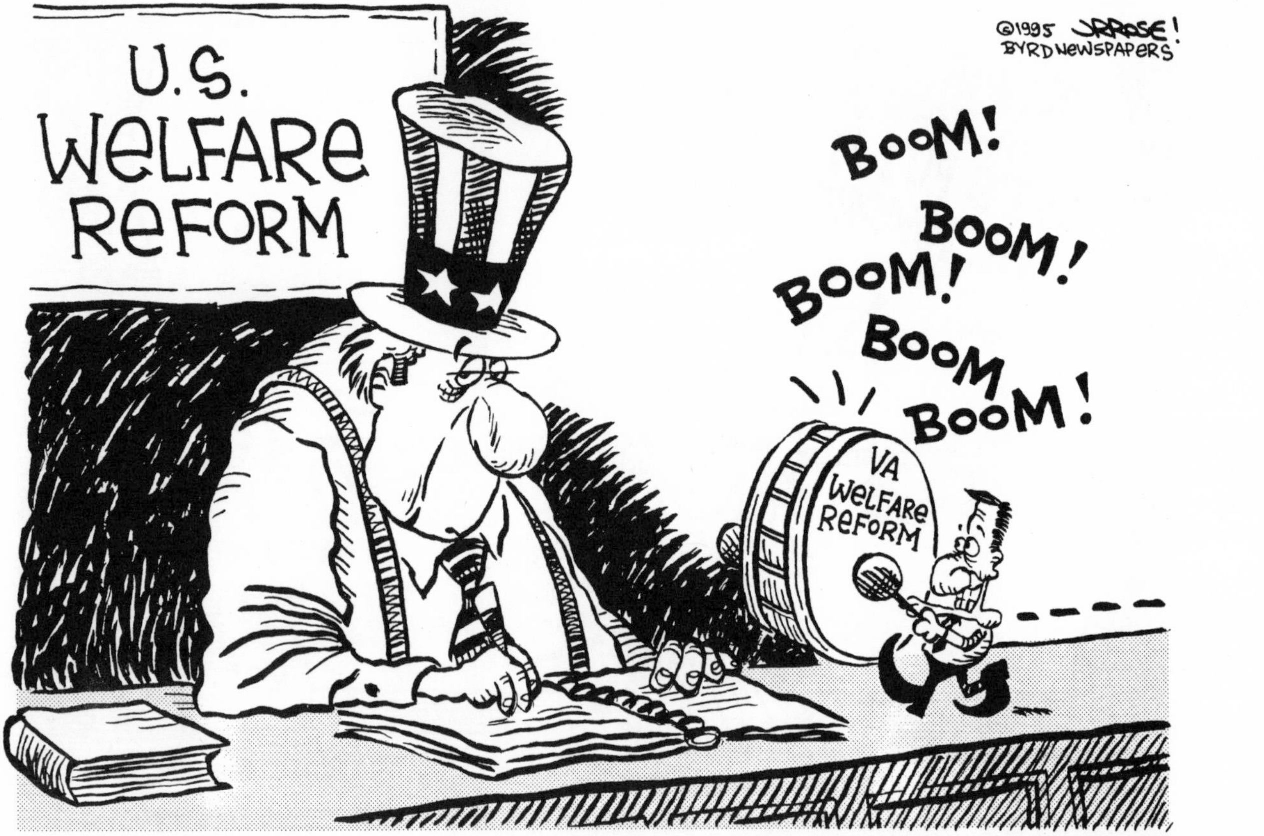
©1995 JRROSE!
BYRD NEWSPAPERS
U.S. WELFARE REFORM
BOOM!
BOOM!
BOOM!
BOOM
BOOM!
VA WELFARE REFORM

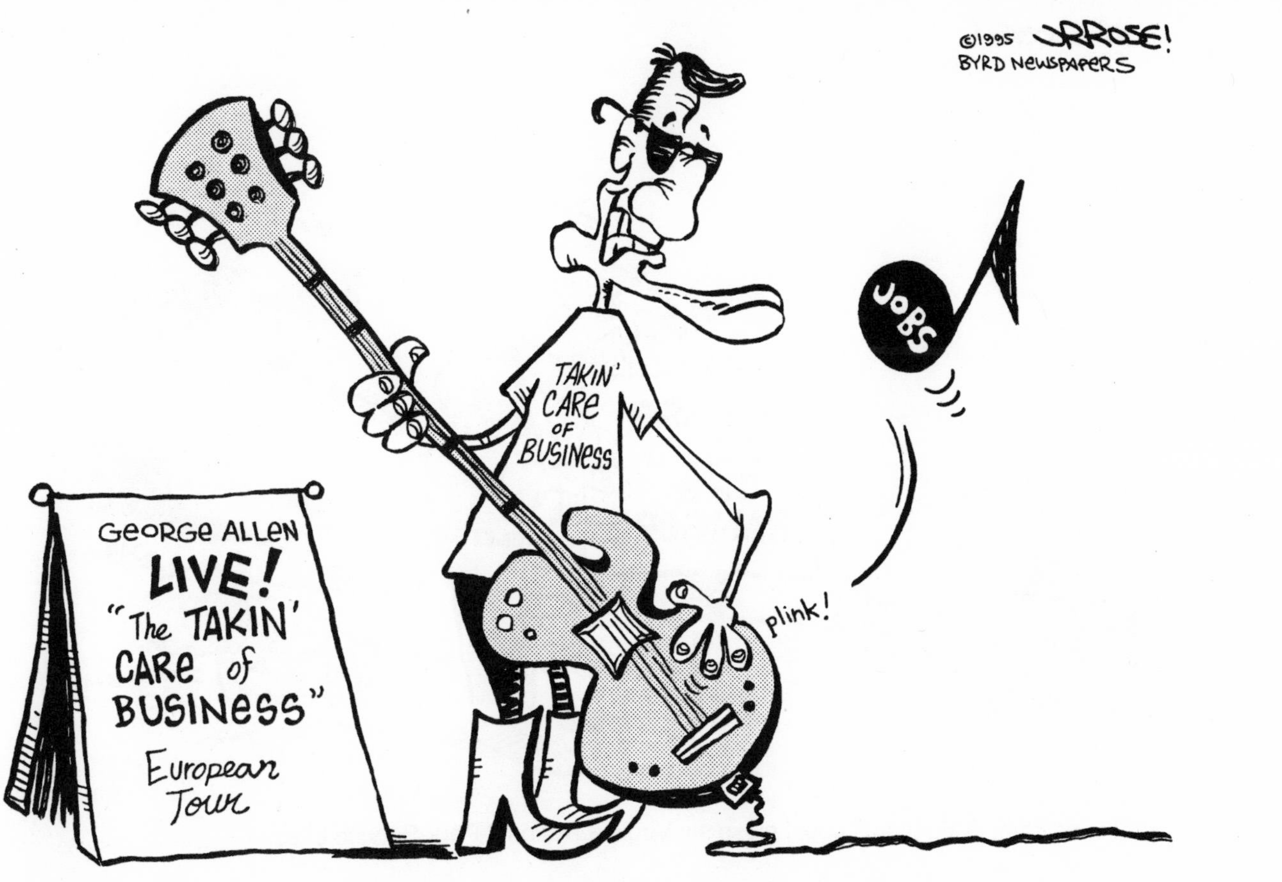
©1995 JRROSE!
BYRD NEWSPAPERS
TAKIN' CARE OF BUSINESS
JOBS
plink!
GEORGE ALLEN
LIVE!
"The TAKIN' CARE of BUSINESS"
European Tour

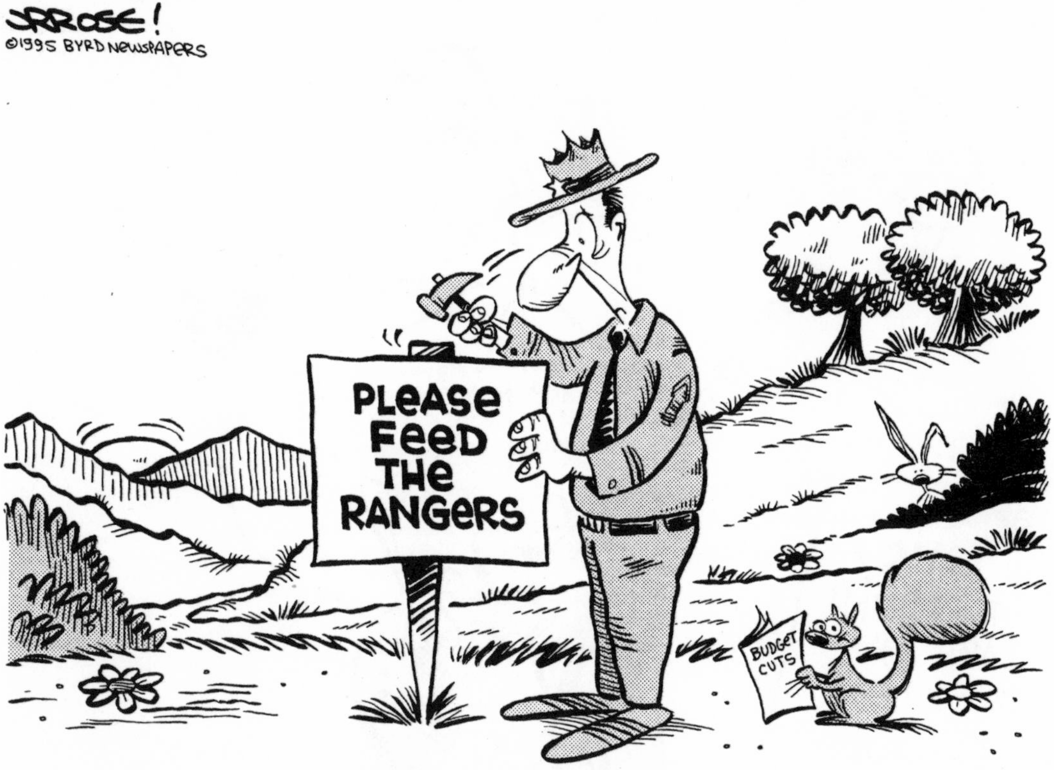
JRROSE!
©1995 BYRD NEWSPAPERS
PLEASE FEED THE RANGERS
BUDGET CUTS

News Item: Budget cuts could close six Virginia National Park Service sites.

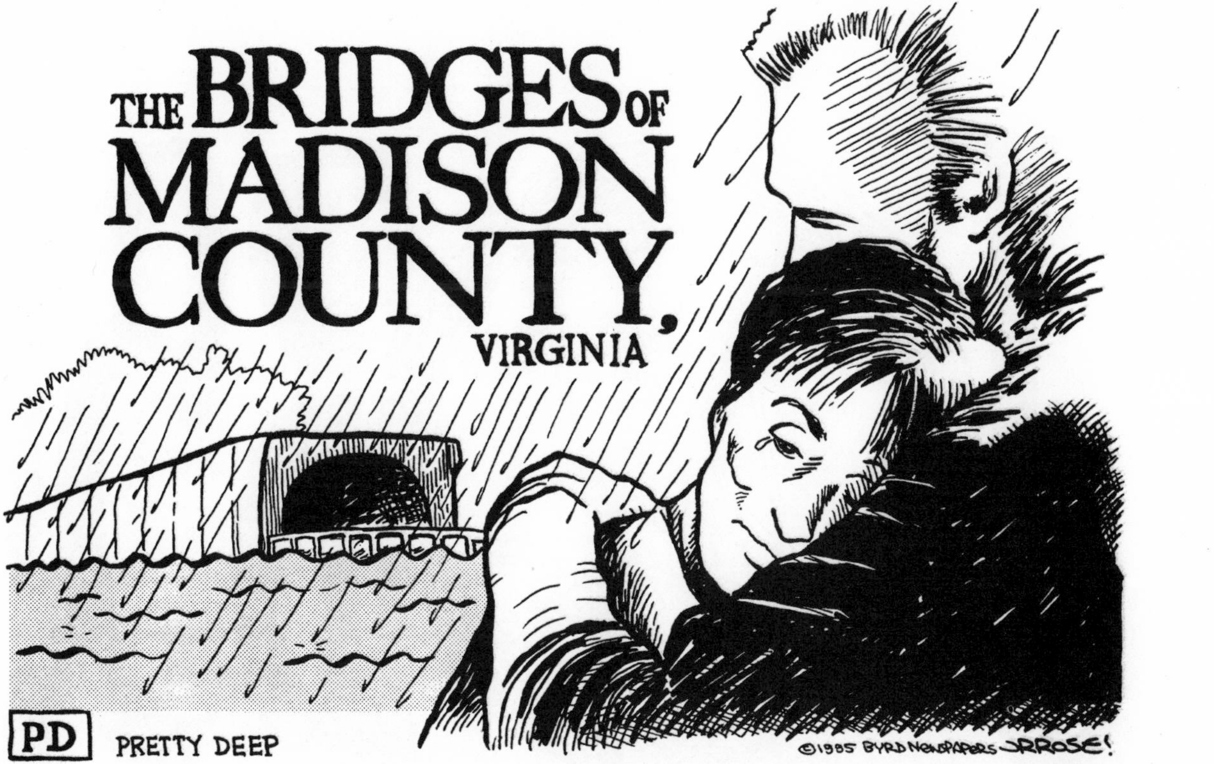
THE BRIDGES OF MADISON COUNTY, VIRGINIA
PD
PRETTY DEEP
©1995 BYRD NEWSPAPERS JRROSE!

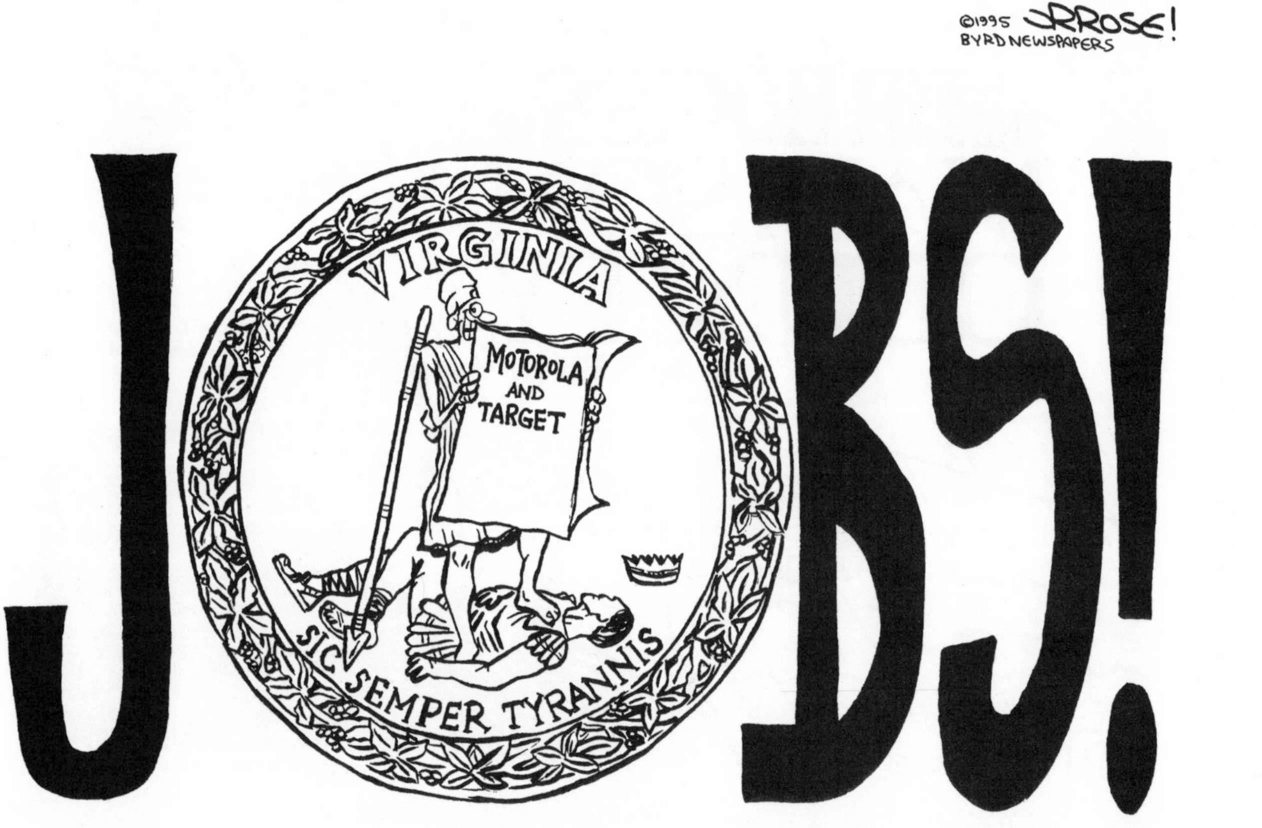
©1995 JRROSE!
BYRD NEWSPAPERS
J
BS!
VIRGINIA
MOTOROLA AND TARGET
SIC SEMPER TYRANNIS

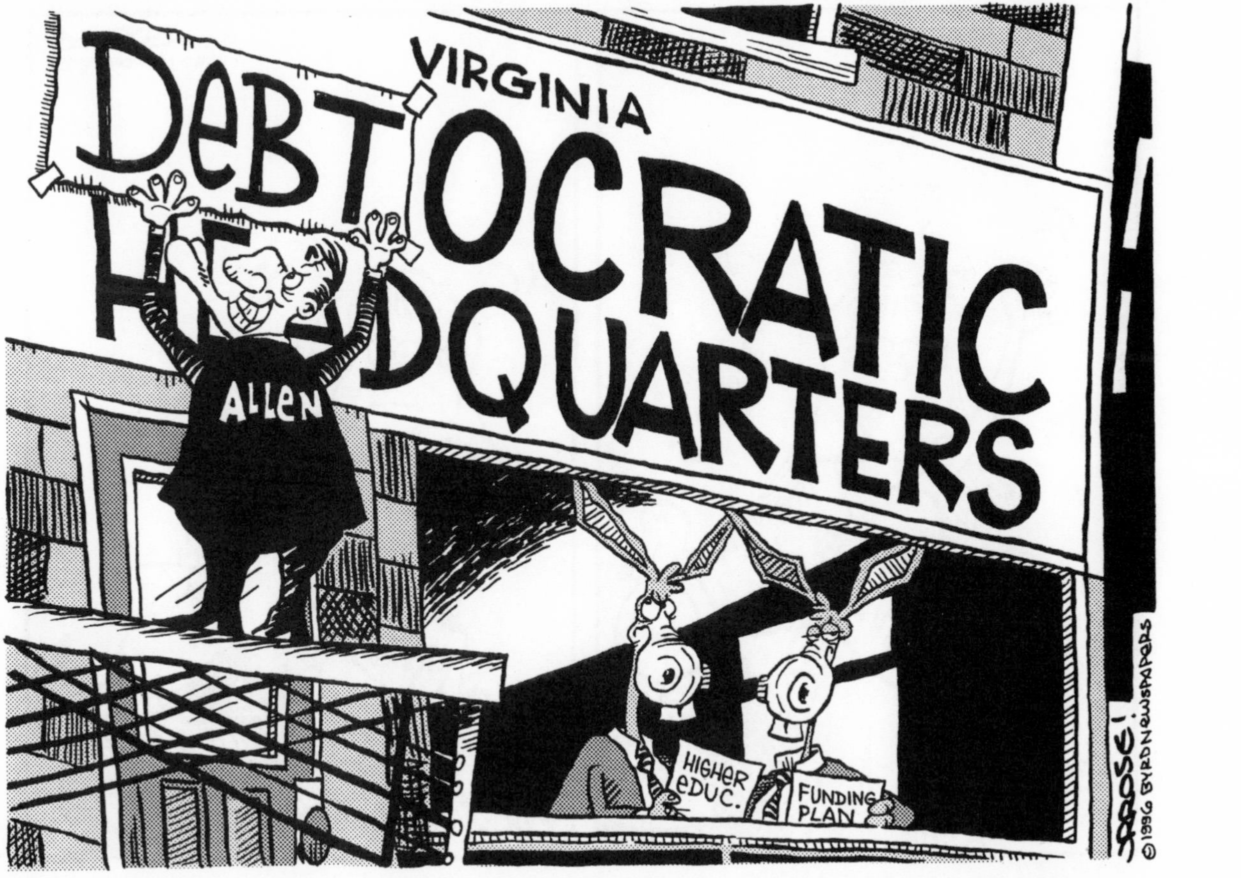

VIRGINIA
DEBT
OCRATIC
H
DQUARTERS
ALLEN
HIGHER EDUC.
FUNDING PLAN
©1996 BYRDNEWSPAPERS

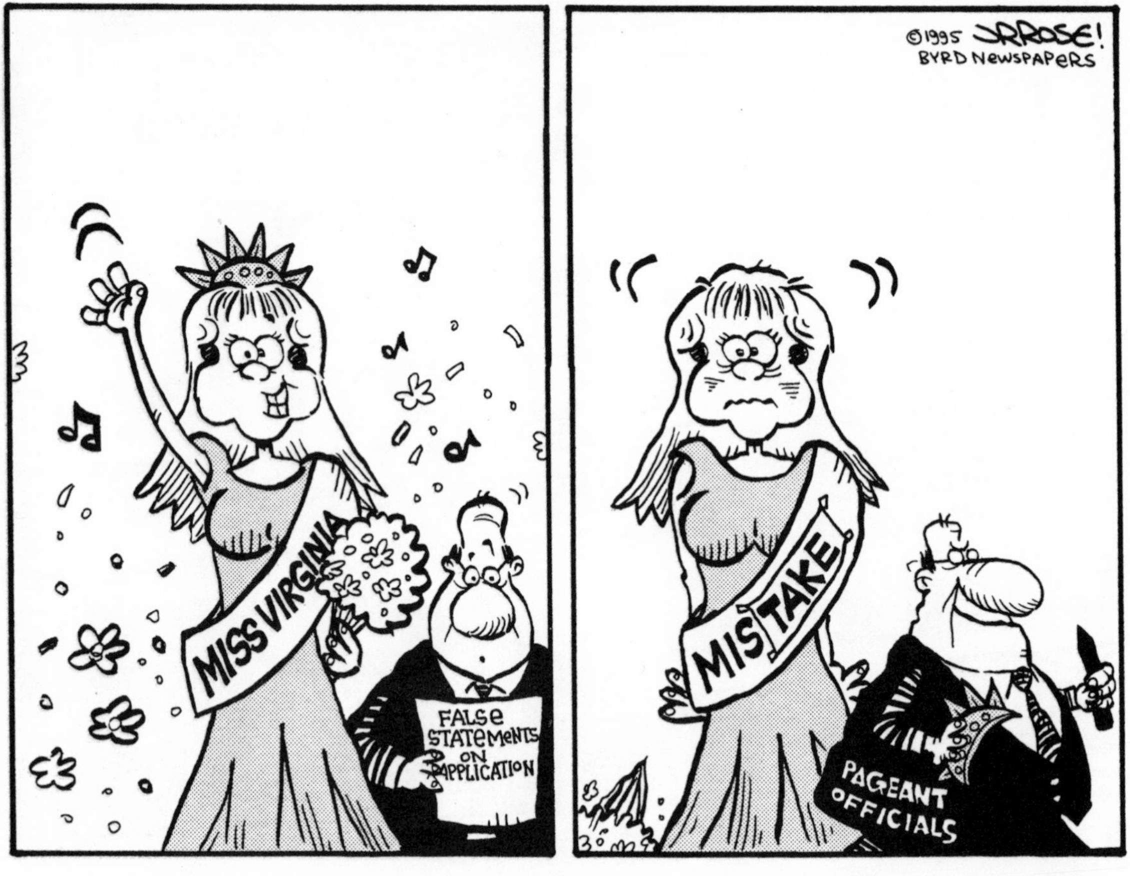
MISS VIRGINIA
FALSE STATEMENTS ON APPLICATION
©1995 JRROSE!
BYRD NEWSPAPERS
MIS TAKE
PAGEANT OFFICIALS

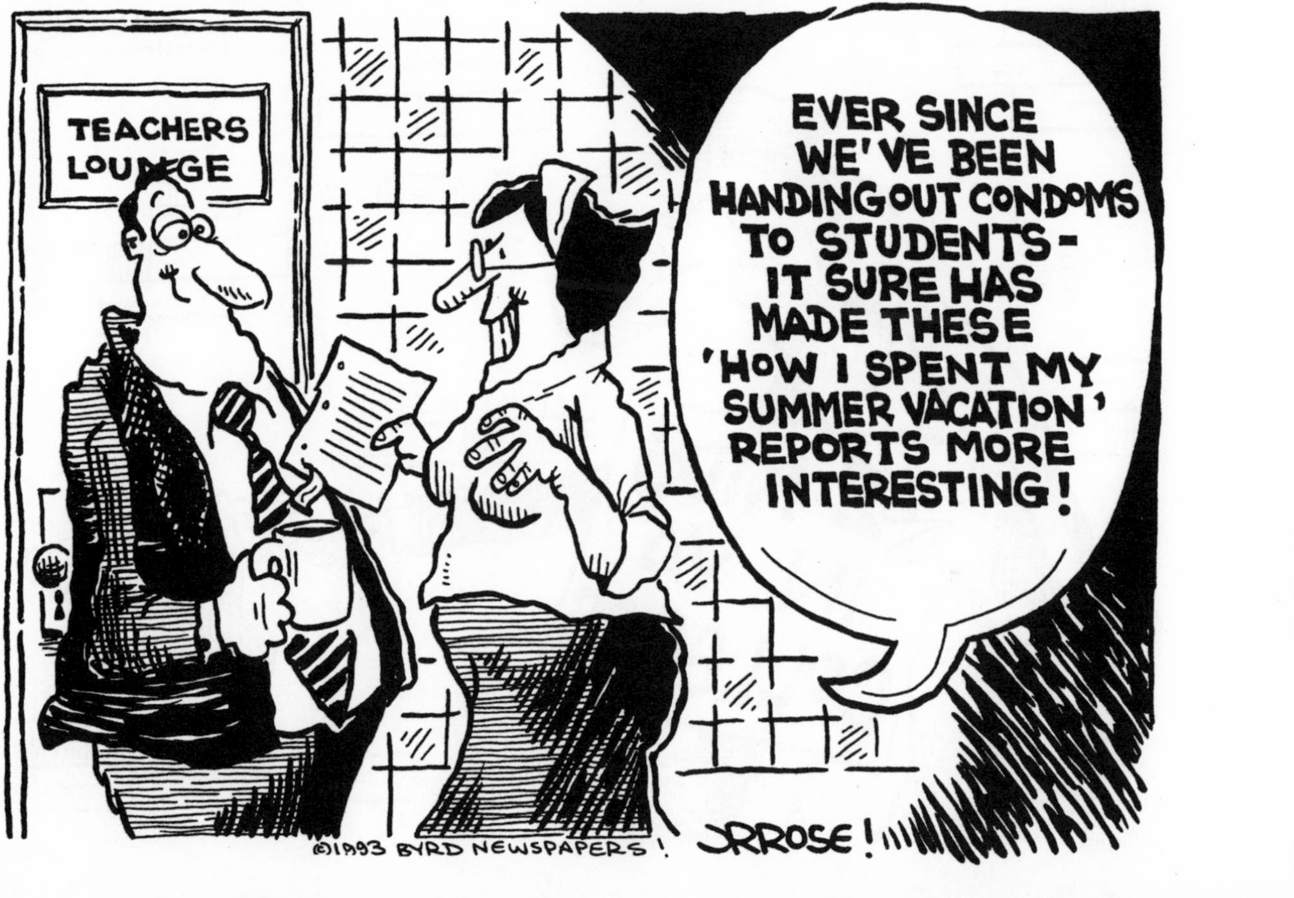
TEACHERS LOUNGE
EVER SINCE WE'VE BEEN HANDING OUT CONDOMS TO STUDENTS - IT SURE HAS MADE THESE 'HOW I SPENT MY SUMMER VACATION' REPORTS MORE INTERESTING!
©1993 BYRD NEWSPAPERS!
JRROSE!

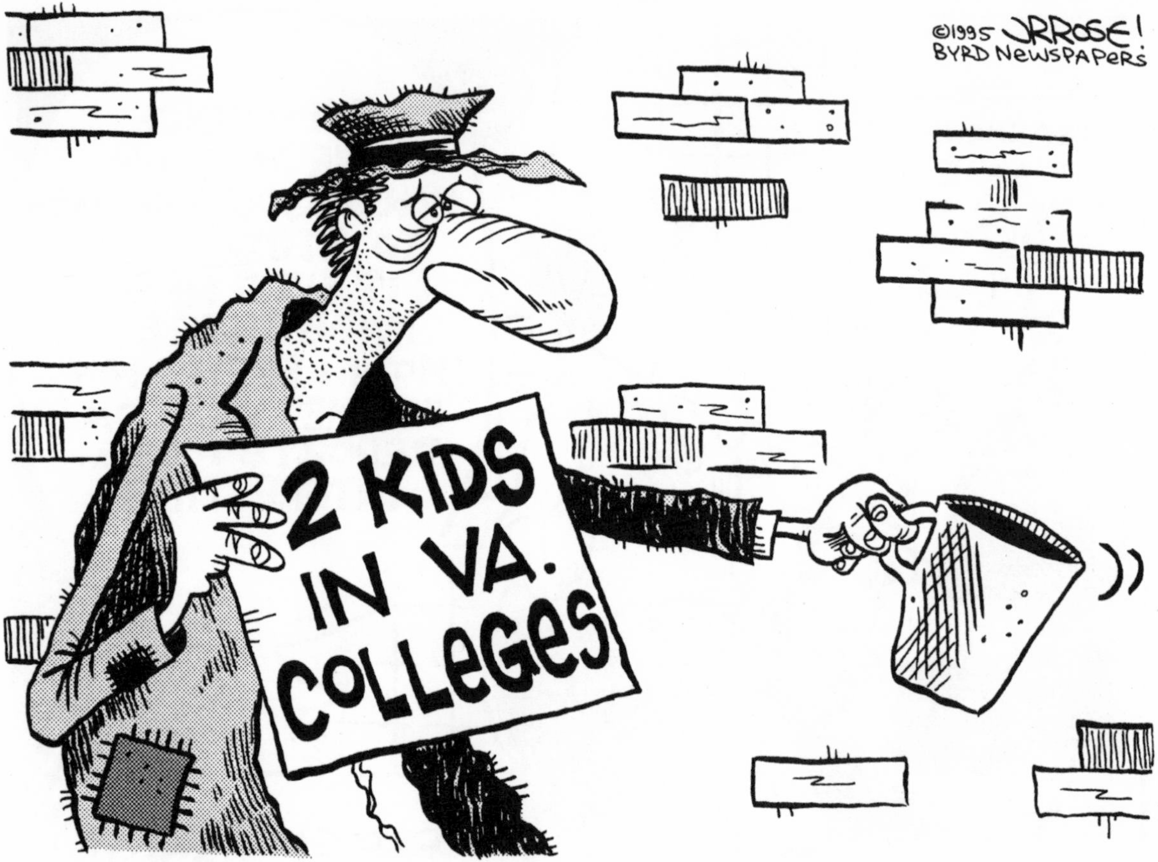
©1995 JRROSE!
BYRD NewsPAPers
2 KIDS
IN VA.
COLLeges

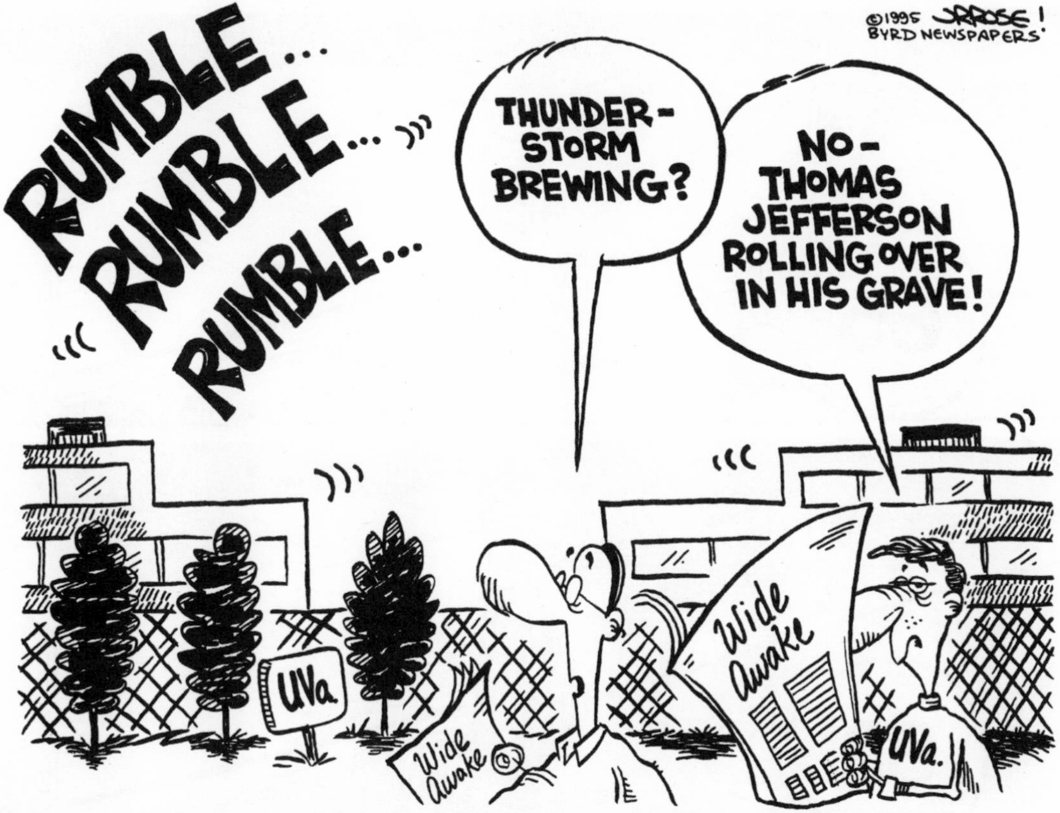
©1995 JRROSE!
BYRD NEWSPAPERS'
RUMBLE... RUMBLE... RUMBLE...
THUNDER-STORM BREWING?
NO- THOMAS JEFFERSON ROLLING OVER IN HIS GRAVE!
UVa.
Wide Awake
Wide Awake
UVa.

News Item: UVa. discriminates against religious expression in funding of student publications.

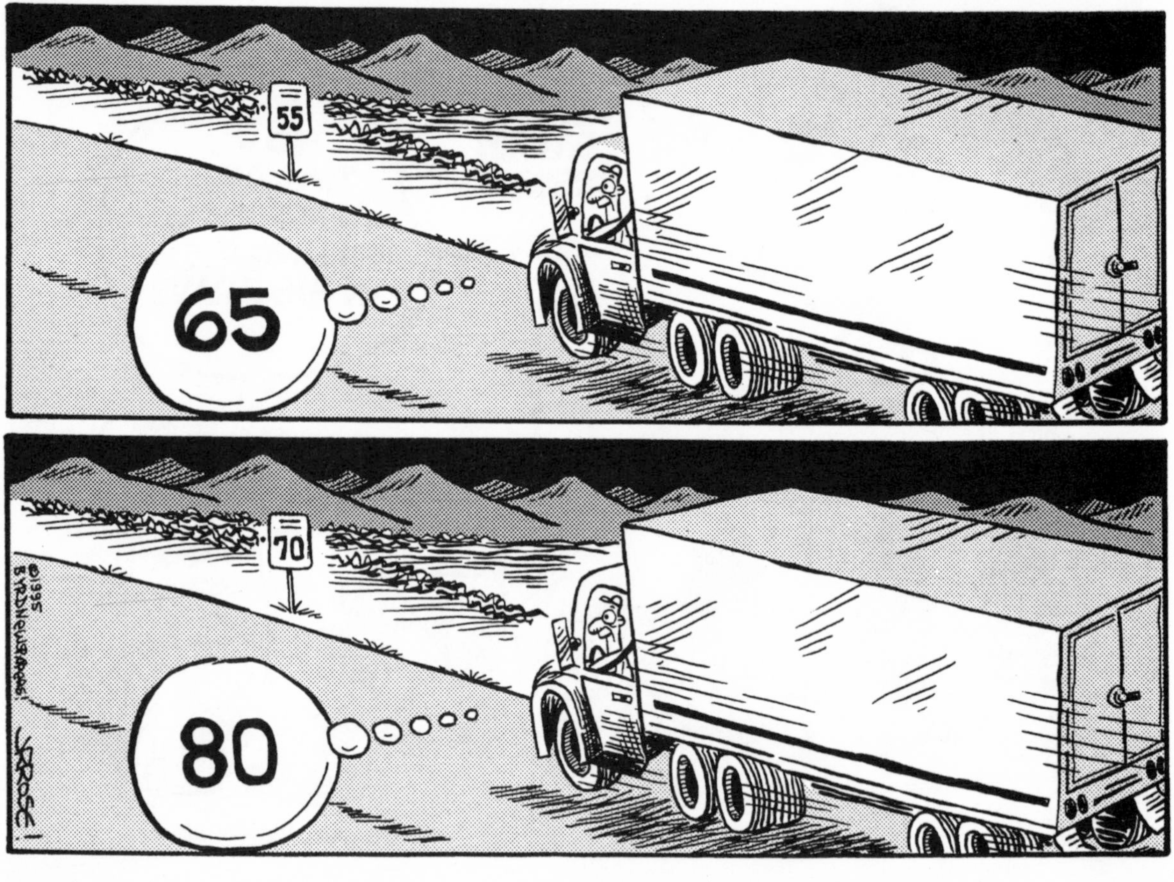
55
65
70
80
©1995
BYRD NEWSPAPERS

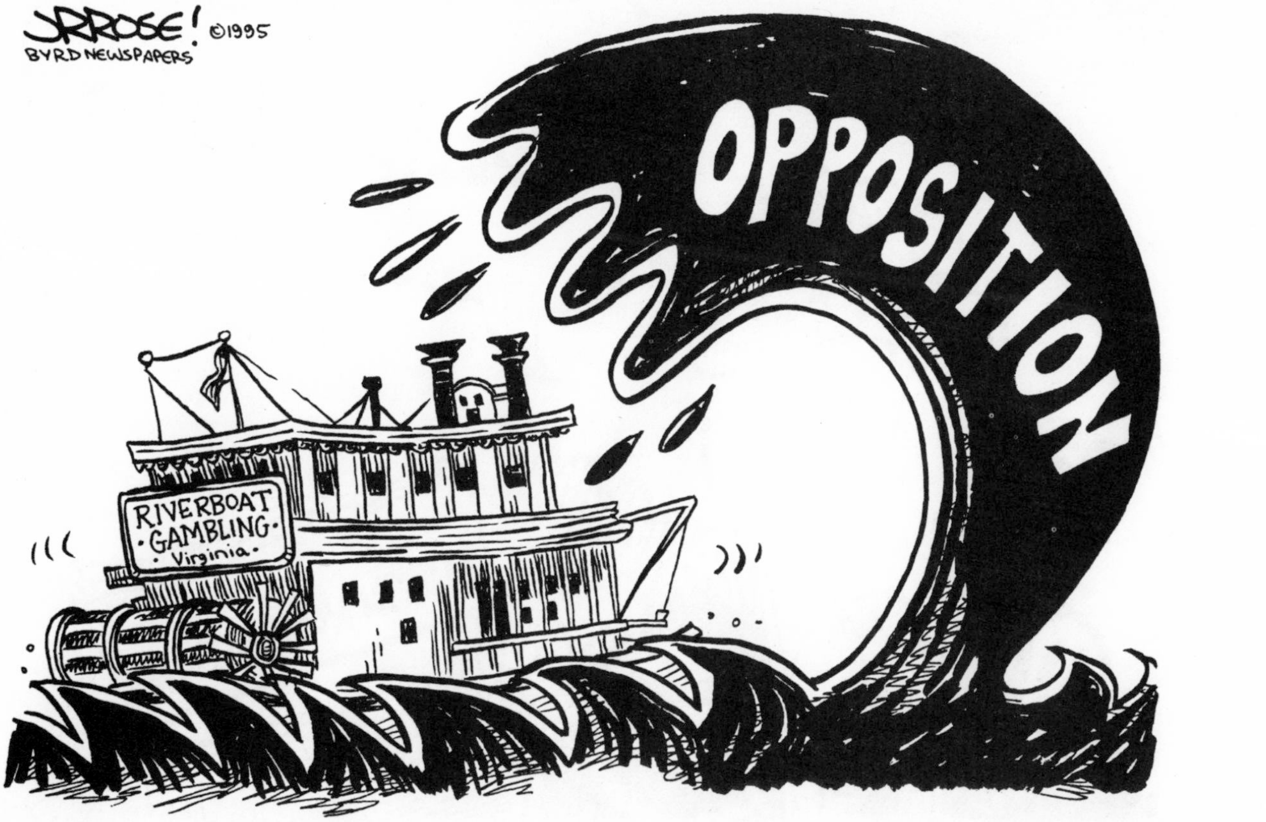

JRROSE! ©1995
BYRD NEWSPAPERS
OPPOSITION
RIVERBOAT
·GAMBLING·
·Virginia·

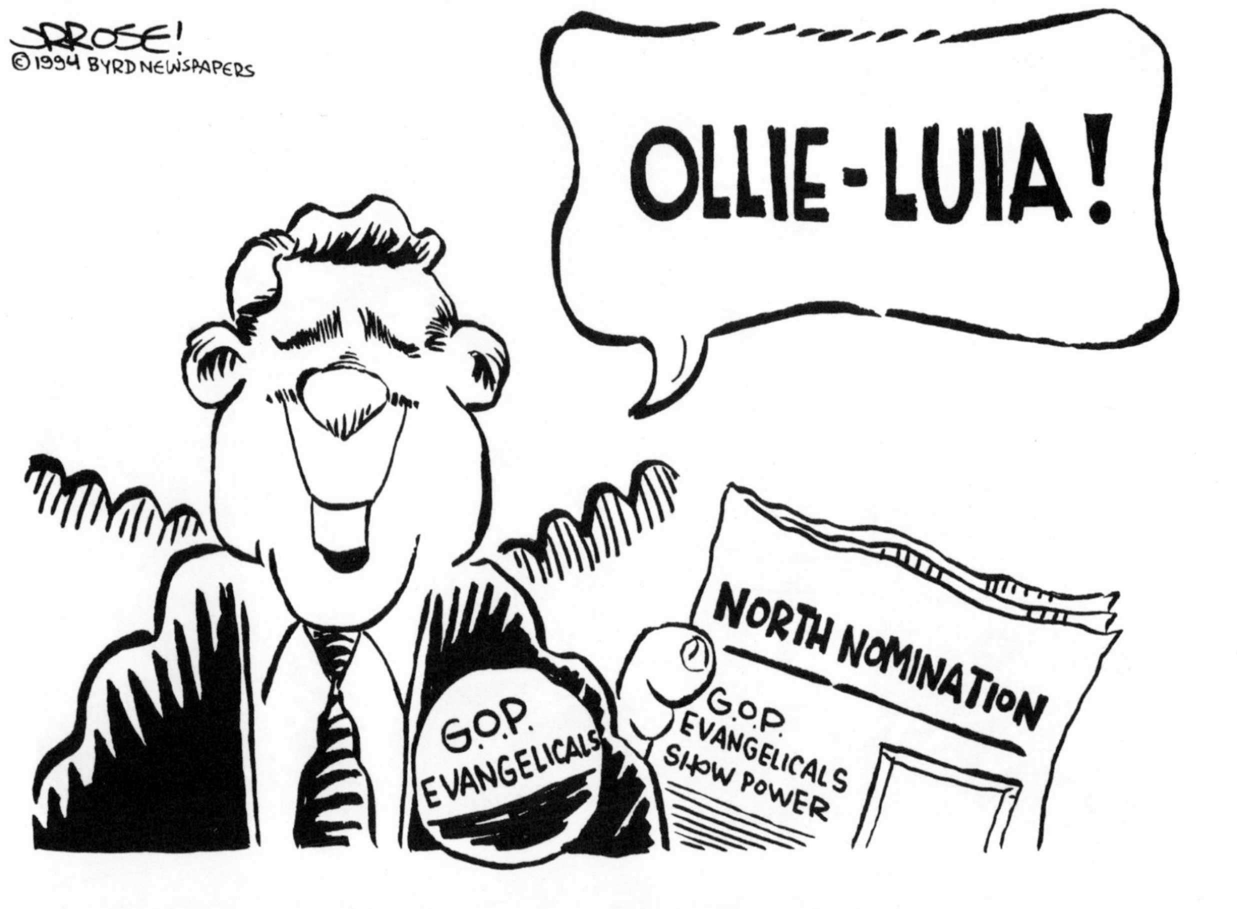
JRROSE!
©1994 BYRD NEWSPAPERS
OLLIE-LUIA!
G.O.P. EVANGELICALS
NORTH NOMINATION
G.O.P. EVANGELICALS SHOW POWER

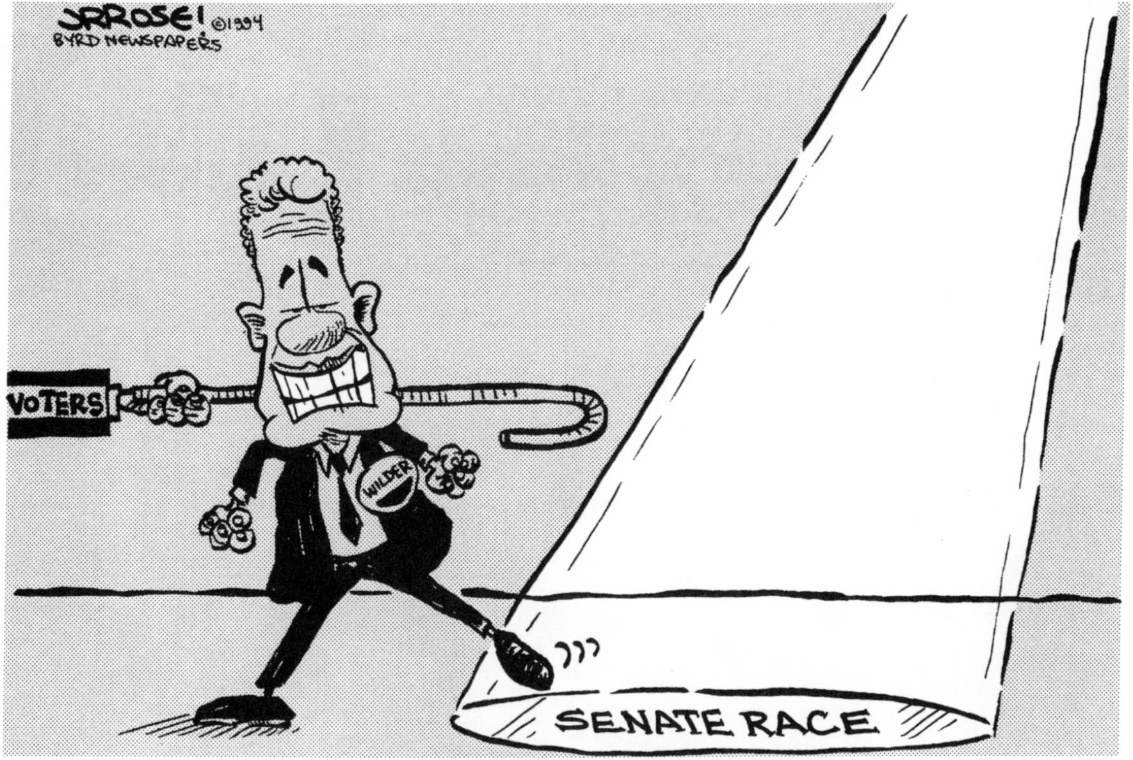
JRROSE! ©1994
BYRD NEWSPAPERS
VOTERS
WILDER
SENATE RACE

LOVING THAT SPOTLIGHT

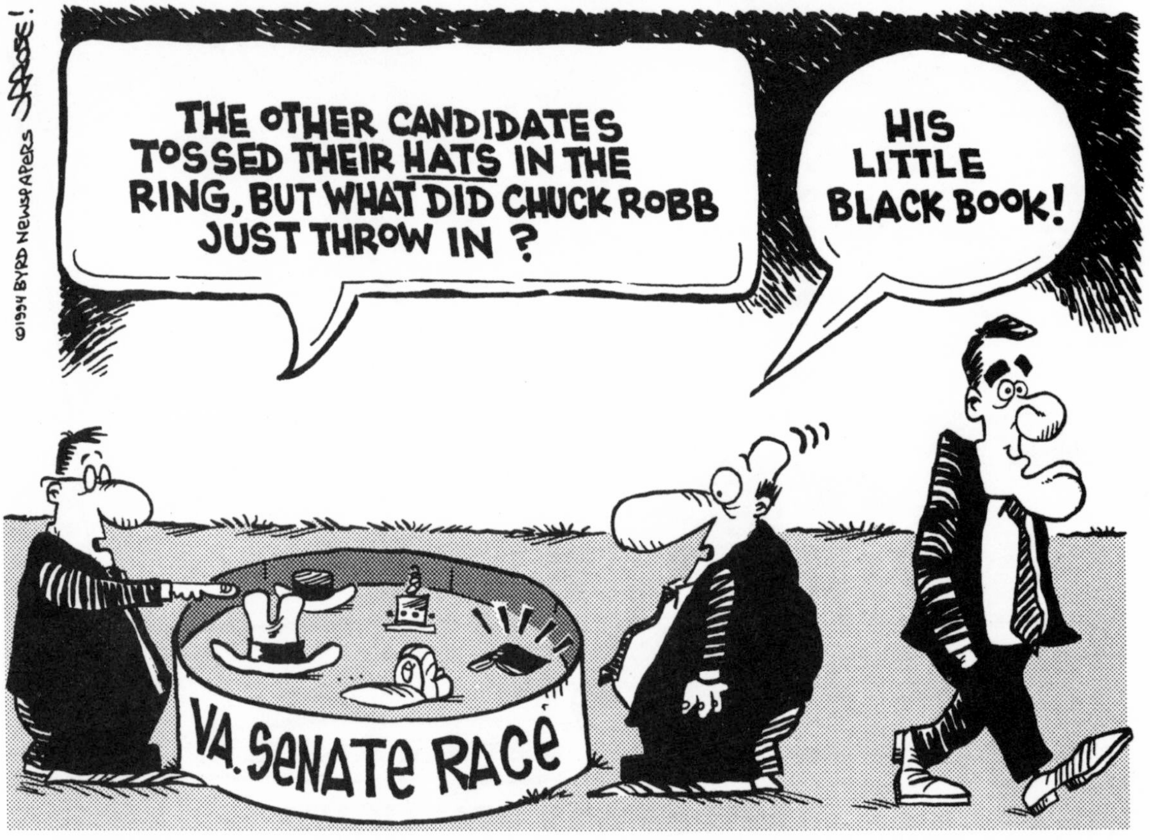
THE OTHER CANDIDATES TOSSED THEIR HATS IN THE RING, BUT WHAT DID CHUCK ROBB JUST THROW IN ?
HIS LITTLE BLACK BOOK!
VA. SENATE RACE
©1994 BYRD NEWSPAPERS

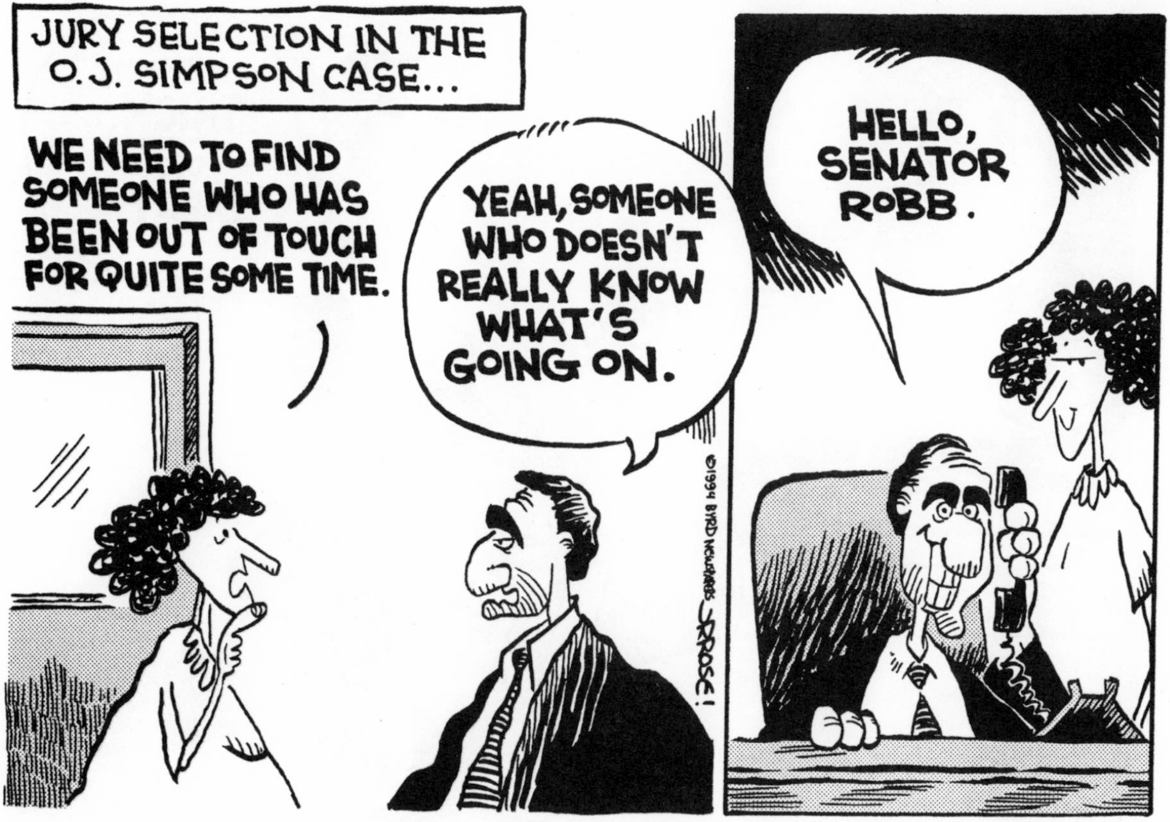

JURY SELECTION IN THE O.J. SIMPSON CASE...
WE NEED TO FIND SOMEONE WHO HAS BEEN OUT OF TOUCH FOR QUITE SOME TIME.
YEAH, SOMEONE WHO DOESN'T REALLY KNOW WHAT'S GOING ON.
HELLO, SENATOR ROBB.
©1994 BYRD NEWSPAPERS
JRROSE!

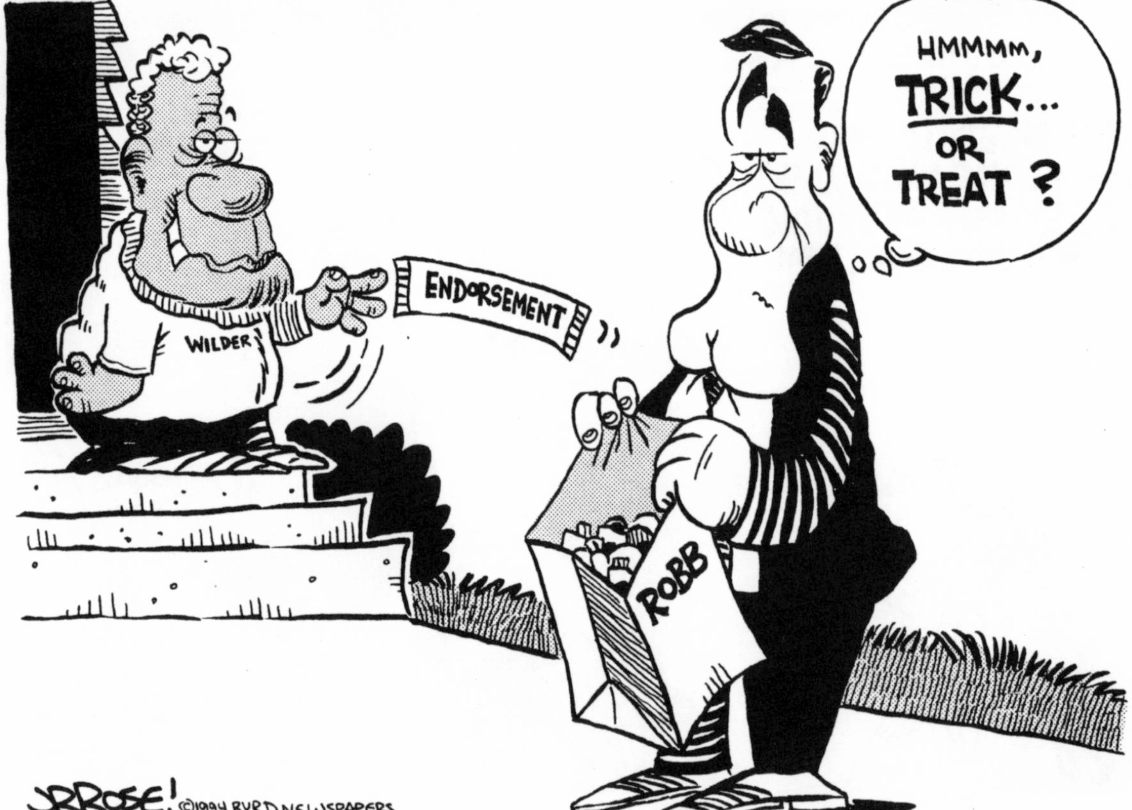

HMMMM,
TRICK...
OR
TREAT ?
ENDORSEMENT
WILDER
ROBB
JRROSE!
©1994 BYRD NEWSPAPERS

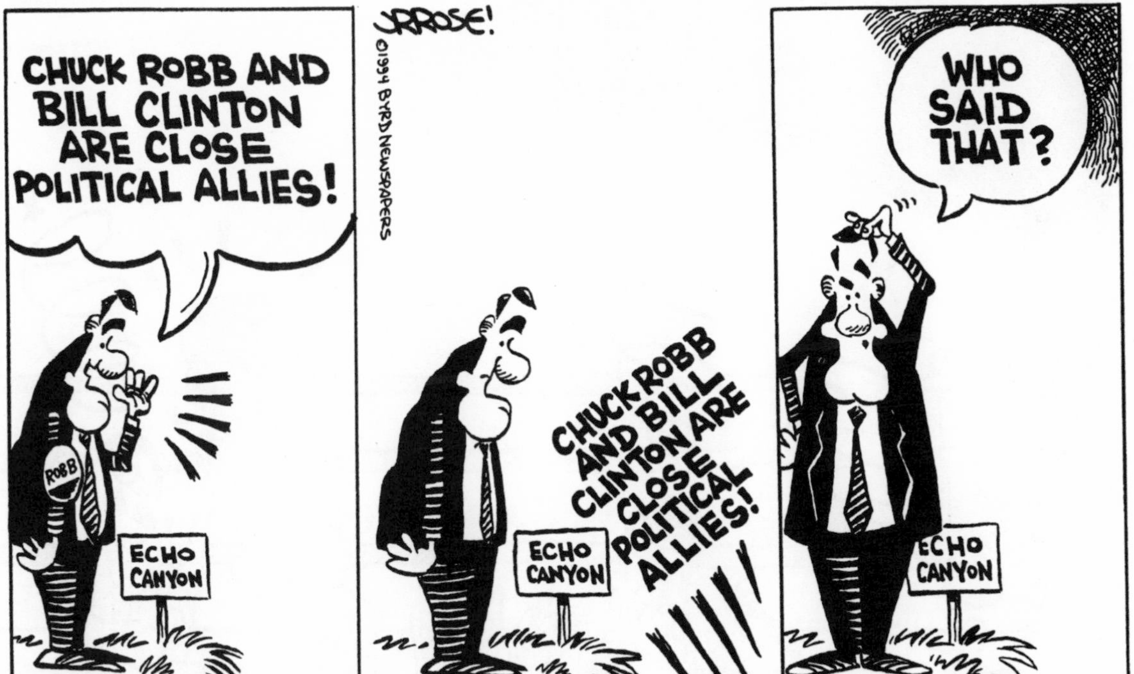
CHUCK ROBB AND BILL CLINTON ARE CLOSE POLITICAL ALLIES!
ROBB
ECHO CANYON
JRROSE!
©1994 BYRD NEWSPAPERS
ECHO CANYON
CHUCK ROBB AND BILL CLINTON ARE CLOSE POLITICAL ALLIES!
WHO SAID THAT?
ECHO CANYON

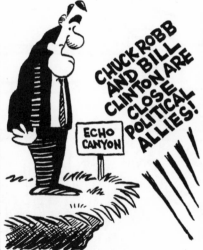

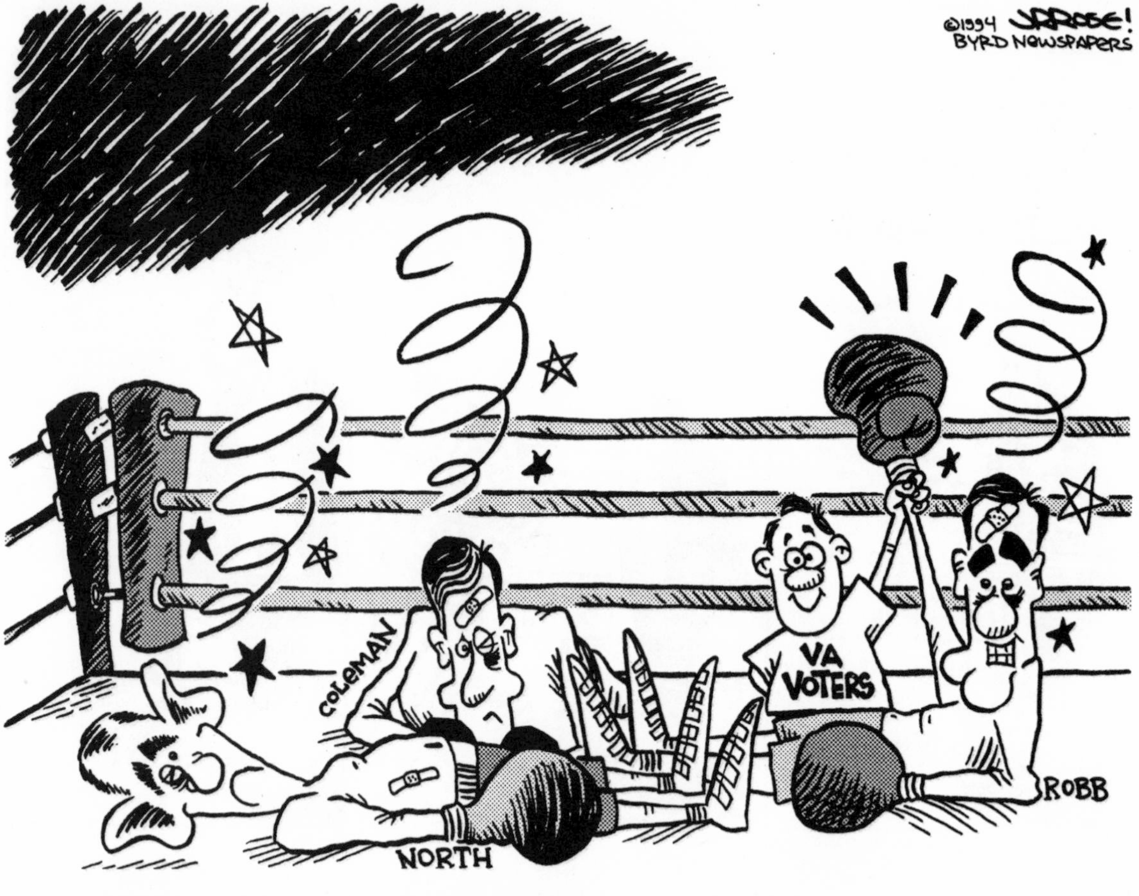
©1994 JRROSE!
BYRD NEWSPAPERS
COLEMAN
VA VOTERS
NORTH
ROBB

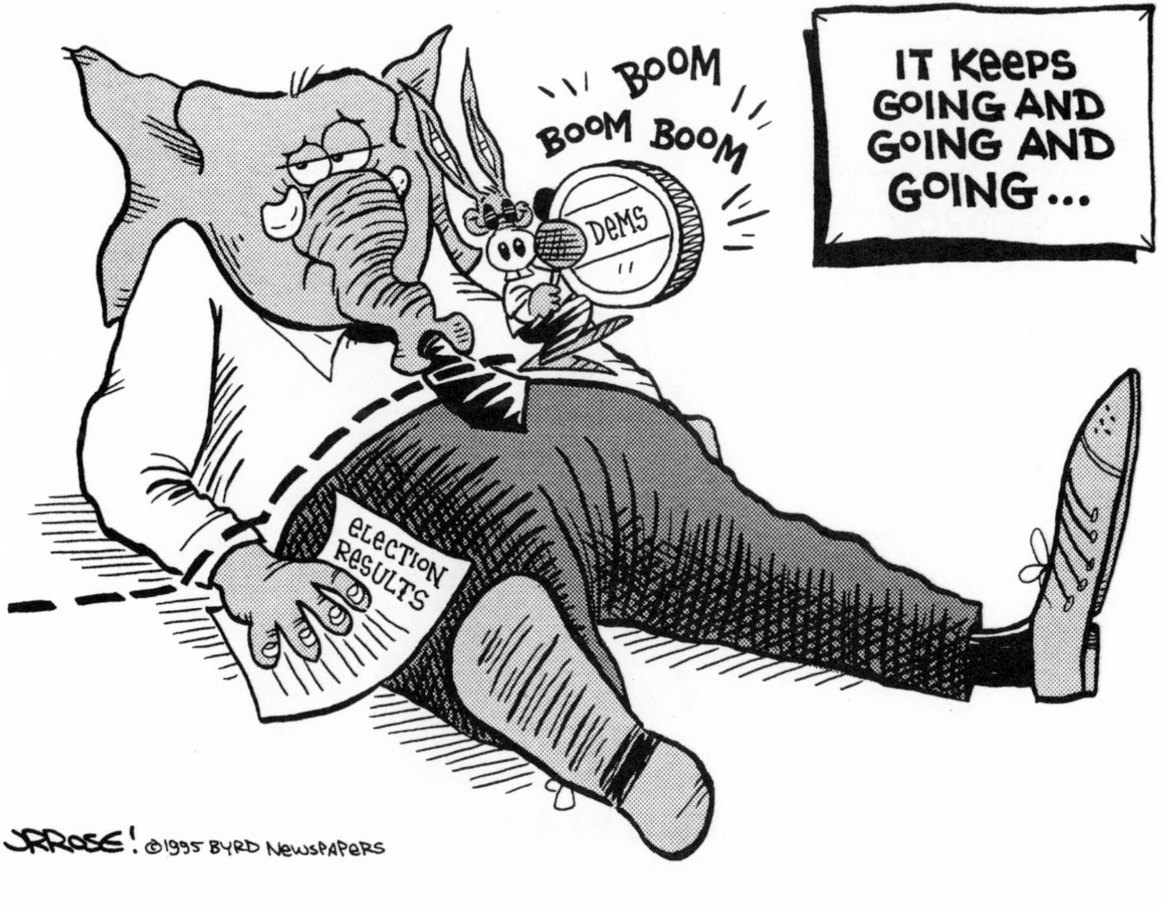

BOOM
BOOM BOOM
DEMS
ELECTION RESULTS
IT KEEPS GOING AND GOING AND GOING...
JRROSE! ©1995 BYRD NEWSPAPERS

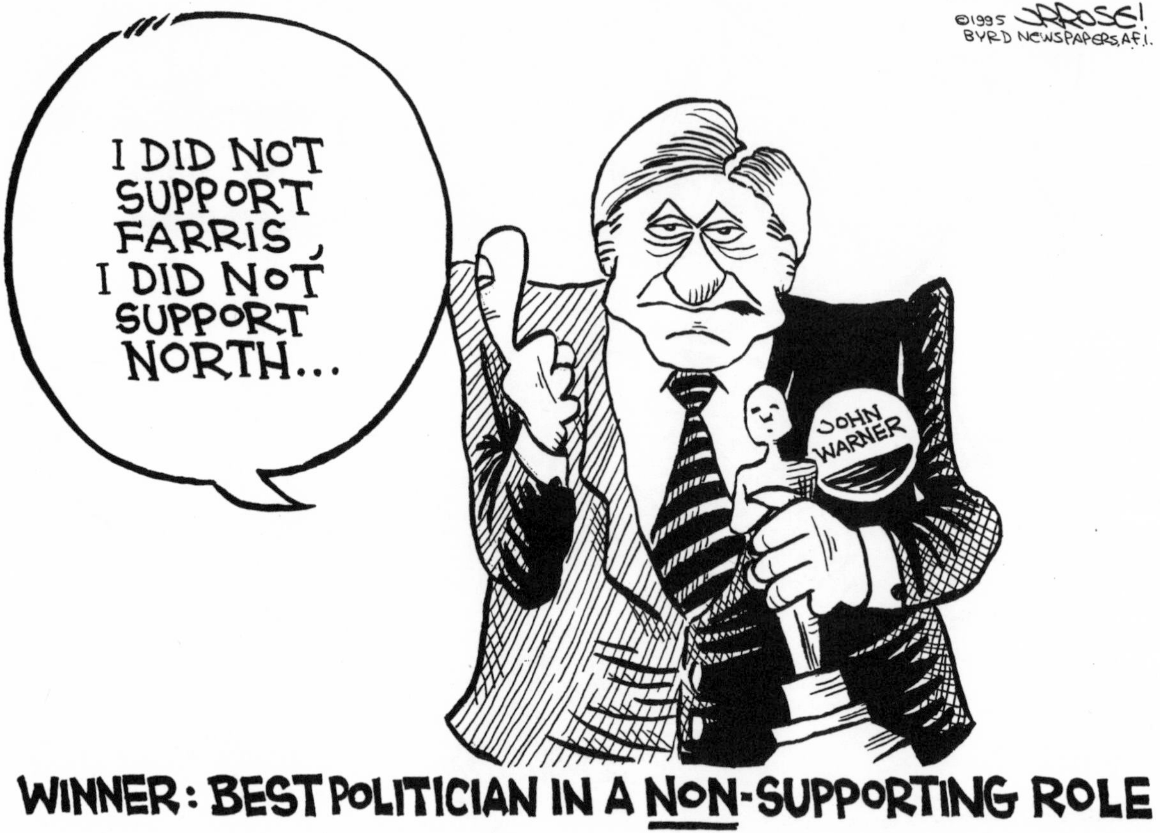
©1995 JRROSE!
BYRD NEWSPAPERS, AF.I.
I DID NOT SUPPORT FARRIS, I DID NOT SUPPORT NORTH...
JOHN WARNER
WINNER: BEST POLITICIAN IN A NON-SUPPORTING ROLE

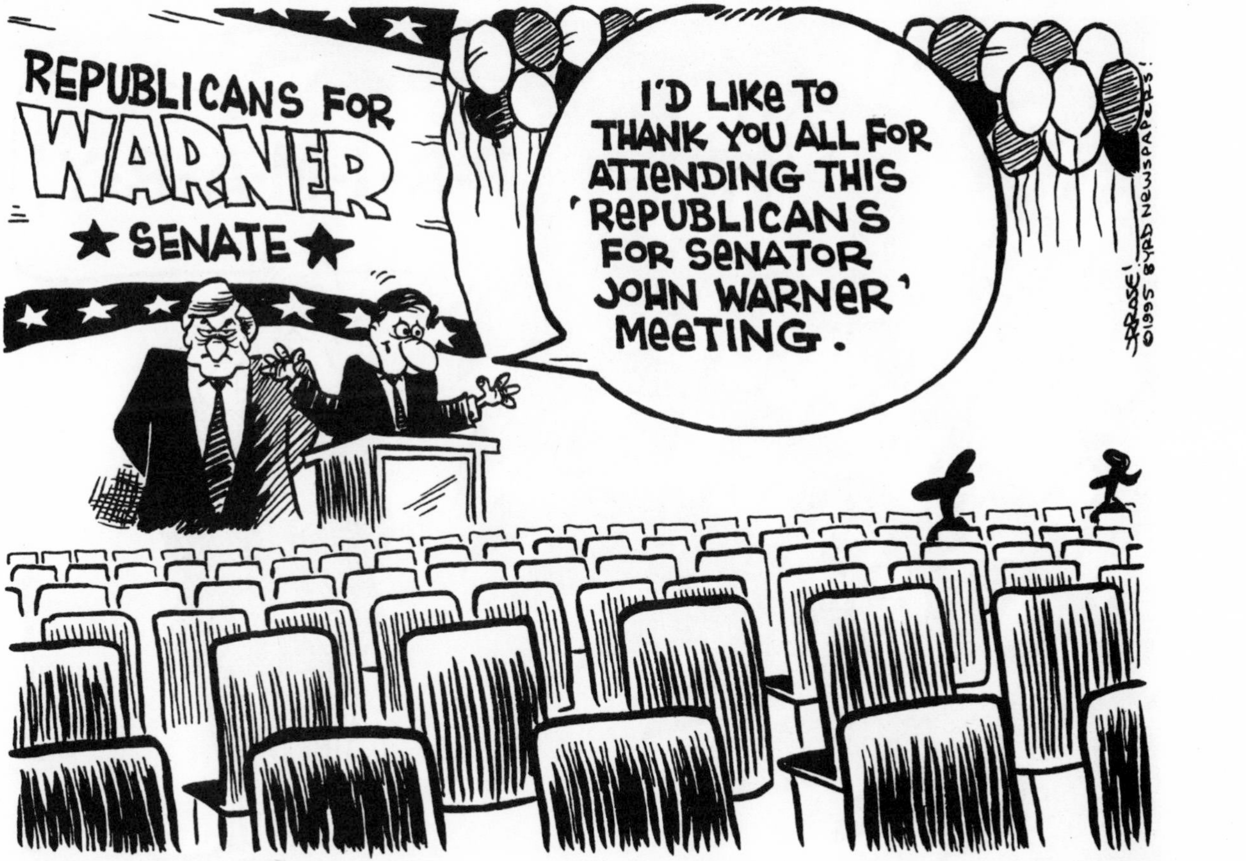
REPUBLICANS FOR WARNER SENATE
I'D LIKE TO THANK YOU ALL FOR ATTENDING THIS 'REPUBLICANS FOR SENATOR JOHN WARNER' MEETING.
©1995 BYRD NEWSPAPERS!

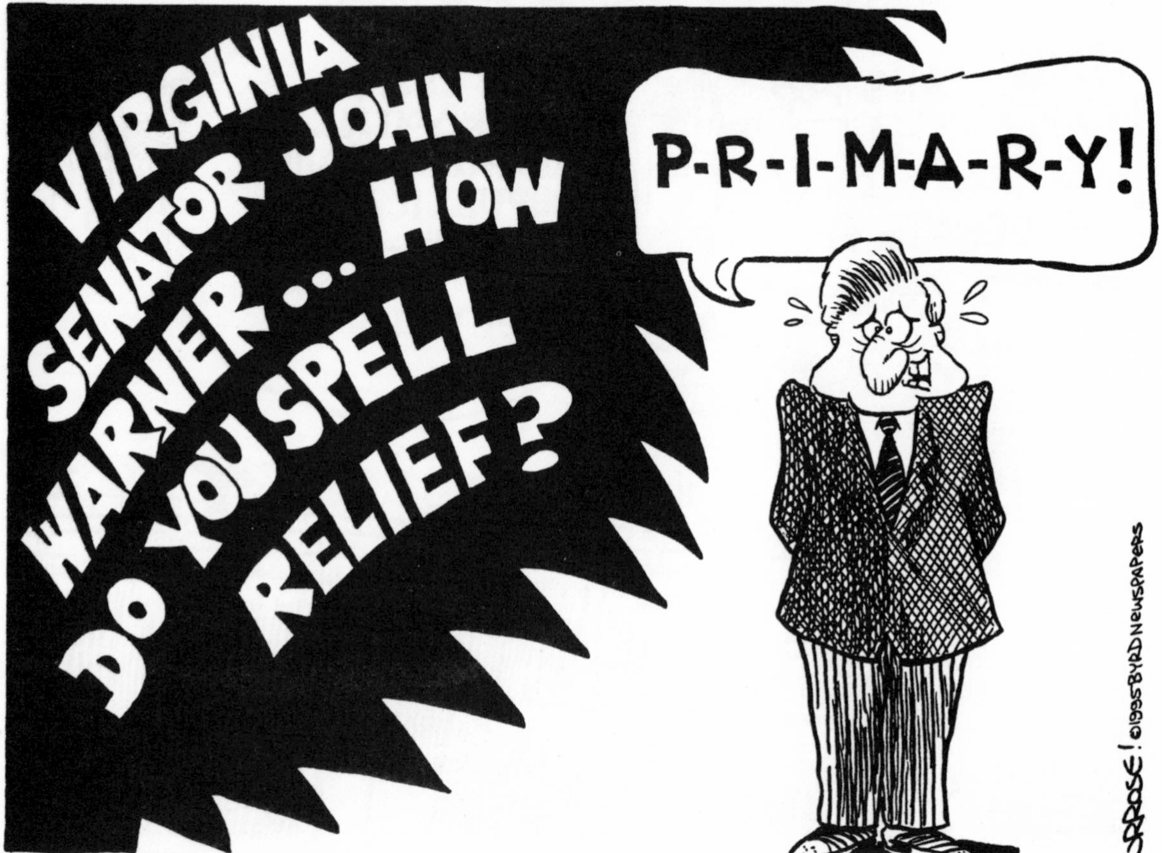
VIRGINIA SENATOR JOHN WARNER... HOW DO YOU SPELL RELIEF?
P-R-I-M-A-R-Y!
SDROSE! ©1995 BYRD NEWSPAPERS

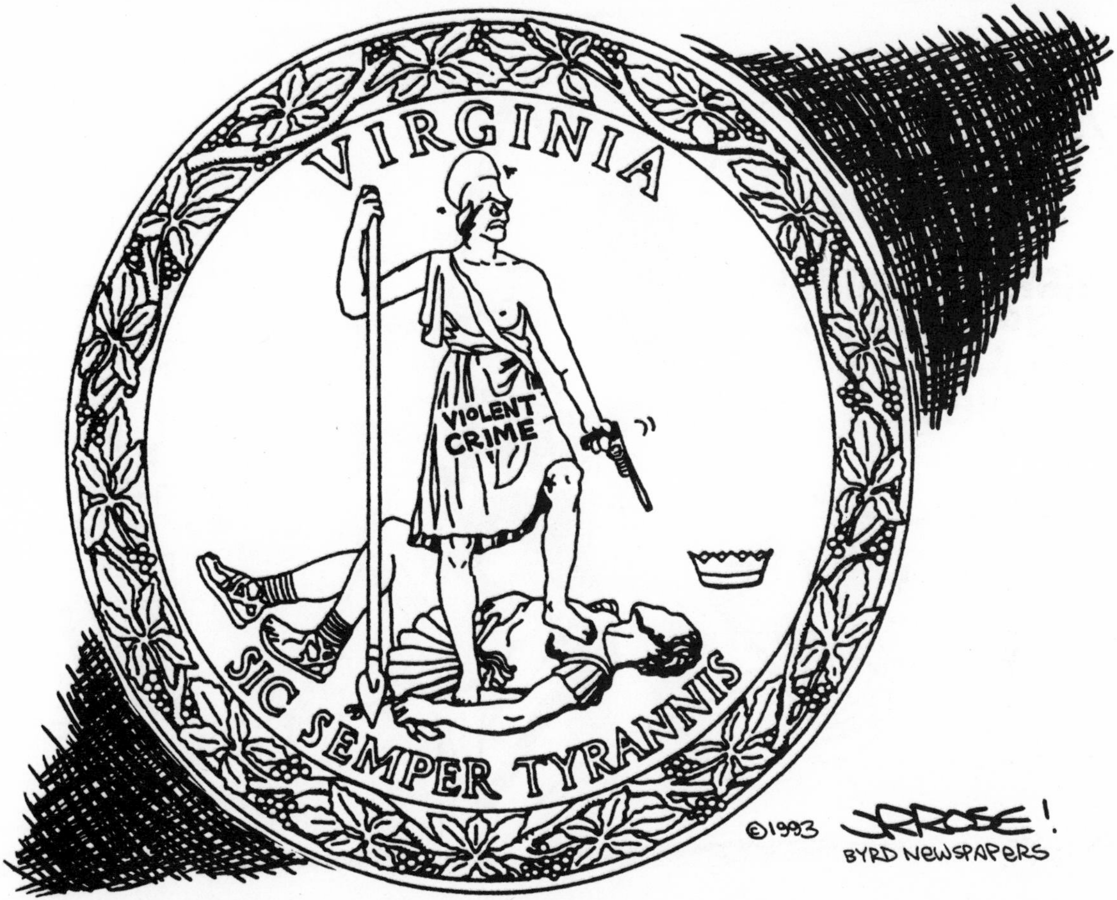
VIRGINIA
VIOLENT CRIME
SIC SEMPER TYRANNIS
©1993
JRROSE!
BYRD NEWSPAPERS

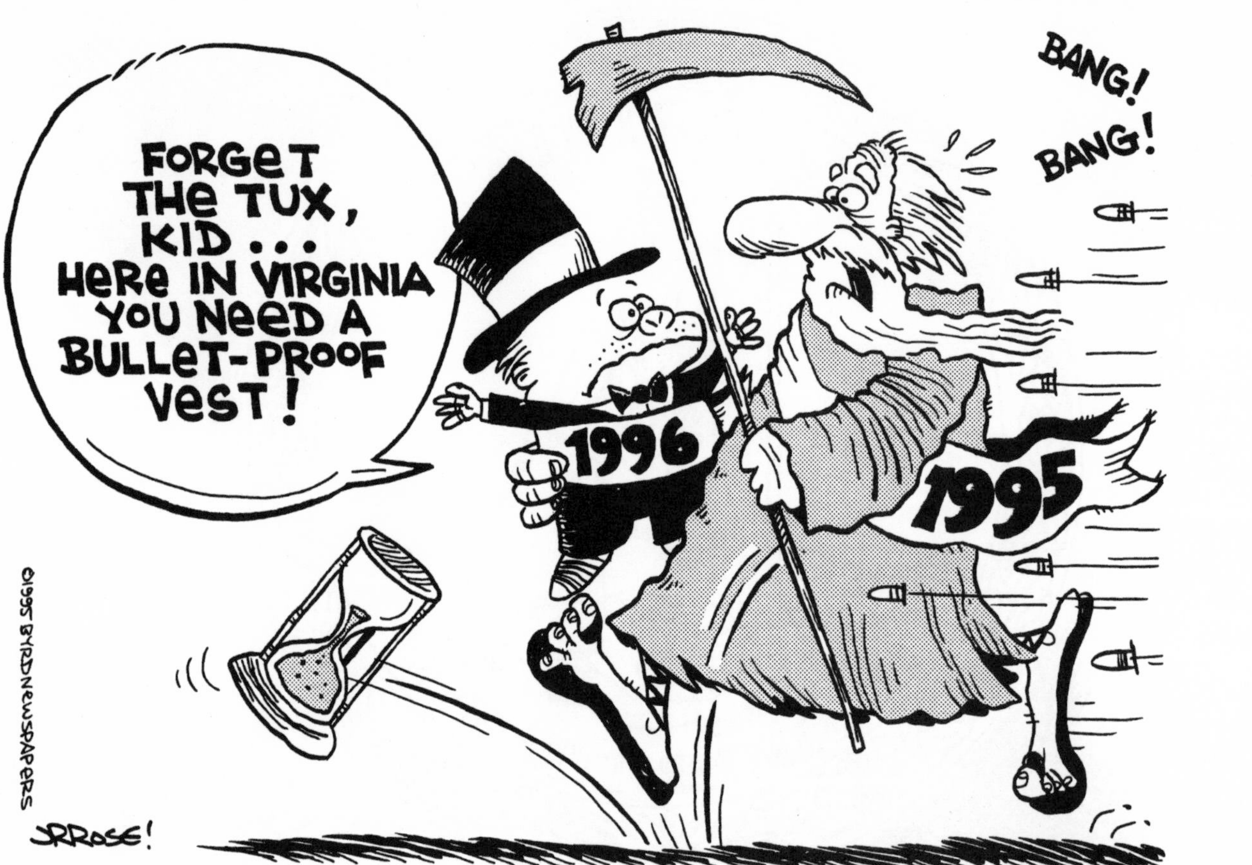
FORGET THE TUX, KID ... HERE IN VIRGINIA YOU NEED A BULLET-PROOF VEST!
BANG!
BANG!
1996
1995
©1995 BYRDNEWSPAPERS
JRROSE!

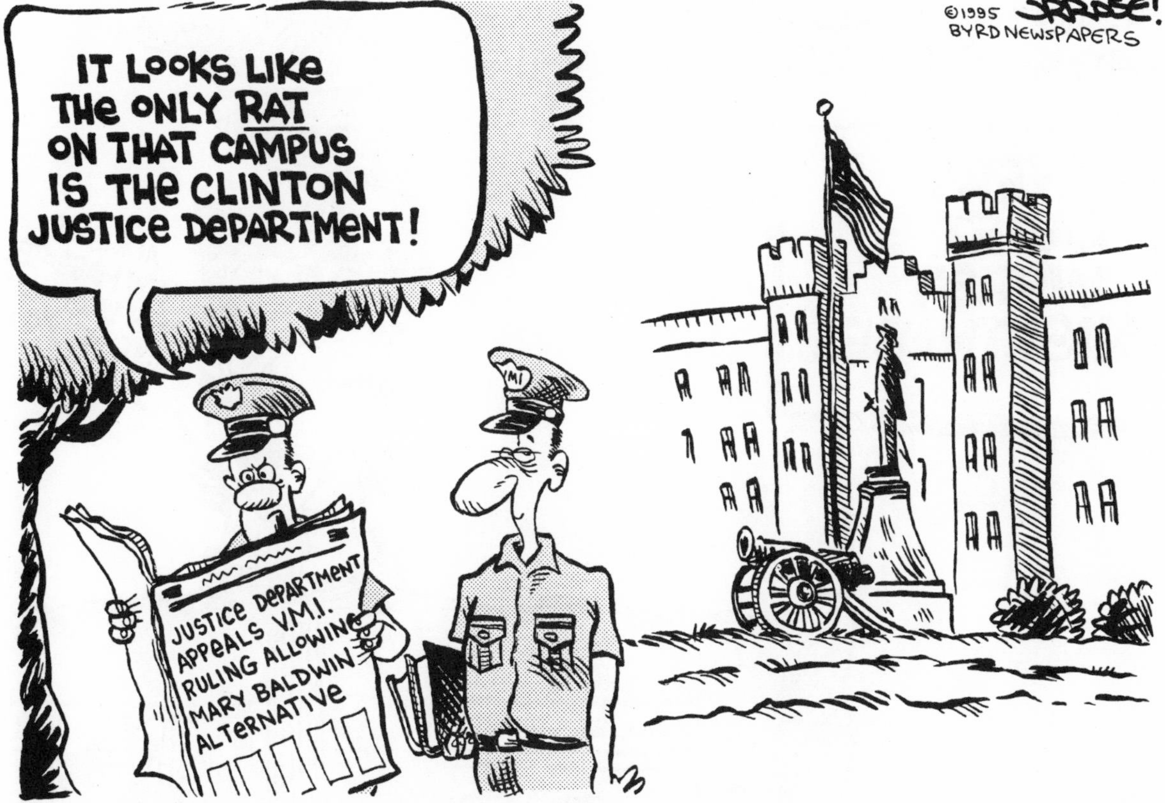

©1995 JRROSE!
BYRD NEWSPAPERS
IT LOOKS LIKE THE ONLY RAT ON THAT CAMPUS IS THE CLINTON JUSTICE DEPARTMENT!
JUSTICE DEPARTMENT APPEALS V.M.I. RULING ALLOWING MARY BALDWIN ALTERNATIVE
VMI

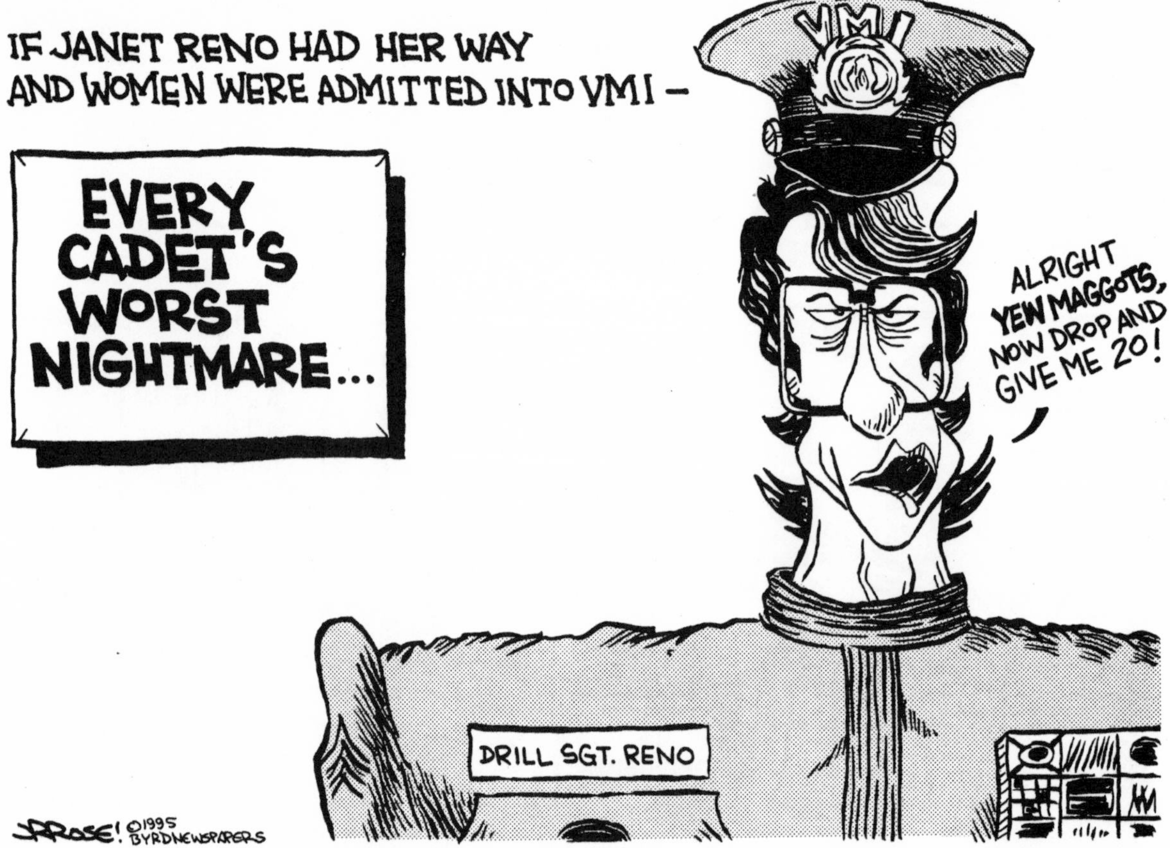

IF JANET RENO HAD HER WAY
AND WOMEN WERE ADMITTED INTO VMI –
EVERY CADET'S WORST NIGHTMARE...
VMI
ALRIGHT YEW MAGGOTS, NOW DROP AND GIVE ME 20!
DRILL SGT. RENO
JRROSE! ©1995 BYRDNEWSPAPERS

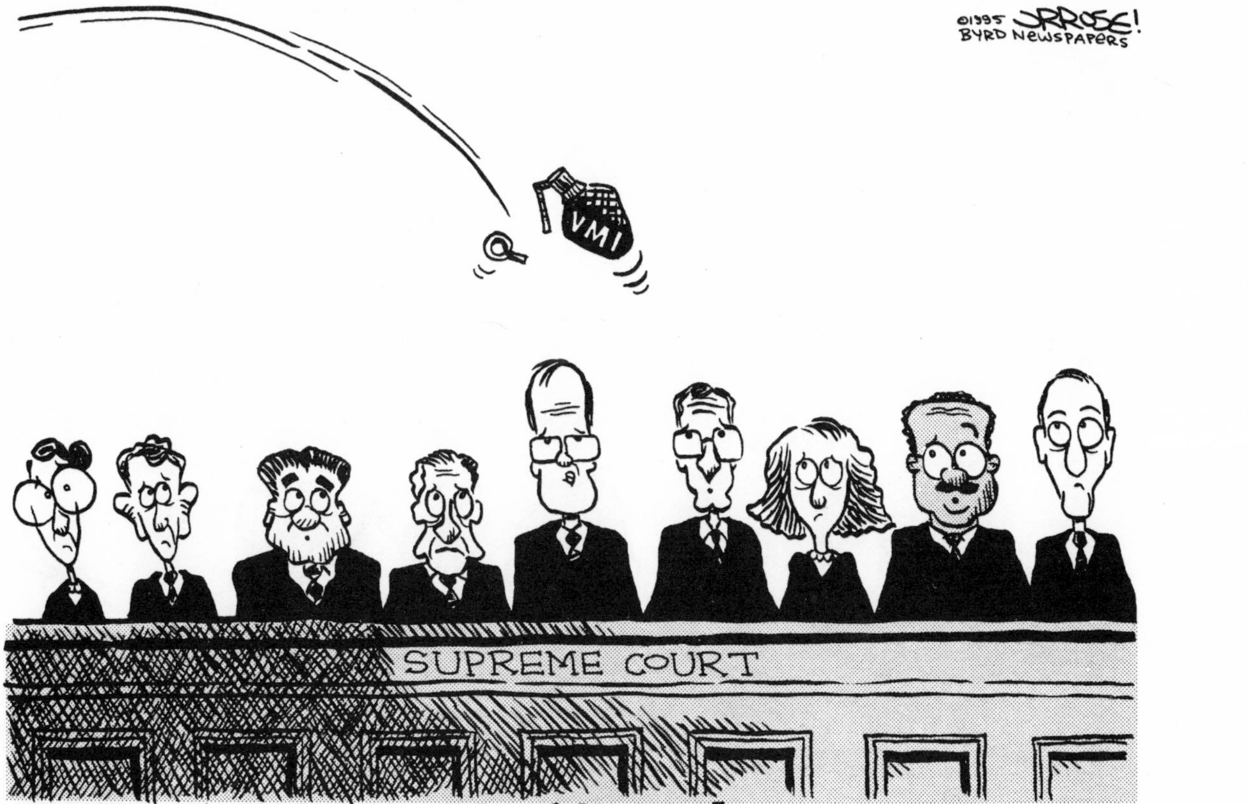
©1995 JRROSE!
BYRD NEWSPAPERS
VMI
SUPREME COURT

INCOMING!

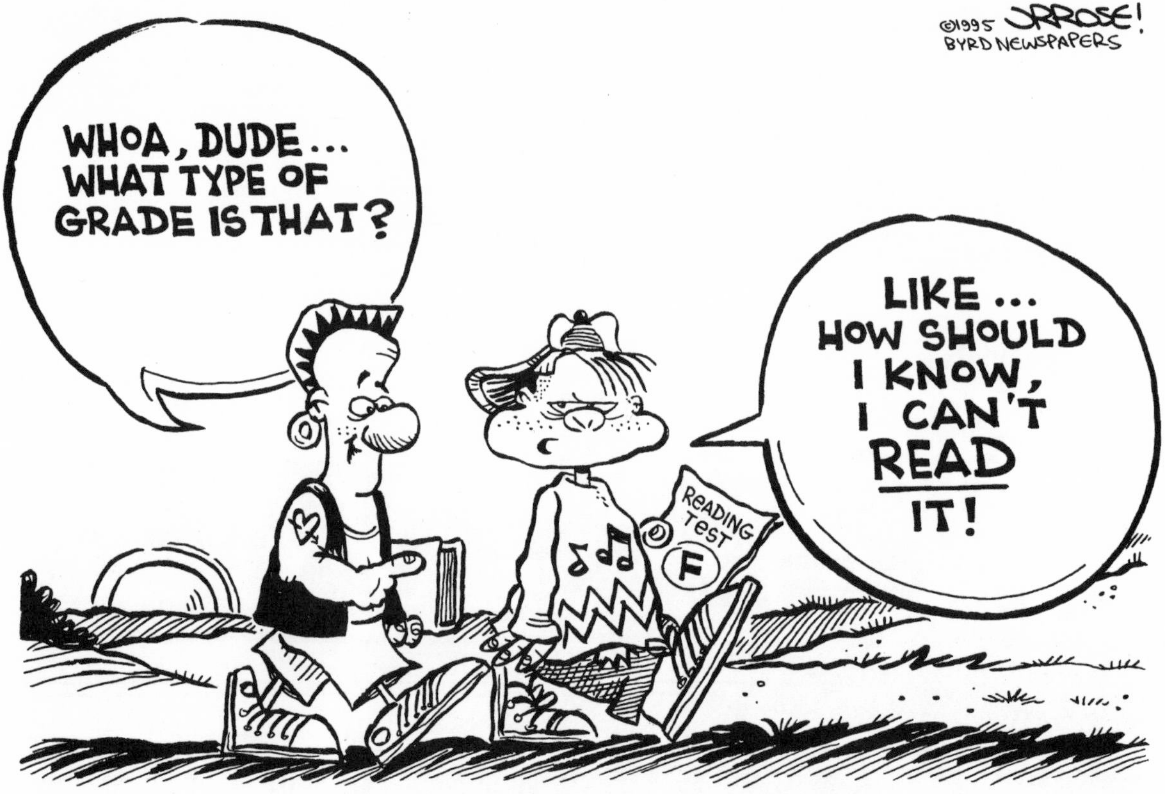
©1995 JRROSE!
BYRD NEWSPAPERS
WHOA, DUDE...
WHAT TYPE OF
GRADE IS THAT?
LIKE ...
HOW SHOULD
I KNOW,
I CAN'T
READ
IT!
READING
TEST
F

News Item: Reading skills of Virginia fourth-graders take big plunge.

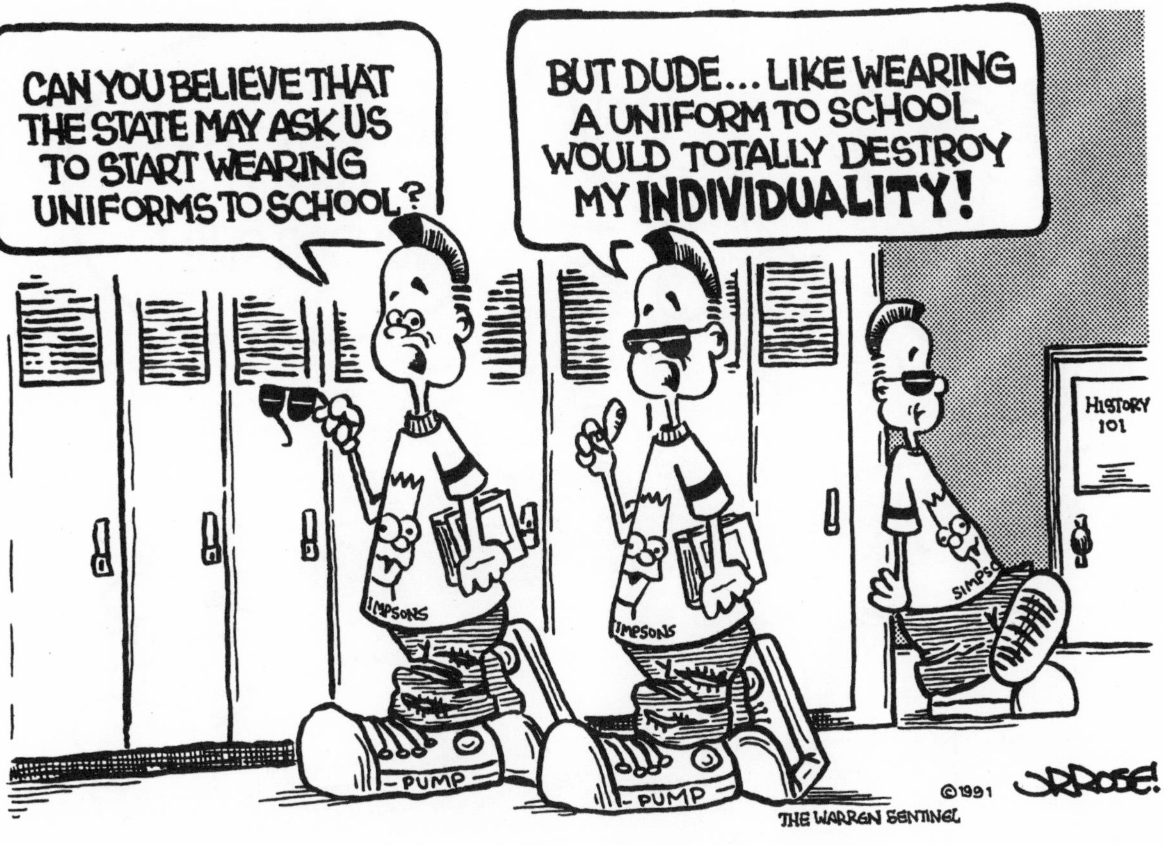

CAN YOU BELIEVE THAT THE STATE MAY ASK US TO START WEARING UNIFORMS TO SCHOOL?
BUT DUDE... LIKE WEARING A UNIFORM TO SCHOOL WOULD TOTALLY DESTROY MY INDIVIDUALITY!
HISTORY 101
IMPSONS
IMPSONS
SIMPS
PUMP
PUMP
©1991
JRROSE!
THE WARREN SENTINEL

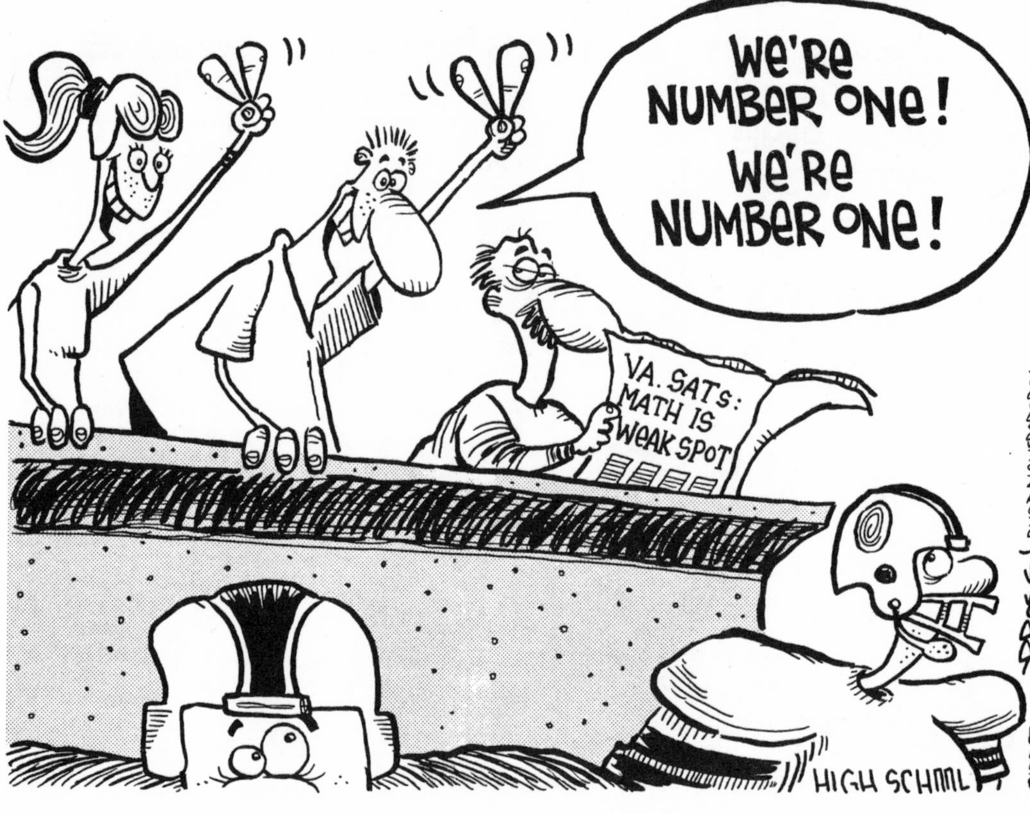

WE'RE NUMBER ONE! WE'RE NUMBER ONE!
VA. SATS: MATH IS WEAK SPOT
HIGH SCHOOL
©1995 JRROSE! BYRD NEWSPAPERS!

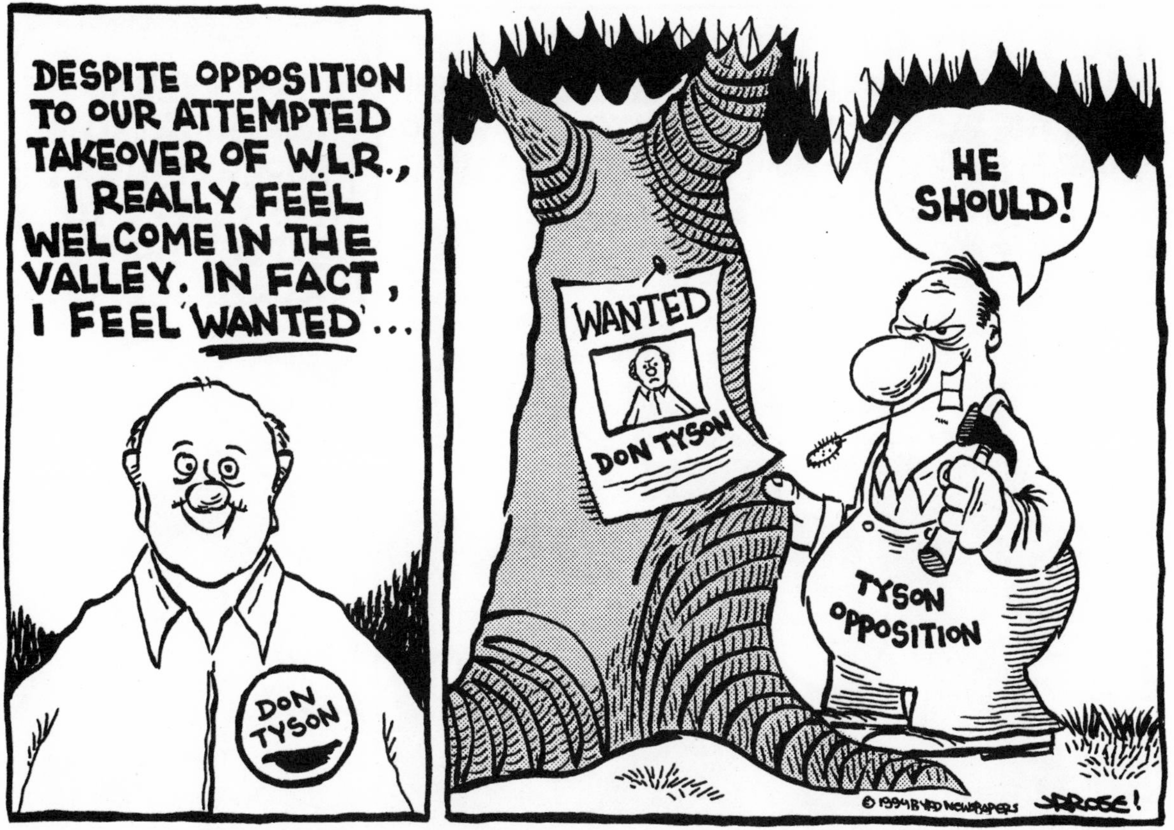
DESPITE OPPOSITION TO OUR ATTEMPTED TAKEOVER OF W.L.R., I REALLY FEEL WELCOME IN THE VALLEY. IN FACT, I FEEL 'WANTED'...
DON TYSON
WANTED
DON TYSON
HE SHOULD!
TYSON OPPOSITION
© 1994 BYRD NEWSPAPERS
JRROSE!

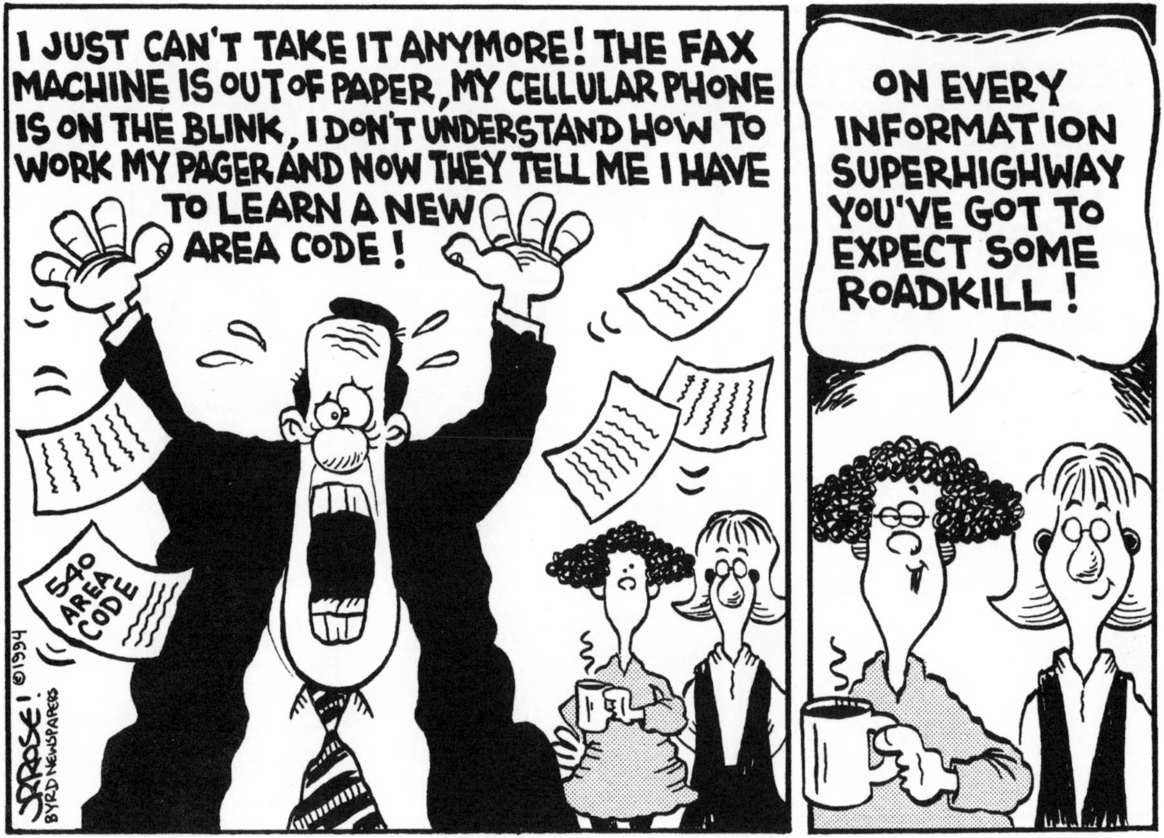
I JUST CAN'T TAKE IT ANYMORE! THE FAX MACHINE IS OUT OF PAPER, MY CELLULAR PHONE IS ON THE BLINK, I DON'T UNDERSTAND HOW TO WORK MY PAGER AND NOW THEY TELL ME I HAVE TO LEARN A NEW AREA CODE!
540 AREA CODE
©1994
SDROSE!
BYRD NEWSPAPERS
ON EVERY INFORMATION SUPERHIGHWAY YOU'VE GOT TO EXPECT SOME ROADKILL!

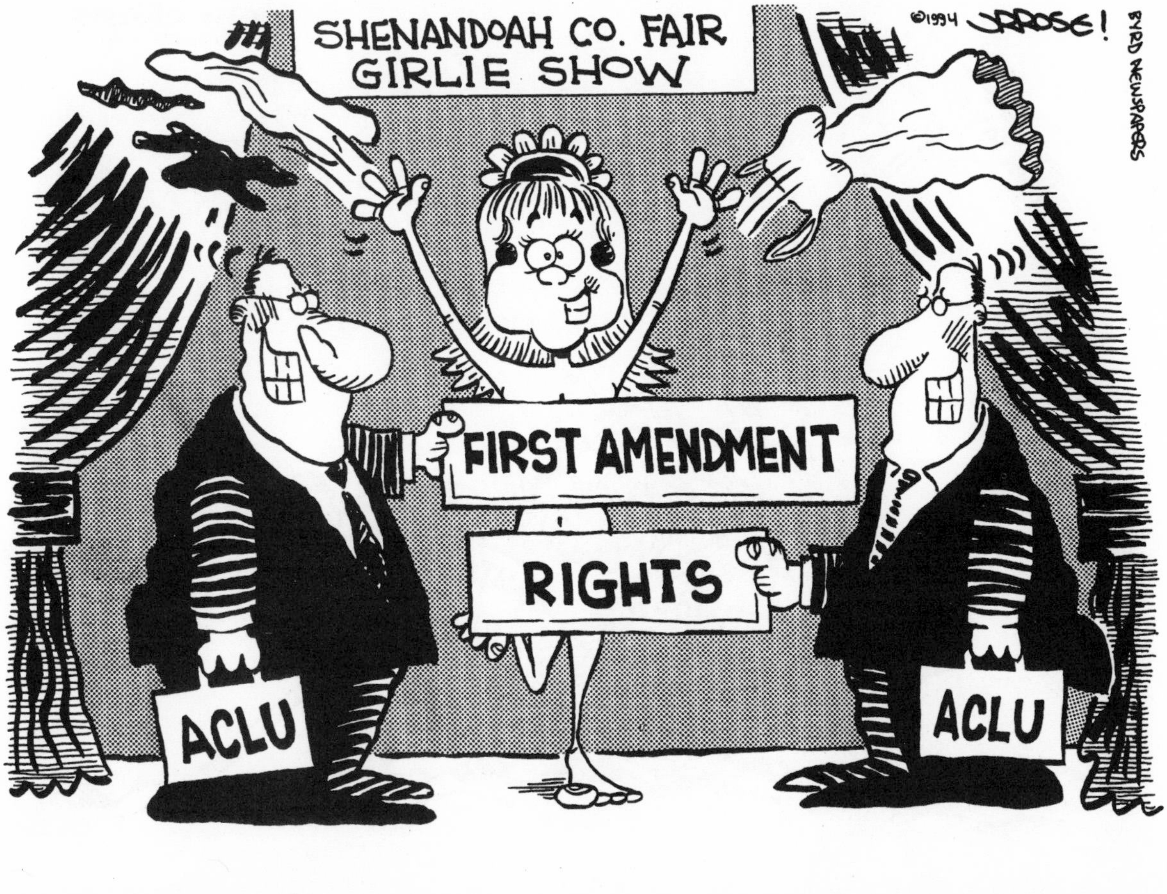
SHENANDOAH CO. FAIR
GIRLIE SHOW
©1994 JRROSE!
BYRD NEWSPAPERS
FIRST AMENDMENT
RIGHTS
ACLU
ACLU

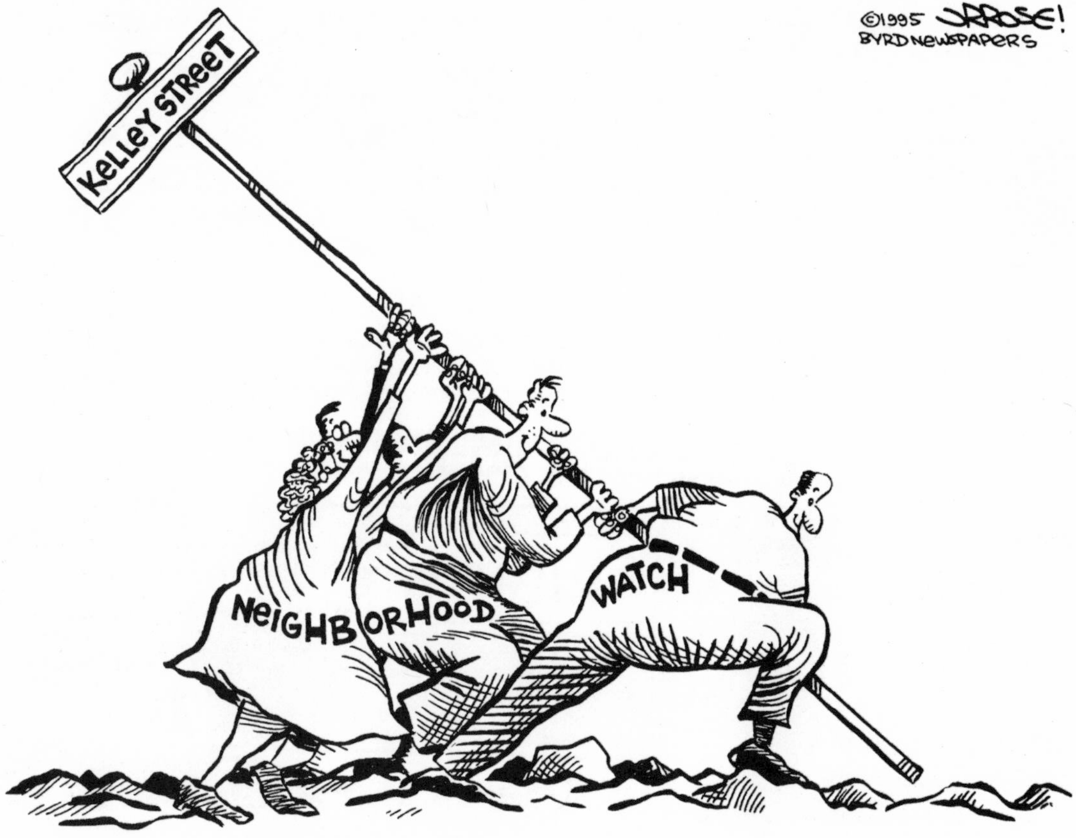
©1995 JRROSE!
BYRD NEWSPAPERS
KELLEY STREET
NEIGHBORHOOD
WATCH

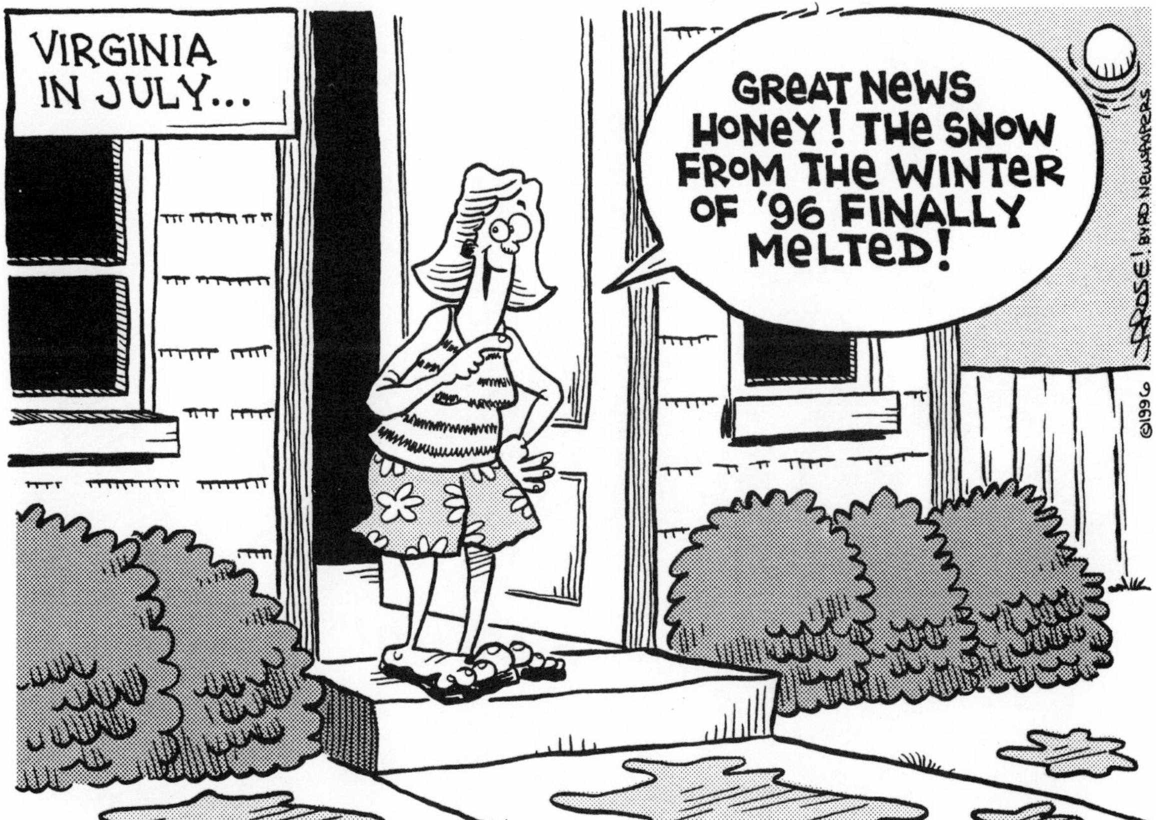
VIRGINIA IN JULY...
GREAT NEWS HONEY! THE SNOW FROM THE WINTER OF '96 FINALLY MELTED!
©1996 ROSE! BYRD NEWSPAPERS

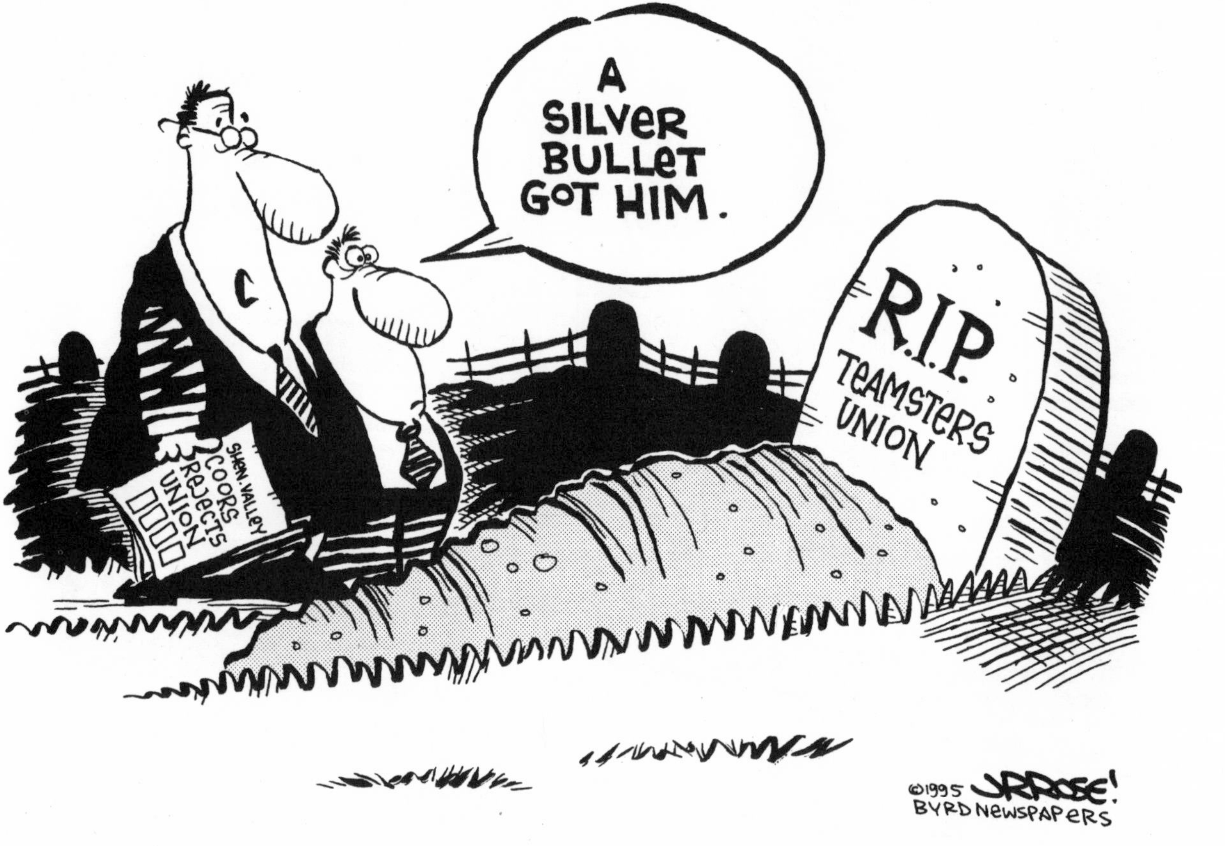
A SILVER BULLET GOT HIM.
R.I.P. TEAMSTERS UNION
SHEN. VALLEY COORS REJECTS UNION
©1995 JRROSE!
BYRD NEWSPAPERS

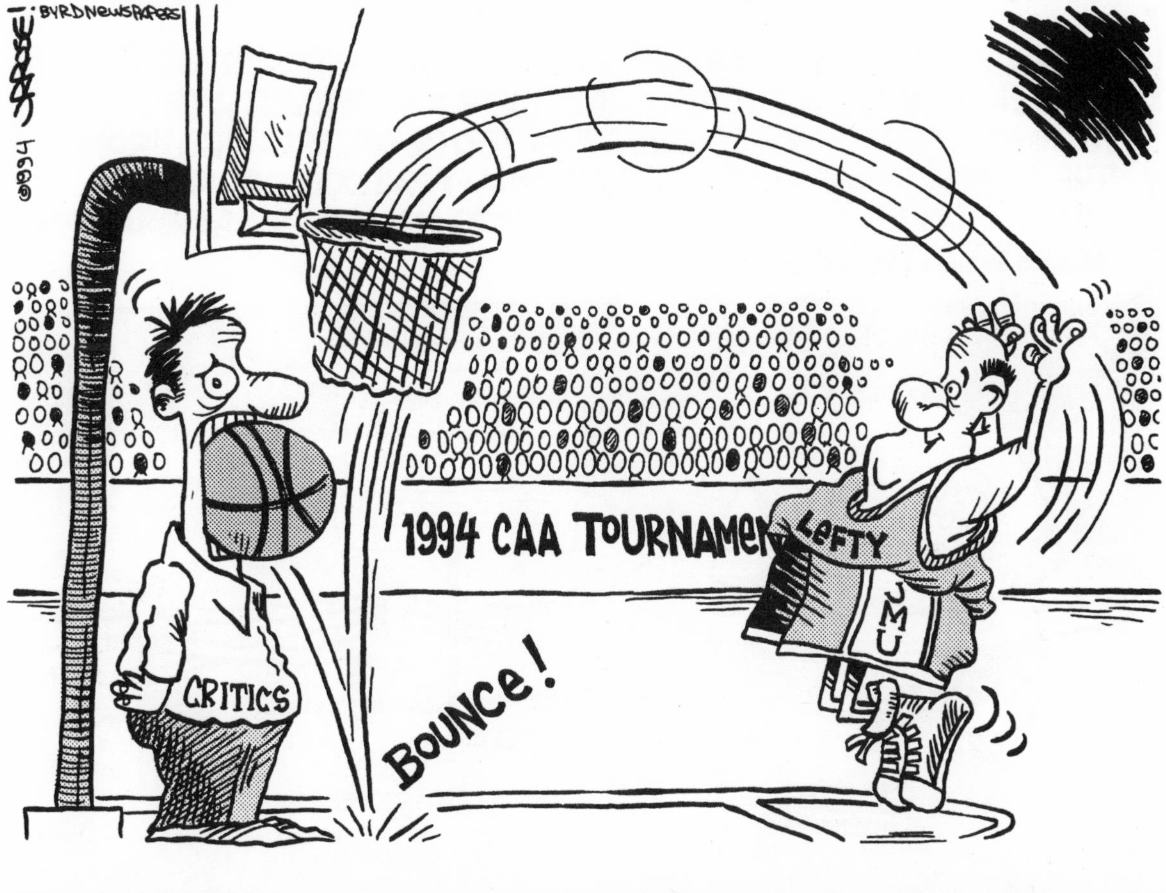

BYRDNEWSPAPERS
1994 CAA TOURNAMEN
LEFTY
JMU
CRITICS
BOUNCE!

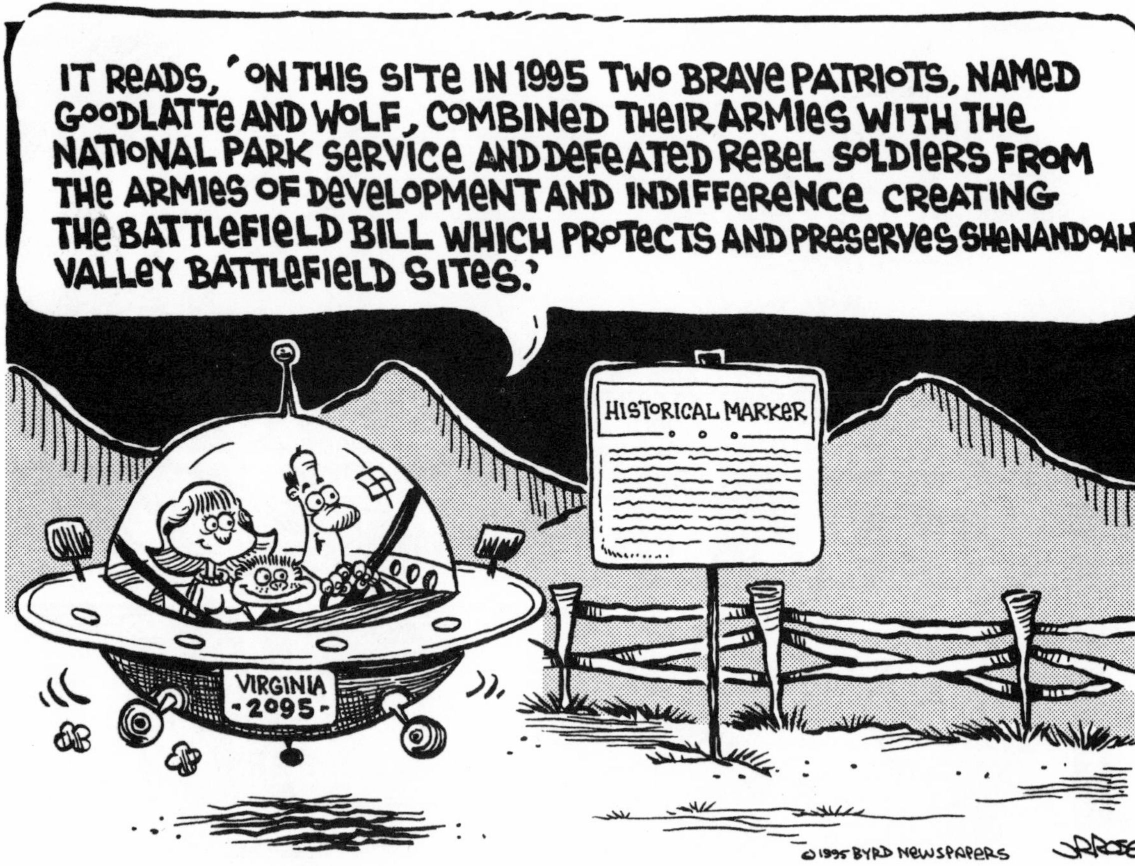
IT READS, 'ON THIS SITE IN 1995 TWO BRAVE PATRIOTS, NAMED GOODLATTE AND WOLF, COMBINED THEIR ARMIES WITH THE NATIONAL PARK SERVICE AND DEFEATED REBEL SOLDIERS FROM THE ARMIES OF DEVELOPMENT AND INDIFFERENCE CREATING THE BATTLEFIELD BILL WHICH PROTECTS AND PRESERVES SHENANDOAH VALLEY BATTLEFIELD SITES.'
HISTORICAL MARKER
VIRGINIA
-2095-
©1995 BYRD NEWSPAPERS
JRROSE!

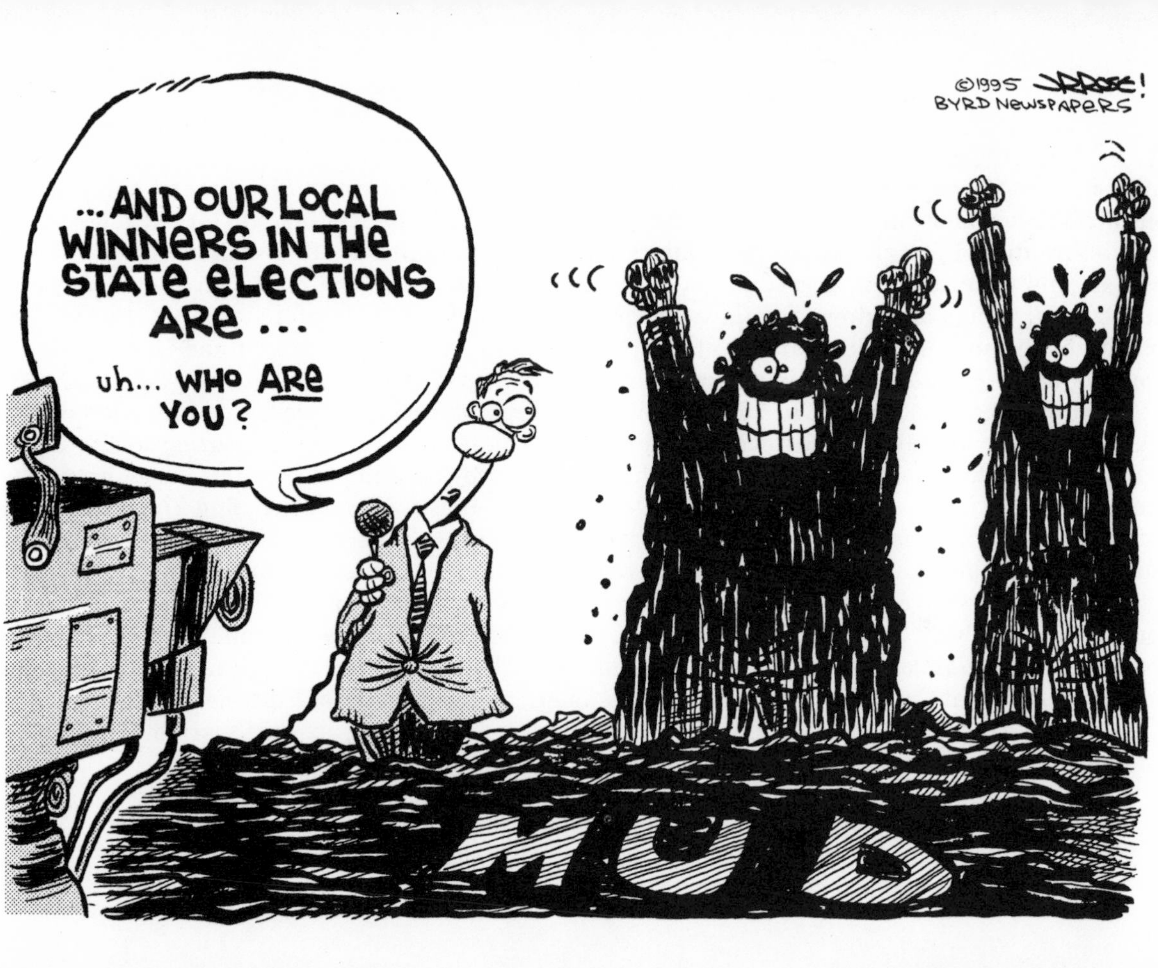

...AND OUR LOCAL WINNERS IN THE STATE ELECTIONS ARE ...
uh... WHO ARE YOU?
MUD
©1995 JRROSE! BYRD NEWSPAPERS

# About the Cartoonist

John R. Rose has always wanted to be a cartoonist. He started drawing on his parents' living room walls and continued throughout his school years in the margins of his test papers (hoping for extra credit).

A native Virginian, Rose graduated from James Madison University in 1986 with a bachelor of fine arts degree in art and art history. After graduation, he worked as a graphic artist for a sign and display company in Manassas, Virginia, and drew free-lance sports cartoons for the local newspaper. He joined Byrd Newspapers of Virginia in 1988, starting at *The Warren Sentinel* in Front Royal and then moving to the Harrisonburg *Daily News-Record*. His cartoons have won awards from the National Newspaper Association and the Virginia Press Association. In 1991, the Virginia Press Association presented him with the Best-in-Show Art Award for an editorial cartoon he did on school uniforms. Besides appearing in the eight Byrd Newspapers, his cartoons are syndicated throughout Virginia by Associated Features. They have also been reprinted in *The Washington Times, The Washington Post* national weekly edition, and *The National Forum*. He has also been featured in the *Best Editorial Cartoons of the Year* collections for the past several years.

In addition to his duties at the *Daily News-Record,* Rose also creates *Kids' Home Newspaper,* a weekly childrens' cartoon/activity page that has been syndicated by Copley News Service since 1991. *Fun with Pup,* a childrens' cartoon/activity book based on this feature, will be published by Pelican. He has illustrated one childrens' book, *Learning to Slow Down and Pay Attention* (Chesapeake Psychological Publications), and is a member of the National Cartoonists Society and the American Association of Editorial Cartoonists.

He lives with his wife, Karen, and daughters, Meredith and Sarah, in the heart of Virginia's scenic Shenandoah Valley. His cartoons can be found displayed on refrigerators everywhere.